The Economic and Business History of Occupied Japan

The Occupation era (1945-1952) witnessed major change in Japan and the beginnings of its growth from of the ashes of defeat towards its status as a developmental model for much of the world. The period arguably saw the sowing of the seeds of what some term the 'postwar Japanese economic miracle'. However, some scholars dispute this position and argue that the Occupation's policies and impacts actually hindered Japan's recovery. This volume addresses this question and others surrounding the business and economic history of this crucial period.

This chapters presented in *The Economic and Business History of Occupied Japan* are authored by major scholars of the Occupation from the U.S., Japan, and Europe. The chapters are divided into three sections: 'Planning, reform and recovery', 'Industries under the Occupation', and 'Legacies of the Occupation era'. Following an introduction focusing on the historiographical background, the first section examines zaibatsu dissolution and its significance, the role of Japanese businessmen within the Occupation's reforms, the crucial impact of Japan's postwar Materials Crisis, and, the impact of reform at the local level in Hokkaidō. Part two looks at a number of individual industries and their development during the era, including the fishing, automotive, and cotton spinning industries. The final section looks at the human impact of the changes of the initial postwar years, including the reintegration of repatriates into the Japanese labour force and the impact of changing working patterns on society and family life.

This book covers a key period of the economic and business history of Japan and presents numerous new approaches and original contributions to the scholarship of the Occupation era. It will be of interest to scholars of modern Japan, economic history, business history, development studies, and postwar U.S.-Japan relations.

Thomas French is an Associate Professor of Modern Japanese History at the College of International Relations, Ritsumeikan University, Japan. He is a specialist on the Occupation of Japan, and his broader research interests include U.S.-Japan relations, the Japanese automotive and arms industries, and the Japanese Self Defense Forces.

Perspectives in Economic and Social History

Series Editors: Andrew August and Jari Eloranta

For a full list of titles in this series, please visit www.routledge.com/series/PESH

The Economic and Business History of Occupied Japan

New Perspectives

Edited by Thomas French

LONDON AND NEW YORK

First published 2018 by Routledge

2 Park Square, Milton Park, Abingdon, Oxfordshire OX14 4RN
52 Vanderbilt Avenue, New York, NY 10017

Routledge is an imprint of the Taylor & Francis Group, an informa business

First issued in paperback 2019

British Library Cataloguing-in-Publication Data
A catalogue record for this book is available from the British Library

Library of Congress Cataloging-in-Publication Data
A catalog record for this book has been requested

ISBN: 978-1-138-19589-9 (hbk)
ISBN: 978-0-367-87710-1 (pbk)

Typeset in Times New Roman
by Apex CoVantage, LLC

Contents

Illustrations

Contributors

Steven Ericson (Associate Professor, Dartmouth College) earned his B.A. at Michigan State University and his A.M. and Ph.D. at Harvard. A specialist on the Occupation of Japan, he is the author of *The Sound of the Whistle: Railroads and the State in Meiji Japan* (Harvard, 1996), articles on the Matsukata financial reform of the 1880s, and co-editor of *The Treaty of Portsmouth and Its Legacies* (University Press of New England, 2008).

Thomas French is an Associate Professor of Modern Japanese History in the College of International Relations, Ritsumeikan University. He is a specialist on the Occupation of Japan, and his broader research interests include U.S.-Japan relations, the Japanese automotive and arms industries, and the Japanese Self Defense Forces. He is the author of *National Police Reserve: The Origin of Japan's Self Defense Forces* (Global Oriental, 2014).

Steven Ivings is an Assistant Professor of Cultural Economic History at the Cluster of Excellence 'Asia and Europe in a Global Context' at Heidelberg University, having completed his Ph.D. in Economic History at the London School of Economics and Political Science. His research examines colonial settlement, migratory labour, and postcolonial migration in the Japanese empire, with a particular focus on Hokkaidō and Karafuto (Southern Sakhalin), and the history of the Japanese empire in comparative perspective. He is currently working on a monograph entitled *Japan's Place in the Snow: The Making and Unmaking of Karafuto* (Japanese Sakhalin).

Mark Metzler is a Professor of History and Asian Studies at the University of Texas at Austin. His book *Capital as Will and Imagination* (Cornell, 2013) is a study of financial capital, inflation, and deflation focused on Japan's postwar recovery and transition to high speed growth, 1945 to 1960. It forms the second part of a long-period history of prosperity and depression begun in *Lever of Empire* (California, 2006), which investigates how liberal financial orthodoxies brought on Japan's interwar depression and destroyed liberalism as a political order. The study is extended in *Central Banks and Gold: How Tokyo, London, and New York Shaped the Modern World* (Cornell, 2016), co-authored with Simon Bytheway. Professor Metzler is now also working on a history of Japanese industrialisation from long term material and ecological perspectives.

Takahiro Ohata (Assistant Professor, Hiroshima University) received his doctor-ate from Kyoto University in 2011 and previously worked as a junior researcher in the Graduate School of Economics, Kyoto University. He is the author of *GHQ no Senryō Seisaku to Keizai Fukkō: Saikō Suru Nihon Menbōsekigyō* ('GHQ's Occupation Policy and Economic Recovery: The Rehabilitation of the Japanese Cotton Spinning Industry', 2012).

Zsombor Rajkai, Ph.D. (2008, 2010), is an Associate Professor in the College of International Relations, Ritsumeikan University. He specialises in the fol-lowing research fields: Japanese society and culture, the modernisation of non-Western societies seen through family change and individualisation, as well as Sino-Central Asian historical relations in the early Ming era. His main publi-cations include *Kyōgō Suru Kazoku Moderuron* ('The Theory of Competing Family Models', 2014), and *The Timurid Empire and Ming China: Theories and Approaches Concerning the Relations of the Two Empires* (2015).

Juha Saunavaara is an Assistant Professor at the Hokkaidō University Arctic Research Center. He earned his Ph.D. at University of Oulu, and his research fields include Japan's postwar political history, the regional development of Hokkaidō, and relations between Arctic and non-Arctic actors. Besides being the author of *GHQ/SCAP to Sengo no Seiji Saiken* ('GHQ/SCAP and the Post-war Political Reconstruction', 2015), he has published various peer-reviewed journal articles concerning the Allied Occupation of Japan.

William Tsutsui (President and Professor, Hendrix College) is the author or edi-tor of eight books, including *Manufacturing Ideology: Scientific Management in Twentieth-Century Japan (1998)* and *Banking Policy in Japan: American Efforts at Reform under the Occupation* (1988), as well as numerous articles and chapters, including (most recently) 'The Pelagic Empire: Reconsidering Japanese Expansion' in Brett Walker, Julia Thomas, and Ian Miller, eds., *Japan at Nature's Edge: The Environmental Context of a Global Power* (2013). He has received Fulbright, ACLS, and Marshall fellowships and was awarded the John Whitney Hall Prize of the Association for Asian Studies in 2000 and the Newcomen Society Award for Excellence in Business History Research and Writing in 1997. He is currently conducting research on the development of the modern Japanese fishing industry and the cultural history of the phrase 'made in Japan'.

Preface

The contents of this volume are largely based on papers presented at a series of conferences attended by the editor and the contributors in Kyoto between 2015 and 2016, specifically: *The XVIIth World Economic History Congress*; *The Economic and Business History of Occupied Japan Conference*; and *The Association of Asian Studies Conference in Asia*. The chapters which make up this book explore a number of new dimensions and original perspectives within the business and economic history of the Occupation of Japan (1945–1952).

The eight chapters are presented in three sections entitled: 'Planning, reform, and recovery', 'Industries under the Occupation', and 'Socioeconomic changes in the Occupation era'. The roles of economic and resource frontiers are explored in the first section, as are the influences of Japanese actors inside GHQ's reform programs. The industries examined in the second section include two bedrocks of Japan's pre-war economy, namely fishing and cotton spinning, and one which would later be seen as indicative of the postwar 'success' of Japan – the automotive industry. The impacts of social and demographic changes on the economy are also examined with the shifts in the family and gender roles and their influence on the economy, and the role of colonial repatriates in the economy, each explored in a chapter in the third section.

The content of the chapters present numerous new interpretations and pieces of evidence related to individual aspects of the business and economic history of the era and also contribute to several wider debates within the broader historiography of the period.

Editor's acknowledgements

Numerous individuals assisted in the preparation of this volume, and the editor would first like to thank the contributors, who were, of course, essential for its production.

David Newbold also deserves my thanks for the thoroughness and professionalism he demonstrated while assisting in the finalisation of the manuscript. Thank you too to Blake Foster for his assistance in this regard.

Thank you to Laura Johnson and Emily Kindleysides at Routledge for their advice and support in bringing the book to publication as well as Kevin Kelsey and his team.

To my colleagues in the College of International Relations at Ritsumeikan University, I express my heartfelt thanks for providing such a stimulating and rewarding working environment and for their decision to offer me a permanent home within such a wonderful team.

Finally, without the patience, support, and understanding of my wife Kaori, my parents, parents-in-law, and son, George, this volume would not have been possible, so it is to them that I dedicate my contributions to it.

Thomas French
Toji-in, Kyoto
April 2017

Note on conventions

Adhering to standard conventions, Japanese names are given in their Japanese style, i.e. family name first, except when cited or mentioned as an author. All dates are presented in the British calendar style (day/month/year). American spellings such as 'defense' are employed where sources use them.

Introduction

Thomas French

Introduction

A key, perhaps fundamental, indicator used to assess the impact and legacy of the Allied Occupation of Japan (1945-1952) is the condition of the Japanese economy. The extent to which the Occupation was 'responsible' for Japan's so-called postwar economic 'miracle' is a central question here, as is the extent to which such postwar growth indicates whether the Occupation itself was a 'success'.[1] The exploration of these questions and the broader impact of the policies of the General Headquarters of the Supreme Commander of Allied Powers (GHQ) on the economy have been influenced by a number major debates within the historiography of the period. Prominent among these, and directly addressed within the content of this volume are: the level of continuity which existed with Japan's past, the interconnected idea of a 'reverse course' in GHQ policy circa 1948, and the roles and 'agency' of Japanese actors during the period.

Situated, as it is, in the immediate aftermath of the war and before the 'era of high speed growth', the Occupation is central to our understanding of the history of modern Japan. However, what the Occupation represented within this centrality could be assessed by asking whether the period did indeed represent a 'period', a 'comma', or a 'hyphen' within that history, i.e. to what degree the Occupation era represented a break from the past, a pause within ongoing trends, or a direct continuation of these trends. This question of the depth of continuity or change also has interconnected implications for analyses of both the level of impact of the Occupation itself, and the broader political, economic, and social character of postwar Japan. The 'punctuation' of Japan's history by the Occupation and what influence is assigned to it also connect here to the 'periodisation' of the era in the scholarship, with studies often framing the outcomes and influence of the Occupation, both deliberately and not, through their positions on whether the period was a postscript to the war itself, or a prelude to the postwar era that followed. Early American studies of the Occupation generally stressed discontinuity with the past and democratising influence of GHQ's policy. In the English language-based literature, this was followed, especially from the late 1960s onwards, by studies stressing the continuities with the pre-1945 era, a trend which had long been established in much of the Japanese scholarship. Within the economic history of the Occupation, examples of studies which stress either continuity or change are numerous, with the works of Noguchi Yukio and his concept of the '1940 system' being an example of the former, and Aaron Forsberg's arguments that the Cold War and U.S. policy were as significant of an influence as the legacy of the war, being an example of the latter.[2] The idea of there being deep and genuine similarity between the pre and post-1945 systems has been contested from many dimensions, and this criticism has led to some innovative interpretations of the dynamics of a period in which both patterns of change and continuity clearly co-existed. A good example here is the work of Andrew Gordon, who argues that the years from around 1920 to 1960 formed a 'transwar' era, which within itself contained 'a recurring dynamic of change' but was distinct in many ways from the periods which preceded and followed it.[3]

The existence of a 'reverse course' within GHQ policy is another debate which is partially interlinked with the level and character of continuity and/or change. Originally a Japanese term (*gyaku kōsu*), with its supposed origins in a series of articles appearing in the *Yomiuri Shimbun* during the Occupation period, the original meaning of the term has been debated, especially whether it first referred to the position of the Japanese Communist Party (JCP), GHQ, or the Japanese government.[4] Whatever its original meaning, the role of the JCP in relation to the 'reverse course' (except as a supposed 'victim' of it) soon faded as the concept was first taken on by Marxist Japanese scholars and then the 1960s generation of more critical U.S. scholars. Both of these groups used it to refer to the alleged reversals of GHQ's democratic and progressive reforms and the revival of conservative political dominance within Japan from around 1948, principally due to the onset of the Cold War. The concept's usefulness both as an accurate description of GHQ's policy direction in the latter half of the Occupation and its applicability to certain elements of Occupation policy have been frequently contested, although the idea still survives as a point of reference and discussion within the scholarship.[5]

The desire to reflect the role of Japanese actors at all levels of society, the economy, and politics within the history of the era has also been a major focus within the scholarship in recent years. The idea of Japanese 'agency' in terms of exercising influence over, and/or holding responsibility for, some of the changes and continuities of the period, has greatly enhanced the scholarship of the Occupation. These efforts have also done much to challenge some earlier accounts of the period which contented that the GHQ bore virtual sole responsibility for Japan's postwar 'success'. Accounts of Japanese experiences within the Occupation era have also helped scholars broaden their fields of inquiry and better understand the grassroots impacts of, and influence on, the Occupation. However, the concept of 'agency' itself has been criticised by some due to disagreements over what forms and character 'agency' actually took, and the occasional stresses on reductive binary dichotomies of resistance/oppression and Japanese/American roles it can encourage.[6]

All of these concepts have relevance within different layers and contexts inside the history of the era, and they provide frameworks and concepts to enhance our understanding of the period, but none of them could be genuinely said to accurately model GHQ policy or the Occupation experience *as a whole*, with all its myriad origins, forms, manifestations, permutations, and legacies. Nevertheless, they have contributed to the great leaps forward the scholarship has made since the 1960s, and when employed together, they provide fresh perspectives and deeper levels of analysis of the history of the period. The chapters of this volume weave into this complex fabric of debate and analysis, interacting with, and occasionally challenging, the key debates noted above.

Planning, reform, and recovery

The first section of this work consists of three chapters: 'Japanese agency and business reform in Occupied Japan: the Holding Company Liquidation Commission and zaibatsu dissolution', by Steven J. Ericson, 'Japan's postwar social metabolic crisis', by Mark Metzler, and 'The role of the frontier: GHQ's economic policies and Hokkaidō', by Juha Saunavaara. The first chapter by Steven J. Ericson examines a hitherto neglected area of Japanese agency and influence inside GHQ's zaibatsu (large industrial conglomerate) dissolution program, an area of reform long thought to have been almost totally dominated by the Occupation. Ericson's chapter illustrates the key role played by the Holding Company Liquidation Commission (HCLC), a Japanese governmental body. The chapter demonstrates that the HCLC, which has not been the target of much scholarly attention to date, acted as an intermediary between GHQ and Japanese businesses, advocating their cases, occasionally delaying reform and achieving some moderate adjustments to GHQ policy. The chapter also highlights that simplistic narratives of Japanese resistance and delay versus GHQ drives for reform are inaccurate in this case, with the relations between the HCLC, GHQ, and the Deconcentration Review Board being dynamic, shifting, and with collaboration and division on all sides. In terms of the 'reverse course', Ericson again shows that an emphasis solely on external Cold War influences in determining the direction of GHQ policy ignores the key influence and advocacy of Japanese actors on the curtailment of the dissolution program. Finally, in relation to continuity, Ericson illustrates some of the limitations of the long term influence of GHQ's reforms by describing how banned trademarks were often readopted after 1952 and showing how many dissolved enterprises also later reconstituted themselves. However, Ericson does state that GHQ's anti-zaibatsu reforms had some lasting merit in that the increase in employee stock ownership they encouraged helped to improve labour relations and led to a wider distribution of wealth in Japanese society.

In the chapter titled 'Japan's postwar social metabolic crisis', Mark Metzler also describes a field where active cooperation between members of GHQ and the Japanese government occurred, both in terms of sharing ideas and developing policy. Adding depth and original insights to the already well established narrative of Japanese bureaucratic influence, Metzler argues that Ōkita Saburō and Edward A. Ackerman shared ideas about measuring and reconstructing the Japanese economy based on concepts of energy usage and output. This new 'calorific' frame of analysis greatly enhances our understanding of the economic policies of the Occupation era and the economic conditions in Japan at the time. In terms of the dynamics of continuity and change, the chapter argues that Japan suffered a temporary regression to earlier forms of production within the fishing, fertilizer, shipping, and transport industries, before surging forward from the economic frontiers at which Japan had stood at in 1941. The chapter itself presents a highly original analysis of the crisis and recovery of the Japanese economy from 1945 to 1955 and stands at several frontiers itself in terms of scholarship, connecting with new ideas about ecological economic history, having links to material and energy flow accounting, and even borrowing concepts from electrical engineering, linked to Ōkita's work in in colonial Manchuria.

The concept of dynamism along Japan's economic frontiers is also carried forward in the third chapter, which explores Hokkaidō's position within GHQ policy and the role of its industries during the Occupation. Juha Saunavaara argues that the impetus to develop the island increased after 1945 due it its potential to help solve the energy and food supply crises and accommodate some of the rapid population growth resulting from repatriation from the empire. After the loss of the empire, the potential of Hokkaidō as an internal resource frontier was increasingly focused upon, and GHQ had both direct and indirect influences on the attempts to further develop the island. Saunavaara also argues that although GHQ did not form a comprehensive policy towards Hokkaidō, arms of it, in particular Natural Resources Section, advocated and heavily supported its development. The chapter indicates that GHQ was pushing for the recovery and development of the industries of this part of Japan, especially food and coal production, well before the alleged 'reverse course' of latter years. In terms of continuity, the chapter also states that although wartime strategies to increase coal production were continued until 1946, these came to be changed relatively quickly due to labour unrest, financial difficulties and infrastructure issues. The chapter also describes how GHQ, despite its support for Hokkaidō, did not seek to diversify its industries, sticking largely with pre-1945 concepts of what the island was best used for, and even arguably undermining some of the previous efforts to move beyond primary resource collection through the suspension of much of the heavy chemical industry on the island during the early Occupation.

Industries under the Occupation

The second section of this volume includes the following chapters: 'An empire reborn: the Japanese fishing industry during the Occupation', by William M. Tsutsui, 'Fiats and jeeps: the Occupation, jeeps, and the postwar automotive industry', by Thomas French, and 'The Japanese cotton spinning industry and economic recovery under SCAP', by Takahiro Ohata. In 'An empire reborn: the Japanese fishing industry during the Occupation', William M. Tsutsui argues that the Occupation period is neglected in the history of Japan's fisheries, being seen as something of a discontinuous aberration between two eras of global Japanese fishing industry dominance. Tsutsui, adopting a transwar perspective, claims that continuity existed in terms of the general principle of governmental intervention to support the industry, but the origins of this pre-dated 1940, and the forms of such support were by no means identical in the postwar period. The chapter also contests some elements of the broader applicability of the 'reverse course' concept in presenting an industry which was revived very rapidly and with GHQ assistance from the start and *then* partially reformed from around 1949.

The fifth chapter, 'Fiats and jeeps: the Occupation, jeeps, and the postwar automotive industry', takes the position that despite the heavy focus of the scholarship to date on the cultural importance of the jeep, a full examination of its influence is only possible once its economic impacts are also taken into account. The automotive industry saw continuity with the war years during the Occupation in continuing to almost exclusively produce trucks for a military customer, albeit GHQ rather than the Imperial Japanese military. However, the era did crucially also see the beginnings of change from a purely truck to a car focused industry, from military to civilian-focused production, and from internal procurement towards export targeted products. The Occupation also continued the pattern of government intervention in the industry although without any real continuity in terms of the methods or aims of such intervention. The revival of the industry based upon the increase in procurement linked to the Korean War, and the creation of the National Police Reserve, are also often linked to the 'reverse course', but this chapter presents the argument that GHQ procurement related to vehicles, although greatly expanded in 1950, was already well established and making a positive contribution to the industry well before that date. In relation to agency, the chapter takes an approach of actually playing down the interpretation that the postwar success of the industry owed nothing to GHQ and was a purely Japanese endeavour. As the chapter states, although Occupation policy was occasionally technically 'restrictive', its procurement and support made GHQ more of a help than a hindrance to the automotive industry between 1945 and 1952.

The sixth chapter, by Takahiro Ohata, focuses on the revival of the cotton industry during the Occupation period. Almost entirely based on primary sources, this chapter argues that, like the fishing industry, the cotton spinning industry was one which was directly and heavily supported by GHQ almost from the start. Parts of GHQ directly assisted the industry, arranging for supplies of raw cotton and credit, acting as a guarantor for loans, and even negotiating trade deals on the industry's behalf overseas. The parts of the Occupation closest to the industry actually also protected it against other sections of GHQ and even occasionally from the U.S. government itself. The role of GHQ in reviving the cotton spinning industry (which was fully back on its feet by 1950) is also argued by Ohata to represent a challenge to the 'reverse course' in that GHQ fully and actively supported the industry almost from the start, and a focus on the 'reverse course' undervalues the contribution of GHQ towards Japan's economic reconstruction prior to 1948.

Socioeconomic changes in the Occupation era

The final section of this book contains two chapters: 'The economic reintegration of former colonial residents in postwar Japan', by Steven Ivings, and 'Good wife, wise mother, and Americanised consumer: the forced social democratisation of the private sphere in Occupied Japan', by Zsombor Rajkai. The chapter by Steven Ivings looks at the previously neglected topic of the reintegration of Japanese repatriates into working life in Japan. Focusing on former colonial residents of South Sakhalin, this study moves beyond the standard popular narrative of successful repatriation to Japan after a grievous journey by examining in detail the successes and failures of South Sakhalin repatriates in finding work and housing in northern Japan after their return. The chapter reveals that while there was no typical experience for these repatriates, many returned to the sectors in which they previously worked, albeit at a generally lower rank; some fell into severe poverty, although not all; and the elite largely maintained their professions and status. This analysis clearly focuses on an almost entirely Japanese element of the history of the Occupation and, in doing so, also indicates directly some of the grassroots experiences of continuity and change during the era and the complexities which can make such binary definitions of limited value.

The final chapter, by Zsombor Rajkai, focuses on GHQ's social reforms and their indirect impacts on the economic sphere. The chapter, largely employing Japanese works, details how the family, the fundamental socio-economic unit in Japan, was remodelled under GHQ, based on U.S. conceptions of the nuclear family tied to consumerism. Charting the continuity and change in family relations, and the high degree of Japanese agency within the development of postwar education and gender equality policies, the chapter details the origins of Japan's middle classes and the pre-war and postwar development of the ideals of the family, housewife, and 'salaryman', all of which formed key elements within the emerging patterns of consumerism and work in the subsequent 'high growth era'.

Conclusion

The chapters of this volume thus present a range of original perspectives on the Occupation itself and its interaction with Japan's economy, businesses, politics, people, and environment. A number of initial common themes emerge linking some of the chapters presented here. In terms of continuity and change, the chapters present the general picture that, although there was continuity between the pre-war and postwar regimes in terms of a willingness to intervene in the economy and business, there was little continuity, at least in a lasting sense, in the means of such intervention.[7] In terms of the broader picture, the chapters reveal an economy staggering back from the massive blows dealt to it in the latter years of the war, but which, once recovered, surged forward again. This sharp but temporary reversal back to older forms of technology and production (Chapters 2, 3, 4, and 6) could be said to indicate a temporarily checked continuity of development, where the broader economy spent a number of years after 1945 regaining its earlier position and then developing rapidly from there. This was not to say though that the industries were reconstituted in identical forms, and as the chapters explain, a large amount of reconfiguration and remobilisation of Japan's resources, both human (Chapters 7 and 8), and natural (Chapters 3 and 4), often took place. The content of this volume also indicates that despite sometimes being viewed as economically underdeveloped or 'catching up' with Western countries in the pre-war era, Japan was in fact highly advanced and competitive in many ways, with a world-leading fishing fleet, cotton industry, level of household electrification, and agricultural yield per hectare.

The chapters of this volume also demonstrate that the idea of a coherent 'reverse course' has major limitations, at least in relation to the industries examined here. Key industries directly linked to stability and security such as the fishing and cotton industries were helped to recover very swiftly by GHQ before later being reformed in a limited fashion (Chapters 4 and 6). The social reforms of workplace and family were also clearly not reversed (Chapter 8). The automotive industry also provides a counter to ideas of clear reversal in favour of recovery in 1948, with GHQ, despite imposing production limits until 1949, also providing assistance and procurement contracts well before that date (Chapter 5). Finally, various reasons besides the impact of the Cold War are presented as to why certain policies were reversed, or adjusted, with Japanese influence being central in many (Chapter 1). Regarding such Japanese agency, the degree of collaboration and influence of Japanese actors with the business and economic history of the period was further revealed. These influences were not always purely those of resistance to GHQ reform efforts, with many chapters indicating a high degree of collaboration between GHQ and various Japanese actors, and even advocacy both internally and internationally on behalf of Japanese industry by elements of GHQ (Chapters 1, 2, and 6).

To conclude, the content of this volume offers the reader a number of original perspectives and makes new contributions to often longstanding debates within the historiography of the Occupation and the business and economic history of the period. The editor and the contributors hope that their research makes a positive contribution to this rich tapestry of interwoven debates around the role and legacy of the Occuaption.

Notes

1 For a fuller analysis of the limitations of employing simple terms such as 'success' or 'failure' to such a complex and multi-layered subject, see: L. E. Hein, "Growth Versus Success, Japan's Economic Policy in Historical Perspective", in A. Gordon, ed., *Postwar Japan as History*, Berkley: University of California Press, 1993. Koikari also suggests that such binary terms are of limited value in assessing the Occupation, see: M. Koikari, "Rethinking Gender and Power in the US Occupation of Japan, 1945–1952", *Gender & History*, Vol. 11, No. 2, July 1999.
2 See: Y. Noguchi, "The 1940 System: Japan Under the Wartime Economy", *The American Economic Review*, Vol. 88. No. 2, May 1998; A. Forsberg, *America and the Japanese Miracle: The Cold War Context of Japan's Postwar Economic Revival, 1950–1960*, Chapel Hill: University of North Carolina Press, 2000.
3 A. Gordon, "Consumption, Leisure and the Middle Class in Transwar Japan", *Social Science Japan Journal*, Vol. 10, No. 1, 2007, p. 3. See also: M. Nakamura, *Sengo-shi* (Postwar History), Tokyo: Iwanami Shoten, 2005, pp. 5–9.
4 See: H. M. Kramer, "Just Who Reversed the Course? The Red Purge in Higher Education During the Occupation of Japan", *Social Science Japan Journal*, Vol. 8, No. 1,

2005; E. Takemae, *Inside GHQ, The Allied Occupation of Japan and Its Legacy*, London: Continuum, 2002, p. 473.

5 See Frost's work for an early and significant challenge to the 'reverse course' concept. P. Frost, "Nippon Senryō ni Okeru 'Gyaku Kōsu'" (The "Reverse Course" within the Occupation of Japan), in R. A. Moore, ed., *Tennō ga Baiburu o Yonda Hi* (The Day the Emperor Read the Bible), Tokyo: Kodansha, 1982.

6 See: L. Hein, "Revisiting America's Occupation of Japan", *Cold War History*, Vol. 11, No. 4, November 2011; Koikari, "Rethinking Gender and Power", p. 316.

7 This conclusion supports the position taken by Bai Gao. It is also the case that state intervention in the economy was hardly a uniquely Japanese phenomenon from the 1930s to the 1960s. See: B. Gao, "Arisawa Hiromi and His Theory for Managed Economy", *Journal of Japanese Studies*, Vol. 20, No. 1, Winter 1994; B. Gao, "The Postwar Japanese Economy", in W. M. Tsutsui, ed., *A Companion to Japanese History*, Malden: Blackwell, 2007.

Part 1

Planning, reform, and recovery

1 Japanese agency and business reform in Occupied Japan

The Holding Company Liquidation Commission and zaibatsu dissolution

Steven J. Ericson

Introduction

To date, studies of the zaibatsu dissolution and business deconcentration programs under the U.S. Occupation of Japan have foregrounded an array of American players. Douglas MacArthur and his subordinates in Tokyo; Washington bureaucrats and Congressmen; U.S. businessmen, diplomats, and journalists in the 'Japan Lobby' – such actors have figured prominently in the literature.[1] Recent work on the Occupation has uncovered previously overlooked input by Japanese individuals and groups into other U.S.-mandated reforms, in particular those of education, labour relations, and the constitution.[2] In the area of business reform, however, most analyses mention only in passing Japanese initiative or agency in the development of Occupation programs for 'democratising' Japanese business.[3]

This chapter focuses on the activities of the Holding Company Liquidation Commission (HCLC), a poorly understood Japanese body that the government of Japan established in August 1946 under SCAPIN 244.[4] Scholars – if they bother to mention the HCLC – have tended to characterise it as a tool of Occupation headquarters (GHQ or 'SCAP' for Supreme Commander for the Allied Powers), an instrument that dutifully carried out SCAP directives on business breakup and reorganisation. Drawing especially on the memoirs of Noda Iwajirō,[5] a central figure in the HCLC, the chapter demonstrates that this agency played a critical role in shaping the Occupation's business reforms and in mitigating their effects. Through skilful negotiation and persuasion, the commission contributed to a scaling back of reforms that previous studies have attributed primarily to American geopolitical, business, and financial concerns after 1947.

The nature of the Holding Company Liquidation Commission

The few scholarly descriptions of the HCLC available in English have been rather equivocal and at times contradictory. T. A. Bisson, for example, termed the commission 'a tightly controlled and pliable instrument of SCAP policy' but then stated at the close of the very same paragraph: 'By the end of 1948 it had become the central agency controlling the full scope of combine dissolution'.[6] Masaru Hosoya, by contrast, claims that SCAP intended from the beginning 'that the

Holding Company Liquidation Commission would wield real power during the actual process of dissolving the four major zaibatsu and other conglomerates'; but he subsequently quotes a member of the commission as declaring, with regard to a decision the agency made in 1948, that 'the HCLC was a "puppet" of the Occupation forces' and 'the commissioners' deliberations were only a "formality"'.[7]

The confusion about the nature of the HCLC stems from what Eleanor Hadley called its 'somewhat peculiar status within the Japanese government – it was of it, yet separate'.[8] Noda explained that the HCLC was 'an American-style commission': though consisting of private citizens, it held executive authority, representing 'a type of organisation that had not previously existed in Japan; its members could be neither politicians nor government officials nor private citizens connected to the zaibatsu'.[9] As Bisson put it, the HCLC 'was a hybrid, marked by a complex and unusual mixture of public and private features'. The cabinet appointed the commissioners and considered them members of the government service, but the commission itself was incorporated under the Commercial Code and 'declared its personnel to be without official status'.[10] As a result of the HCLC's 'peculiar' standing, 'its members were, for the most part, freed from the obstructions of Japanese officialdom'.[11] On the other hand, in contrast to normal Occupation practice whereby SCAP kept Japanese government actions separate from its own, a GHQ observer attended all meetings of the HCLC, guiding its policies and reviewing its decisions, which the commission never made without prior SCAP approval. Hadley noted: 'Such close supervision was not exercised over other parts of the Japanese government'.[12] SCAP rightly assumed that, if it put Japanese government officials directly in charge of the zaibatsu-busting program, they would quickly find ways to obstruct it.[13]

The title of the commission resulted from SCAP's initial acceptance of the Yasuda Plan whereby the four leading zaibatsu agreed to dissolve their top holding companies but left out any mention of combine subsidiaries or intercorporate ownership and management ties. That proposal, which Takemae Eiji labelled 'patently self-serving and full of loopholes, a transparent "easy-out" for the zaibatsu', in effect shifted the focus of 'liquidation' from combine to holding company.[14] The cabinet attempted further to weaken the HCLC's authority by translating the word 'liquidation' as *seiri* or 'adjustment' rather than as *seisan*, the literal equivalent. Nevertheless, as Bisson pointed out, 'SCAP officials were not much interested in terminological subtleties', and, over time, they steadily expanded the functions and powers of the HCLC until by late 1947, it had attained, 'in fact if not in name', the status of a *combine* liquidation commission.[15]

The pre-surrender career of Noda Iwajirō

The HCLC may have required SCAP approval for every action it took, but it was in negotiating that approval or in delaying or refraining from action that the commission exerted its growing influence, and the agency found the ideal man to lead it in Noda Iwajirō (1897-1988). Fluent in English with over 20 years of work experience in the United States before the Pacific War, married to an American, and well connected within Japan's managerial elite through school and business ties – Noda occupied a unique place in SCAP antitrust programs as HCLC's vital intermediary between Japanese corporations and Occupation headquarters. A native of Nagasaki, Noda graduated from Tokyo Commercial School, present-day Hitotsubashi University – an important pipeline of managerial talent for Japanese business and banking circles – and entered *Mitsui Bussan* (Mitsui and Co.) in 1918. The trading firm quickly dispatched him to Seattle, to which Bussan was mainly engaged in exporting raw materials for U.S. wartime production of margarine and vegetable oil. In a surprising move for the time, Noda wed an American woman, Alice Carita Coston (1897-1961), a secretary in the Seattle office; he did so over the vigorous objections of both of their families and of his employer. In those days, recalled Noda, when anti-Japanese sentiment was running high on the West Coast, international marriage was close to a 'prohibition of the house' (*oie no gohatto*) in Bussan;[16] upon their marriage, his wife lost her U.S. citizenship. Recognising that his marital situation had become a handicap, Noda decided to resign from Bussan and seek employment with a more tolerant firm.

He found that employer in *Nihon Menka* or *Nichimen* (Japan Cotton), which sent him to its New York branch in 1926. Nichimen rivalled Mitsui Bussan in the volume of raw silk it imported into the United States; but, unlike other Japanese silk importers, who generally entrusted their product to U.S. agents, Noda's new company engaged in direct sales, dispatching him and other salesmen to meet with potential buyers throughout the United States. In 1931, Nichimen appointed Noda, at the age of 34, to head its New York office.

After the attack on Pearl Harbor, Noda was held for nearly two years at detention centres on the East Coast and at Fort Missoula Internment Camp in Montana. At his first place of detention, fellow Japanese detainees chose him to serve as liaison with the American authorities, an experience Noda found helpful when he later performed a similar role for the HCLC. Repatriated under an exchange program in September 1943, Noda worked part time in the research section of the Navy Ministry translating English-language radio broadcasts and telegrams; others in that section included men who would become top executives in firms he would deal with during the Occupation. Noda also joined a group in the Navy General Staff that investigated conditions in the United States; there, he emphasised the unified, melting-pot nature of American society, which, according to him, the Army tended to think was on the verge of disintegration because of its multi-racial, multi-cultural immigrant character.[17]

Noda and the HCLC

After the war ended and the Occupation commenced, Noda accepted appointment as a founding member and executive commissioner of the HCLC. He explained his decision to join the commission by stating: 'I figured that, if zaibatsu dissolution, one of the terms of Japan's surrender, didn't go well, the Japanese people and I myself would be put in a difficult position'.[18] Besides Noda, the original commission membership comprised three bank executives, the chairman of a securities firm, the managing director of a cement company, a lawyer, a newspaperman, and two professors of economics. Later replacements included the vice-chairman of the Sōdōmei trade union and the president of a brick manufacturing company.

The HCLC got off to a rocky start, as the first nominee for its chairmanship, San'wa Bank president Nakane Sadahiko, was unexpectedly purged. A *waka* enthusiast, Nakane had composed a poem during the war with the playful phrase '*yuru fun* (*rūzu beruto*) [loose belt]', which SCAP deemed anti-American for ridiculing the late president Roosevelt.[19] The purge also befell the next nominee for chairman, a college professor, who, despite being a devout Catholic, was charged with supporting state Shinto for having written a positive essay about visits he had made to shrines and temples in Kyoto and Nara. The third try was the charm, as Noda negotiated with SCAP to appoint Sasayama Tadao, former director of the semi-official Industrial Bank of Japan, as HCLC chairman.[20] When Sasayama resigned in 1949, Noda himself would assume the chairmanship.

The HCLC began operations in August 1946 by embarking on the dissolution of the first group of designated holding companies – those of the big four zaibatsu and Nakajima Aircraft – according to plans that SCAP had already worked out with the Japanese government.[21] For 78 additional firms the HCLC had designated as holding companies by early 1947, as well as 325 companies it named in February 1948 for possible breakup under the 1947 Deconcentration Law, the commission followed the basic policy of 'listening to the wishes and ideas of the companies concerned and moving things as much as possible in the direction they desired'.[22] Some 50 of the 83 designated 'holding companies' were in fact essentially 'operating companies with holding company characteristics'.[23] For the most part, the HCLC successfully argued that it could meet SCAP objectives for holding-company liquidation by eliminating the designated operating companies' ownership and management ties to other firms but actually dissolving only concerns among the 30-odd 'pure' holding companies and transferring their operating branches to 'second companies' whose shares it would offer to the public.[24]

Over the course of its five-year existence, the HCLC held a total of 51 general meetings, which represented the formal decision-making venue. While leading each meeting, Noda would render members' statements into English for the SCAP 'observer' and then the observer's statements into Japanese. Prior to the meetings, he would typically solicit SCAP's opinions on pending matters such as which firms to designate as holding companies or how to break up a particular enterprise. He and other executive members would then meet with the owners and managers of the companies concerned to hear their views or would conduct independent investigations before drafting proposals for submission to the Occupation authorities. After making the rounds to obtain informal consent (*nemawashi*) at SCAP headquarters, Noda would submit a proposal at a general meeting for a decision. Initially, SCAP would often bring proposals to the HCLC meetings based on its own investigations, but over time, 'it became the norm' for the commission to take the initiative.[25]

Though the HCLC employed a staff of 500, including 'excellent bank and company employees' returning from Japan's former empire,[26] its workload grew to enormous proportions: it handled the dissolution of holding companies, the disposal of the assets of zaibatsu owner-family members, the divestiture of intercorporate stockholdings among former combine subsidiaries, and, eventually, the deconcentration of large operating companies. Noda and other HCLC members conducted detailed studies of the hundreds of designated firms and visited offices, factories, and mines throughout Japan. Many firms fell under both the holding-company liquidation ordinance and the later Deconcentration Law,[27] and in each of those cases, the commission had to draw up two different reports, further complicating its work. What seemed like maddeningly slow progress to some SCAP officials, therefore, resulted from more than just the 'game' of obstruction and delay that, according to Eleanor Hadley, the Japanese government 'played again and again'.[28]

Noda claimed that the HCLC, sandwiched among SCAP, the Japanese government, and business, 'was misconstrued' by all three as 'an adversary', but by and by they all came to trust the commission.[29] SCAP expressed its growing confidence in the HCLC by continually adding to its responsibilities, though the commission, when also asked to reorganise financial institutions and draft an anti-monopoly law, declined on the grounds that it had plenty to do concentrating on the industrial and non-financial service sectors and that its job was to establish the conditions for fair competition, not to plan for its enforcement. Meanwhile, political and corporate leaders came to recognise that although the HCLC was, for the most part, dutifully carrying out Occupation directives, it was also able both to modify those directives before their issuance through negotiation with SCAP and to manage their implementation so as to 'protect the interests of the businesses' (according to Noda).[30]

Despite its accommodation with SCAP, the HCLC still faced a major nemesis there, the committed 'New Dealer' Edward Welsh, who arrived in Tokyo in April 1947 to head the Antitrust and Cartels Division of the Occupation's Economic and Scientific Section (ESS). In Noda's view, Welsh 'pursued zaibatsu dissolution far too faithfully and by the book'.[31] Welsh for his part inserted into his memoranda the stock complaint that the HCLC lacked 'understanding of Occupation policy' whenever the commission found no evidence of 'restraint of trade' for a company that, in Welsh's view, was patently guilty of restricting competition.[32] The HCLC, however, was often able to use persuasion and the mediation of Welsh's less radical assistants to moderate their superior's demands. As Noda explained:

> Rather than confront Welsh directly, we would first make his subordinates our allies and . . . get them to advise him; and, since it was the advice of his own subordinates, Welsh would sometimes accept it. We would also influence them at the stage of collecting information on which Welsh would make decisions.[33]

Trust-busting and business deconcentration

One of the HCLC's first major tasks, as directed by SCAP, was to take physical custody of the stocks owned by the holding companies of the big four zaibatsu and Nakajima. Noda initiated this action on 8 October 1946, when he took a group of HCLC members to the main offices of the Mitsui and Mitsubishi holding companies in Tokyo, loaded on to two trucks 46 sealed wooden boxes containing ¥1.25 billion in stock and bond certificates and, escorted by armed MP guards, brought the securities to the Hypothec Bank of Japan, next to the HCLC offices, for storage pending their disposal.[34] Following this dramatic photo opportunity, the commission proceeded over the next three weeks to secure the stocks of the other three holding companies in this first round of designations.

After eventually designating well over 300 firms as holding companies or 'excessive concentrations of economic power' or both, the HCLC strove to create a reasonably level playing field in each economic sector. Whenever possible, it accepted the voluntary proposals of designated firms, dropped from the lists companies for which it determined dissolution or reorganisation was unwarranted and 'defended' firms from SCAP plans it considered too severe.

Of enterprises designated under both the holding-company and deconcentration orders, for example, the HCLC obtained SCAP approval to remove from the lists both Matsushita Electric and Furukawa Electric after visiting their factories and conferring with their executives. Matsushita, as a manufacturer of home appliances, was fortunate that SCAP was targeting makers of heavy electrical goods such as Hitachi and Toshiba. Toshiba, by contrast, seems to have been an exceptional case of a firm that took a separate hit under each dissolution measure: as a designated holding company, it had to spin off 13 new enterprises, while as an 'excessive concentration of economic power' it also had to dispose of 27 factories and one research laboratory.[35] Meanwhile, the HCLC found that Furukawa Electric, a subsidiary of the Furukawa combine's holding company and a producer mainly of electric cables, did not have an excessive share of the electric-cable market; as a result, the firm, whose president was a classmate and close friend of Noda, escaped reorganisation other than voluntarily liquidating its holdings in electric utilities.[36] The HCLC, however, failed to get SCAP to accept the request of another dual designee, *Nihon Seitetsu* (Japan Iron and Steel), that it be split into two companies; instead, SCAP ordered the firm's division into four enterprises.[37] By contrast, Noda claimed that, following the wishes of Mitsubishi Heavy Industries, the commission convinced SCAP to divide that firm into three companies, presenting the firm's proposal as its own. 'Of course', Noda slyly remarked, 'we didn't tell SCAP that Mitsubishi Heavy Industries desired that outcome'.[38]

In the Mitsubishi case, Occupation records somewhat contradict Noda's account of how matters unfolded. According to memoranda in SCAP files, the HCLC proposed that Mitsubishi Heavy Industries be divided into two new companies, but Welsh wanted to go further with a four-company reorganisation. In the end, the Deconcentration Review Board (DRB), which Washington sent to Japan in 1948 to advise on the breakup of businesses under the 1947 Deconcentration Law, essentially split the difference by recommending the firm's own plan for a three-way division. Noda, however, may well have been instrumental in persuading Welsh to go along with that plan.[39]

Daiken Industries was yet another enterprise that ended up on both dissolution lists. SCAP initially viewed Daiken, formed in 1934 by the merger of a textile company and two trading firms, as being on par with the huge trading subsidiaries of the Mitsui and Mitsubishi combines, companies that had handled 70 percent of Japan's foreign trade before the war. Noda negotiated directly with Welsh on Daiken's behalf and finally got him to agree to the removal of the holding-company designation by arguing that, if Welsh were to group the much smaller Daiken with those giants, it would only 'subject SCAP to ridicule'. Nonetheless, Daiken Industries remained among the 18 companies ultimately designated for reorganisation under the Deconcentration Law, and the firm itself requested that it be broken up. Following its policy of complying with the wishes of designated firms, the HCLC thereupon approved Daiken's division into four companies: Kureha Textile, Marubeni and C. Itoh (now Itochu) trading firms, and Amagasaki Nail Manufacturing Works.[40]

Mitsui Bussan and Mitsubishi Shōji were not so fortunate. The drastic breakup of those trading firms was the one glaring exception to SCAP's policy of working through the HCLC and relying on the voluntary dissolution of designated holding companies. In their cases alone, SCAP issued in July 1947 a special directive demanding the companies' dissolution, an action that came as 'a bolt from the blue' for Noda and his fellow commissioners. In Noda's view, Bussan and Shōji were the epitome of companies that bungled direct negotiations with the Occupation authorities. After the HCLC had named the two firms as holding companies in December 1946, it had entered into negotiations with SCAP on how and to what extent they should be broken up. In informal discussions with Mitsui Bussan's president and a subordinate of Welsh, Noda believed that they had reached a consensus on dividing Bussan into no more than nine units but had decided that they needed to do more research on whether to break up the firm by region or by commodity. Thereafter, however, Bussan began to negotiate directly with SCAP, which stopped consulting the HCLC on the matter. In mid-1947, Welsh summoned Noda and informed him that he had received a petition from Bussan detailing reasons why the company should be exempted from dissolution and that this brazen action had made Welsh more convinced than ever that the firm should be dissolved. A few days later, Welsh called Noda back to his office and abruptly handed him a memorandum ordering the HCLC to take immediate steps to break up – or, as Theodore Cohen puts it, 'to pulverize' – Bussan and Shōji into hundreds of firms. The directive called for additional harsh measures: no more than one person who had been a manager at or above the level of branch-office or department head over the previous decade could enter a successor firm, nor could more than 100 of the thousands of Bussan or Shōji employees do so, and they could no longer use their current offices or the same trade names as before.[41]

Noda speculated that Britain was responsible for the harsh treatment of the two trading companies. Whereas before the war, Japan had enjoyed a reciprocal trade relationship with the United States centring largely on the exchange of silk for cotton, Britain and Japan had been rivals in trade. Furthermore, the British representative on the advisory Allied Council on Japan had constantly complained about the leniency of the HCLC's programs.[42] This attitude contrasted sharply with British resistance to U.S. deconcentration efforts in occupied Germany, as British firms 'had well-established relations with German industry and had participated actively with German firms in pre-war cartels'.[43] A simpler explanation is that Bussan's manoeuvring to evade dissolution, as Morikawa Hidemasa suggests, incurred 'the wrath of the Occupation authorities', above all the hardliner Edward Welsh. Noda himself recorded Welsh as stating: 'The dissolution [of Bussan and Shōji] was my own decision'.[44]

Welsh also drove the decision-making process that led to the December 1947 promulgation of the Deconcentration Law, which empowered the HCLC to designate and eliminate 'excessive concentrations of economic power'.[45] Before the Diet enacted the law, Welsh had projected that it would cover as many as five thousand companies. The HCLC, however, insisted that SCAP add the word 'excessive' to the proposed bill to prevent its reckless application, although, as John Haley notes, the measure in fact 'closely tracked' the earlier U.S. deconcentration statute for Germany with its prohibition against 'excessive concentrations of German economic power'.[46] Welsh eventually submitted to the HCLC for possible dissolution under the law a list of 450 companies, which the commission then reduced to 325, a number that included 51 firms it had previously designated under the holding-company liquidation directive.[47] Even this trimmed-down group comprised almost all of Japan's large corporations, accounting for 66 percent of the country's total paid-up capital.[48] Within two months of the arrival in early May 1948 of the DRB, which Washington had dispatched at MacArthur's request to determine whether dissolution of designated firms would retard Japan's economic recovery, the HCLC had further cut the deconcentration list to 100 companies.[49]

Scholars often cite Kazuo Kawai's inaccurate assertion that 'the Deconcentration Review Board quickly found one reason or another to whittle down the number of corporations to be dissolved from 1,200 to 325, then to 30, then to 19, and finally when nine corporations had been dissolved it announced that the deconcentration program had been satisfactorily completed'.[50] In fact, shortly before the board landed in Japan, the HCLC had already removed 50 companies from its list of 325 and notified another 144 firms that they would have to make only minor changes, then dropped 31 additional enterprises to reach the 100 company mark. At the direction of the Review Board, the commission finally narrowed the list of designated companies to 18; it ordered 11 of them broken up into two or more firms and had the remaining seven dispose of various assets.[51] Only four of the 11 dissolved companies were new to designation, the other seven having already been on the list of designated holding companies.

The standard view of the 'whittling down' process is that the U.S. government, through the DRB, effectively forced SCAP to abandon the deconcentration program as part of the Cold War driven 'reverse course' in Occupation policy. This interpretation, however, obscures the active part the HCLC played in the process. Given the vagueness of the criteria for determining 'excessive concentrations' and the paucity of available business data, the commission cast a wide net, then proceeded to investigate all 325 designated concerns and, in Noda's words, 'one after another removed from designation firms that did not seem concentrated'.[52] From the start, the HCLC resisted what it saw as a program of 'severe business dismemberment', one that, if carried out as SCAP envisaged, might cause the Japanese economy to collapse.[53] According to Noda, in deliberations on the final 100 companies, 'the five members of the Deconcentration Review Board lined up in the middle as the judge, while Welsh and members of the Antitrust and Cartels Division sat on one side as the prosecution and HCLC Chairman Sasayama and I on the other side as the defense, arguing for and against dissolution and presenting evidence'.[54] Noda admitted that 'a big factor' behind the containment of business deconcentration was 'the change in U.S. policy as the Cold War intensified' but claimed that the decision to reorganise only 18 companies 'was also due to our intense advocacy'.[55]

Noda offered examples illustrating how the HCLC defended the interests of businesses designated under the Deconcentration Law. For instance, *Tōyō Seikan* (Tōyō Canning Company), which had absorbed Hokkaidō Canning in 1941, asked the commission if it could spin off its Hokkaidō operation as a way of pre-empting more extensive dissolution. Noda at once set off to inspect the firm's factories in Kyūshū, Tokyo, and Hokkaidō and found that, although the Hokkaidō plant accounted for only 28 percent of the company's business, its production capacity amounted to 40 percent of the total, and on that basis, he persuaded SCAP that cleaving off Tōyō's Hokkaidō division would result in a competitive second firm. In the case of *Nippon Tsūun* or *Nittsū* (Japan Express), which dominated express delivery, SCAP had decided to break it up into several regional companies. The HCLC, however, countered that such a division of Nittsū, which mainly handled delivery of rice at the time, would disrupt the orderly distribution of that staple. Ultimately, SCAP accepted the commission's opinion, and Nittsū avoided dismemberment, though Occupation authorities ordered it to sell or lease to national and private railways its station facilities and to dispose of about a fourth of its 300 ships and directed the government to promote local transport companies to foster competition at the regional level.[56]

Two cases in the food and beverage industry demonstrate the HCLC's efforts to nurture competition on a limited scale but not to the extent that SCAP's trustbusters desired. In the highly concentrated beer industry, Dai Nippon Beer held about a 70 percent share of Japan's total production capacity, and Kirin Beer the remainder. The president of Dai Nippon approached SCAP and the HCLC to have his firm split in two. Welsh wanted to break up Kirin as well – most Japanese observers expected a total of five new companies, three out of Dai Nippon and two out of Kirin[57] – but Noda got Welsh to agree that, if they left Kirin alone and divided Dai Nippon into two concerns, the result would be three competitive firms of roughly equal size. Consequently, Dai Nippon was split into Asahi and Nippon Beer (later renamed Sapporo Beer), with Asahi initially accounting for 37 percent of all production capacity, Nippon for 35 percent, and Kirin for 28 percent. In the dairy industry, *Hokkaidō Rakunō* (Hokkaidō Dairy Cooperative) had far greater power than either Meiji or Morinaga. Accordingly, the HCLC negotiated with

SCAP to require that Hokkaidō Dairy divide into two companies, Hokkaidō Butter and Snow Brand, and dispose of two factories on the main island, one to Meiji and the other to Morinaga. The commission then denied a petition by Meiji and Morinaga to have Snow Brand Dairy restricted in its operations to Hokkaidō and encouraged nationwide competition among the three firms.[58]

Designated companies were not the only ones undergoing reorganisation during the Occupation. As Hadley noted, 'almost all major corporations in Japan' were doing so 'because of insolvency or near-insolvency' after the Japanese government in effect cancelled war indemnity payments to them in October 1946; she added that, even among the 83 designated holding companies, '76 were concurrently engaged in drawing up reorganization plans'. Furthermore, many businesses that the government had forced into mergers during the war wanted to undo them and resume independent operation. Such was the case with the only bank to undergo dissolution during the Occupation, the giant Teikoku Bank, which in 1948 reversed the 'unnatural' wartime consolidation of the Mitsui and Daiichi banks.[59]

'Designated Persons'

The HCLC's treatment of zaibatsu family members suggests a need to qualify the standard interpretation that, owing to runaway inflation, the divestiture of family-owned stocks in exchange for ten-year non-negotiable public bonds amounted to virtual confiscation and, together with the March 1947 capital levy and land reform, wiped out the wealth of zaibatsu owner families. Besides disposing of the stocks that zaibatsu family members held through their combine holding companies, the HCLC also gained authority to deal with the members' direct holdings, and in March 1947, it named 56 members of ten zaibatsu families as 'designated persons' who would have to transfer their personally held securities to the commission.[60] Noda made it clear, however, that the HCLC would only dispose of assets that the owner families disclosed to the commission and would not go on 'fishing expeditions' in search of undeclared assets. When some staff members suggested the HCLC should look into the Nomura family's collection of valuable Noh costumes, for instance, Noda insisted: 'Investigating such items is not the job of the commission'.[61] He also held in strict confidence the lists of assets the families submitted, refusing to show the lists even when the Tax Office asked to see them. He attributed the smooth operation of the individual divestiture program to these procedures.[62]

The HCLC took other steps to soften the blow that zaibatsu families sustained as a result of Occupation policies. For one, Noda persuaded SCAP to modify its decision to require that the families sell all their properties other than main residences and instead allow each family to keep one villa (*bessō*) to 'maintain a minimum living standard'.[63] Furthermore, according to Noda, the HCLC strenuously objected to compensating the zaibatsu families with public bonds that were non-negotiable, non-transferable, and ineligible for use as collateral for ten years. How were the families to eat? Arguing that U.S. taxpayers would have to support the zaibatsu households, Noda finally convinced SCAP to switch the compensation from bonds to cash. As he concluded, 'popular opinion tends to be that zaibatsu assets were confiscated, but we HCLC members persuaded SCAP to give the zaibatsu proper compensation in cash'.[64]

In disposing of the individual and holding-company stocks, the HCLC was to give purchase preference first to employees of each issuing firm and then to local residents at the sites of the company's branches and factories.[65] The commission was next to offer shares to brokers for resale to the public and finally to put up for public auction any remaining stocks. Much to Noda's satisfaction, the employee-first policy saved Kawana hotel and golf resort – an Ōkura zaibatsu subsidiary and favourite of Noda – from the clutches of a scrap-iron dealer from Kyūshū. This upstart (*narikin*) businessman had promised to erect a statue of the current owner, Ōkura Kishichirō, if he could acquire the resort. Hotel employees obtained most of Kishichirō's stocks, which he then later bought back, preserving Noda's beloved golf resort.[66]

The trade name and trademark controversy

The HCLC spent much of its final years fending off Welsh's determined effort to prohibit the use of zaibatsu trade names and trademarks by the ten largest combines. Noda asserted: 'It is no exaggeration to say that the HCLC's battle over this issue was the single most important role the commission performed'.[67] In September 1949, under intense pressure from the Antitrust and Cartels Division, the commission instructed Mitsui, Mitsubishi, and Sumitomo to stop using their old trade names and marks until 1958 and to comply by mid-1950. The HCLC specified that the prohibition would apply to 341 companies and affiliates of Mitsui, 205 of Mitsubishi, and 160 of Sumitomo.[68] Despite concerns that this measure would harm the Japanese economy, the commissioners hoped it would forestall extension of the ban to the other zaibatsu. By January 1950 only a few major companies in each of the 'Big Three' combines were still using the zaibatsu name. The corporate holdouts vehemently opposed the prohibition, the president of Mitsubishi Electric denouncing it as a 'plan for total obliteration of the zaibatsu', and the managing director of Osaka Sumitomo Marine and Fire Insurance declaring similarly that the loss of names and trademarks that 'represented "good will"' and 'enjoyed international reputation . . . would condemn the zaibatsu to death'.[69]

That same January, despite the HCLC's effort to limit the ban, Welsh directed the commission to extend the measure to the other seven leading zaibatsu. The commissioners furiously objected, arguing in particular that changing trade names and marks would impose an undue financial burden on the second-tier zaibatsu and would adversely affect Japan's foreign trade. Prime Minister Yoshida intervened on behalf of the businesses concerned and had the cabinet postpone enforcement of the ban until mid-1951. Before Welsh left for the United States in June 1950, he made one last attempt to force the issue, ordering the HCLC to convene an emergency meeting and decide on implementation of the ban for all ten zaibatsu. Bypassing Welsh, Noda successfully appealed to a senior SCAP adviser, who pressured ESS into cancelling Welsh's order. With Welsh's departure from Japan and the outbreak of the Korean War, SCAP shelved the ban indefinitely. In March 1951 the Japanese government put the final nail in the coffin by formally postponing enforcement of the prohibition yet again, until mid-1952, two months after the Occupation was to end. Once Japan regained independence in April 1952, former zaibatsu companies that had adopted new names and trademarks began restoring their old ones in earnest, completing the process within two years.[70]

Banks

Trade-name alteration was one of the few business reforms that affected banks; for instance, Nomura Bank changed its name to Yamato Bank, and Yasuda Bank to Fuji. Other than the voluntary breakup of Teikoku Bank noted above, however, no financial institution underwent dissolution. As William Tsutsui points out, scholars have tended to attribute the general lack of bank reorganisation 'either to concentrated Japanese opposition or to the reorientation of official [US] policy under the "reverse course"', though he himself emphasizes the 'paralysis' of Occupation financial reform resulting from 'factionalism and indecision' within the SCAP bureaucracy, particularly the jurisdictional tug-of-war between the trustbusters in the Antitrust and Cartels Division and the stabilisers in the Finance Division of ESS.[71] Some historians have suggested that the occupiers' preconceptions about the commercial nature of private banks based on U.S. practice led them to downplay the investment activities of Japanese banks; yet precedents in occupied Germany cast doubt on this explanation, for the extensive holdings of corporate stock by German banks 'horrified most Americans' and prompted the occupying powers to dissolve six of the biggest banks there.[72]

The specific part played by the HCLC in the delay and ultimate derailment of bank restructuring, however, is largely absent from studies of occupied Japan. Although MacArthur, in line with policy directives from Washington, had, in November 1945, expressly called for dissolution of financial as well as industrial, commercial, and agricultural combines, and the Antitrust and Cartels Division pushed for inclusion of financial institutions in both the holding-company and deconcentration programs, the HCLC refused to designate any bank or insurance company under either measure. Fully aware of disagreements between SCAP's antitrust and finance officials, the commission insisted that SCAP permit banks to break up or reorganise voluntarily under the aegis of the Finance Division, which, for its part, held that no bank dissolutions should take place until Japan's economy showed signs of stable recovery. Shortly after the Diet promulgated the Deconcentration Law in December 1947, MacArthur indicated to Washington that SCAP would have six banks designated as 'excessive concentrations', yet not one financial institution appeared on the list of 325 designated companies that the HCLC finalised in February 1948. After the DRB recommended the removal of banks from consideration for dissolution, the HCLC publicly announced in late July 1948 that, because former combine banks were no longer tied to holding companies and were subject to the Anti-Monopoly Law, they would not be liable for designation or restructuring under the Deconcentration Law.[73] As both Bisson and Hadley maintained, the omission of zaibatsu banks was crucial, for it meant that SCAP's business reforms left largely untouched 'a major instrument of combine ownership and revival', as commercial banks soon replaced holding companies as 'nuclear centres' of former zaibatsu groups.[74]

The results of Occupation business reforms

Many historians have tended to minimise the long term significance of zaibatsu dissolution under the U.S. Occupation of Japan. The HCLC's part in delaying and containing SCAP programs would seem to offer qualified support for such a view; nonetheless, what the commission did carry out in the way of reform was fairly substantial. Of the 83 designated holding companies, the HCLC completely dissolved 16 companies, broke up another 26 with successor firms, and allowed 41 companies to continue, although it ordered 11 of those companies to spin off new enterprises.[75] The HCLC, 'using 10-percent ownership as its definition of subsidiary',[76] identified nearly 1,200 companies as subsidiaries of the top ten zaibatsu. They, in turn, supplied the majority of the 325 companies the commission put on its list of designated firms under the Deconcentration Law.[77] As one SCAP staff member remarked: 'The list reads like a Who's Who of Japanese business'.[78] Yet, of the 18 companies that ultimately underwent 'deconcentration', as the HCLC had already scheduled eight of them for breakup or reorganisation as designated 'holding companies', only ten additional companies ended up being dissolved or restructured. Still, the actions resulting from the combined application of the two reform measures produced a total of 104 new firms and, subtracting dissolved companies, a net total of 60, not an inconsiderable achievement. Moreover, as Mark Metzler states, 'while U.S. efforts did fall short of the goals of GHQ's "zaibatsu busters", the companies they broke up in fact constituted the industrial and commercial core of Japan's economic order'.[79]

Developments after 1952 undid some of what the Occupation had accomplished in breaking up big business concerns. Besides the 104 newly established enterprises, more than three hundred firms emerged from Welsh's atomisation of Mitsui Bussan and Mitsubishi Shōji. Yet, as Theodore Cohen eloquently wrote: 'within five years, like droplets of mercury coalescing into ever bigger drops on contact with each other, both the Mitsubishi and the Mitsui trading companies were substantially reconstituted as before'.[80] The relaxation of the Anti-Monopoly Law beginning in 1949 paved the way eventually for several of the other dissolved firms, such as Mitsubishi Heavy Industries and the successors to Hokkaidō Dairy, to reassemble as well.

The HCLC had modest results in its program to sever horizontal ties among former zaibatsu subsidiaries and other large companies. Under a 1946 imperial ordinance, the commission ordered 'restricted concerns', some 1,200 companies capitalised at ¥5 million or more, to divest themselves of all shareholdings in other companies; their subsidiaries and affiliates were to do so for shares acquired after 8 December 1945, a requirement designed to prevent the parent firms from avoiding divestiture by transferring shares to their satellite companies. The firms were to draw up disposal plans and, after securing HCLC approval, were to carry out the disposals themselves. As Bisson noted, despite the comprehensiveness of the program to dissolve intercorporate networks, 'the results for stock divestiture were surprisingly meagre. In its *Final Report*, the HCLC reported only 616 companies submitting to the procedure'.[81] The Fair Trade Commission, however, carried out a parallel divestiture program aimed at eliminating group cross holdings, receiving stock disposal plans from six times the number of firms and overseeing the sale of shares with twice the total paid-up value as those recorded by the HCLC. The combined operations of the two commissions led to the disposal of stocks worth nearly ¥5 billion in paid-up value.[82] This figure no doubt represented only a portion of the actual cross holdings of business concerns, for the two divestiture programs did little to impede the emergence of bank-centred enterprise groups after 1952.

Corollary to the goal of breaking up combines and individual big businesses through divestment of securities was the objective of achieving 'the widest possible distribution of such securities'.[83] The disposal of shares by the HCLC and other agencies had mixed results in that regard. The HCLC obtained stocks with a total paid-up value of about ¥9 billion, of which some ¥7 billion came from designated companies, half a billion from zaibatsu family members, and about ¥1.5 billion from corporate cross holdings. In addition, the Ministry of Finance appropriated about ¥2 billion in securities to pay the capital levy, the Fair Trade Commission ¥3.3 billion in intercorporate holdings, and a commission set up to liquidate 'closed institutions' such as wartime control companies another ¥4 billion. These stocks represented 42 percent of the paid-up value of all corporate stocks in Japan at the end of 1946.[84]

A raft of challenges faced the public sale of these stocks: thousands of reorganising companies were simultaneously issuing tens of billions of yen in new stocks, the question of reparations removals bred uncertainty until their cancellation in 1949, and the stock exchanges had been closed from 1945 until that year as well, all in the context of an adverse investment environment with rampant inflation and a generally impoverished populace.[85] Despite these complications, by December 1950 the HCLC had managed to dispose of 64 percent of the roughly ¥7.4 billion in securities that the designated holding companies and zaibatsu family members had transferred to it.[86]

To a considerable extent, the stock sell-off met the goal of 'democratising' corporate ownership. By 1951, the HCLC had sold 51 percent of the stocks it had acquired from 787 companies to 117,125 employees of those firms.[87] For paid-up value, Bisson cited data compiled by Eleanor Hadley in 1949 on HCLC stock disposals for the first quarter of that year.[88] Combined with the 1951 figures for total number of securities sold, they suggest 'a wide distribution' but 'of small-scale purchases': stock sales to employees and local residents accounted for only 28 percent of the shares' aggregate paid-up value that quarter, whereas public bidding, which tended to favour concentrated acquisitions, did so for almost

50 percent of the total.[89] The HCLC and other security disposals did trigger a significant temporary increase in the percentage of the total number of issued stocks held by individuals, which leaped from 53 percent in 1945 to 69 percent in 1949 but thereafter slid back to around 55 percent; by contrast, financial institutions steadily raised their share of all stockholdings from a low of 10 percent in 1949 to well over 20 percent by the late 1950s. On the other hand, the number of individual stockholders climbed dramatically during those years, going from fewer than two million in 1945 to more than 13 million in 1960, nearly a six-fold increase adjusted for population growth.[90]

For all that Noda and the HCLC criticised and resisted aspects of the Occupation's trust-busting program, decades later he could look back positively on the program as a whole. In the early 1980s, he wrote:

> By democratizing the Japanese economy, which a handful of zaibatsu families had dominated, zaibatsu dissolution gave birth to a multitude of investors from the general public, produced an entrepreneurial society in which anyone could become a company president, and laid the basis for Japan's subsequent miraculous recovery and high-speed growth as well as current prosperity.[91]

Undoubtedly, Noda took pride in the role that the Holding Company Liquidation Commission had performed, largely under his leadership, in softening the punitive edges of SCAP initiatives while at the same time helping to restructure Japanese business along more open and competitive lines.

Notes

1 See, for instance, J. Roberts, "The 'Japan Crowd' and the Zaibatsu Restoration", *Japan Interpreter*, Vol. 12, Nos. 3–4, Summer 1979, pp. 384–415, and by H. B. Schonberger: "Zaibatsu Dissolution and the American Restoration of Japan", *Bulletin of Concerned Asian Scholars*, Vol. 5, No. 2, 9/1973, pp. 16–31; "The Japan Lobby in American Diplomacy, 1947–1952", *Pacific Historical Review*, Vol. 46, No. 3, 8/1977, pp. 327–359; and *Aftermath of War: Americans and the Remaking of Japan, 1945–1952*, Kent, OH: Kent State University Press, 1989.

2 See especially the masterful studies by E. Takemae, *The Allied Occupation of Japan*, New York: Continuum, 2003, and by J. W. Dower, *Embracing Defeat: Japan in the Wake of World War II*, New York: W. W. Norton, 1999.

3 One exception is the Yasuda combine's pre-emptive proposal for holding-company dissolution. For the text of the Yasuda Plan, see T. A. Bisson, *Zaibatsu Dissolution in Japan*, Berkeley: University of California Press, 1954, pp. 241–243.

4 One of many SCAP 'instructions' or directives written in a special jargon facetiously referred to as 'SCAPINese'. Other Japanese agencies involved in business reform during the Occupation included the Public Utilities Commission, which directed the dissolution of ten power companies; the Closed Institutions Liquidation Commission, which supervised the dissolution of wartime control companies and colonial or semi-colonial organisations, such as the Bank of Taiwan and the South Manchuria Railway Company; and the Fair Trade Commission, which oversaw enforcement of the Deconcentration Law and the divestiture of intercorporate stockholdings not disposed of 'through other channels'. Bisson, *Zaibatsu Dissolution*, pp. 125, 136–137.

5 I. Noda, *Zaibatsu Kaitai Shiki: Watashi no Rirekisho* (A Private Record of Zaibatsu Dissolution: My Life History), Tokyo: Nihon Keizai Shinbunsha, 1983. I wish to thank Professor Morikawa Hidemasa for alerting me to this book and kindly sending me a copy from his personal library.

6 Bisson, *Zaibatsu Dissolution*, p. 102.

7 M. Hosoya, "Selected Aspects of the Zaibatsu Dissolution in Occupied Japan, 1945–1952: The Thought and Behavior of Zaibatsu Leaders, Governmental Officials and SCAP Officials", Ph.D. Dissertation, Yale University, 1982, pp. 107–108, 185, quoting R. Minobe, " 'Shūhai Hō' Tōji no Omoide" (Reminiscences From the Time of the "Deconcentration Law"), *Keizai Hyōron*, Vol. 1, No. 8, 1952, pp. 83, 87.

8 E. M. Hadley, *Antitrust in Japan*, Princeton: Princeton University Press, 1970, p. 69.

9 Noda, *Zaibatsu Kaitai Shiki*, p. 59.

10 Bisson, *Zaibatsu Dissolution*, p. 99.

11 Ibid., p. 102.

12 Hadley, *Antitrust*, p. 69.

13 Bisson, *Zaibatsu Dissolution*, p. 100.

14 Takemae, *The Allied Occupation*, p. 335; Bisson, *Zaibatsu Dissolution*, p. 75.

15 Bisson, *Zaibatsu Dissolution*, pp. 108–109, 133.

16 Noda, *Zaibatsu Kaitai Shiki*, p. 30. Noda recounts his pre-1945 vita on pages 9–53.

17 Ibid., pp. 51–52.

18 Ibid., p. 60.

19 Ibid., p. 62.

20 Ibid., pp. 62–63.

21 On the designation, dissolution, and reorganisation of holding companies, see General Headquarters, Supreme Commander for the Allied Powers, *History of the Non-Military Activities of the Occupation of Japan*, Vol. 24, *Elimination of Zaibatsu Control*, Tokyo: SCAP, 1952, Chapter 2, "Liquidation of Holding Companies". Available on microfilm, Wilmington, DE: Scholarly Resources, 1989, Reel 4. Morikawa Hidemasa states that, although Nakajima Aircraft (part of which became Fuji Heavy Industries in 1950) may not fit the criteria for a zaibatsu head office, SCAP grouped it with the top four zaibatsu holding companies because all of Nakajima's capital came from one family and 'because it controlled a number of subsidiaries and cooperated in the war effort'. H. Morikawa, *Zaibatsu: The Rise and Fall of Family Enterprise Groups in Japan*, Tokyo: University of Tokyo Press, 1992, p. 237.

22 Noda, *Zaibatsu Kaitai Shiki*, p. 200.

23 Holding Company Liquidation Commission, *Final Report on Zaibatsu Dissolution*, Tokyo: HCLC, 1951, p. 20.

24 Ibid., pp. 21, 28–29.

25 Noda, *Zaibatsu Kaitai Shiki*, pp. 153–154.

26 Ibid., p. 63. The head of one HCLC department, for example, had come from the central bank of Manchukuo. Ibid., p. 61.

27 See Bisson, *Zaibatsu Dissolution*, pp. 256–261, for a list of the 83 enterprises the HCLC designated as holding companies by the type of action the commission took, together with a list of the second companies formed from the 37 dissolved firms that had successors; Kabushiki Kaisha Seiri Iinkai, ed., *Nihon Zaibatsu to Sono Kaitai* (Japan's Zaibatsu and Their Dissolution), Tokyo: Hara Shobō, 1974, Vol. 2, pp. 23–88, for details on the 325 firms the HCLC designated under the Deconcentration Law; and Bisson, *Zaibatsu Dissolution*, pp. 291–292, and Hadley, *Antitrust in Japan*, pp. 178–180, for details on the 18 companies that underwent reorganisation under that law. Hadley also lists the 83 designated holding companies by date of designation, which came in five waves from 7 September 1946 to 30 September 1947; in another appendix, she divides the 83 firms into groups according to HCLC action, though she slightly overinflates the number of second companies for Daiken Industries (five instead of

four) and for Toshiba (14 instead of 13). Hadley, *Antitrust in Japan*, pp. 464–465, 515–517.

28 Hadley, *Antitrust in Japan*, p. 76.
29 Noda, *Zaibatsu Kaitai Shiki*, p. 73.
30 Ibid., pp. 72, 155.
31 Ibid., p. 158.
32 See, for example, E. Welsh, "Designation of Hitachi Engineering Works", 16/12/1948, and "Designation of Furukawa Electric Company", 7/3/1949, in *The Occupation of Japan: Economic Reform, Part 1 Deconcentration and Modernization of Economic Power*, Bethesda, MD: Congressional Information Service and Tokyo: Maruzen, 1994–1995 (hereafter *The Occupation of Japan*), 4–115–01.45 and 4–115–01.34.
33 Noda, *Zaibatsu Kaitai Shiki*, p. 158. Theodore Cohen, who also served in ESS, described Welsh as 'wiry, quick, intelligent, articulate, and contentious' with 'a stubbornness and an inflexibility' about zaibatsu dissolution. T. Cohen, *Remaking Japan: The American Occupation as New Deal*, ed., H. Passin, New York: Free Press, 1987, p. 352.
34 Noda, *Zaibatsu Kaitai Shiki*, p. 65; Bisson, *Zaibatsu Dissolution*, pp. 109–110.
35 Bisson, *Zaibatsu Dissolution*, p. 261; Hadley, *Antitrust*, p. 179.
36 In a proposal to the HCLC in April 1948, Furukawa Electric had requested that, if its breakup was unavoidable, the company be divided into no more than three firms. Nihon Keiei Shi Kenkyūjo, ed., *Sōgyō Hyaku-nen Shi* (Centennial History), Tokyo: Furukawa Denki Kōgyō Kabushiki Kaisha, 1991, p. 113. In a memo to the DRB in January 1949, Welsh had recommended splitting the company in two, but four months later, with the DRB's blessing, the HCLC cancelled Furukawa Electric's designation as an excessive concentration of economic power. E. Welsh, "Reorganization of Furu-kawa Electric Company", 14/1/1949, and T. Sasayama, "Order of Cancellation of Des-ignation", 20/5/1949, in *The Occupation of Japan*, 4–115–01.34.
37 In its proposal for dividing Japan Steel into two firms, the HCLC, in a departure from normal practice, included the dissenting views of two members, newspaper editorial writer Minobe Ryōkichi and economist Wakimura Yoshitarō, who opposed any reor-ganisation of the company on the grounds that iron making in Japan 'intrinsically' had to take a concentrated form and that division of the firm carried the 'danger of raising the cost'. HCLC, "Final Order of Reorganization", 17/12/1948, in *The Occupation of Japan*, 4–115–01.163. On 1 April 1950 Japan Steel was broken up into two steel mak-ers, a shipping firm, and a firebrick manufacturer. Yawata Seitetsujo Shoshi Hensan Jikkō Iinkai, ed., *Yawata Seitetsujo Hachijū-nen Shi: Sōgō Shi* (Eighty-Year History of Yawata Steel Works: General History), Kitakyūshū: Shin Nippon Seitetsu Kabushiki Kaisha Yawata Seitetsujo, 1980, p. 193.
38 Noda, *Zaibatsu Kaitai Shiki*, pp. 202–204.
39 Deconcentration Review Board, "Matter of Mitsubishi Heavy Industries Company", 12/4/1949, in *The Occupation of Japan*, 4–115–1.97.
40 Noda, *Zaibatsu Kaitai Shiki*, pp. 83–84. Cohen, *Remaking Japan*, p. 358 for the 70 per-cent figure. Daiken in fact proposed reorganisation into five new companies, including two textile firms, but the HCLC apparently convinced Welsh that Daiken's textile oper-ation did not constitute an excessive concentration of economic power and should be kept intact. Antitrust and Cartels Division to DRB, "Reorganization of Daiken Com-pany", 21/1/1949, and Welsh to DRB, "Designation of Daiken Company", 15/2/1949, in *The Occupation of Japan*, 4–115–1.11.
41 Noda, *Zaibatsu Kaitai Shiki*, pp. 74–76, 166; Cohen, *Remaking Japan*, p. 358. See also General Headquarters, Supreme Commander for the Allied Powers, *History of the Non-Military Activities of the Occupation of Japan*, Vol. 24, Chapter 6, "Dissolution of Zaibatsu Trading Companies and the East Asia Shipping Company". In April 1947, Mitsui Bussan itself had drawn up plans to split the firm into ten companies on a geo-graphical basis but in subsequent discussions with GHQ officials 'sensed hints of a

more favorable trend' and came to think that division into five or six units might satisfy SCAP. The dissolution order, therefore, was all the more 'stunning in its unexpectedness and shocking in its severity'. *The 100 Year History of Mitsui & Co., Ltd.*, Tokyo: Mitsui & Co., 1977, pp. 4–5, 149–150. Noda exclaimed in the HCLC's 1951 report: that the two trading companies 'should have to be utterly destructed and crushed to the bones and dissolved under conditions unprecedentedly strict and severe' eluded even the commission's explanation. HCLC, *Final Report*, p. 47.

42 G. C. Allen lent credence to Noda's speculation when he wrote that some members of a postwar planning committee he had headed in the British Foreign Office pressed for 'various restrictions' on Japanese industries partly 'with an eye . . . on their future competitive capability in international markets' and that the Board of Trade in particular had called for 'measures to prevent the re-emergence of competition with British textiles in overseas markets'. G. C. Allen, *Japan's Economic Policy*, London: Palgrave Macmillan, 1980, pp. 187, 191. I am grateful to Janet Hunter for pointing out this source.

43 J. O. Haley, *Antitrust in Germany and Japan: The First Fifty Years, 1947–1998*, Seattle: University of Washington Press, 2001, p. 28. On Allied and especially British opposition to U.S. proposals for combine dissolution in Germany, see also W. Wells, *Antitrust and the Formation of the Postwar World*, New York: Columbia University Press, 2002, pp. 148, 167–170.

44 Morikawa, *Zaibatsu*, p. 238; Noda, *Zaibatsu Kaitai Shiki*, p. 170.

45 On the drafting, evolution, and modification of the Deconcentration Law, see General Headquarters, Supreme Commander for the Allied Powers, *History of the Non-Military Activities of the Occupation of Japan*, Vol. 25, *Deconcentration of Economic Power*, Chapters 1–3, Reel 5.

46 Haley, *Antitrust in Germany and Japan*, pp. 33–34.

47 Kabushiki Kaisha Seiri Iinkai, ed., *Nihon Zaibatsu to Sono Kaitai*, Vol. 2, pp. 23–88.

48 Noda, *Zaibatsu Kaitai Shiki*, pp. 80, 180; HCLC, *Final Report*, pp. 58–59.

49 For more on the DRB, see General Headquarters, Supreme Commander for the Allied Powers, *History of the Non-Military Activities of the Occupation of Japan*, Vol. 25, Chapter 4, "The Deconcentration Review Board".

50 K. Kawai, *Japan's American Interlude*, Chicago: University of Chicago Press, 1960, p. 147. See, for instance, Schonberger, "Zaibatsu Dissolution and the American Restoration of Japan," p. 27, and D. C. James, *The Years of MacArthur, Vol. III, Triumph and Disaster, 1945–1964*, Boston: Houghton Mifflin, 1985, p. 251. The figure 1,200 refers to another classification, namely, 'restricted companies' – firms in which the top ten zaibatsu holding companies or their main subsidiaries held ten percent or more of the capital – that were required under a November 1946 ordinance to divest themselves of shareholdings in other firms. Hadley, *Antitrust*, pp. 73–76; Kabushiki Kaisha Seiri Iinkai, ed., *Nihon Zaibatsu to Sono Kaitai*, Vol. 2, pp. 343–395.

51 Bisson, *Zaibatsu Dissolution*, pp. 144, 148; Hadley, *Antitrust*, pp. 178–180.

52 Noda, *Zaibatsu Kaitai Shiki*, p. 80.

53 Ibid., pp. 78, 80.

54 Ibid., p. 81.

55 Ibid., p. 81. Economist Wakimura Yoshitarō, a 'part-time' member of the HCLC, suggested that the commission played an even bigger role in these deliberations; according to him, the DRB and the HCLC made the decisions while Welsh simply offered his 'opinions for reference' (*sankō iken*). Y. Andō, ed., *Shōwa Keizai Shi e no Shōgen* (Witness to Shōwa Economic History), Tokyo: Asahi Shinbunsha, 1966, Vol. 2, p. 191. My thanks to Laura Hein for recommending this source.

56 Noda, *Zaibatsu Kaitai Shiki*, pp. 84–85.

57 Y. Miyake, *Bīru Kigyō Shi* (History of the Beer Industry), Tokyo: Mitakisha, 1977, p. 150.

58 Noda, *Zaibatsu Kaitai Shiki*, pp. 85–86, 200; Hadley, *Antitrust*, p. 179; K. Kimura, *Hokkaidō Rakunō Hyaku-nen Shi* (Centennial History of Hokkaidō Dairy Cooperative),

Tokyo: Jusonbō, 1985, p. 89. The HCLC had originally recommended the division of Hokkaidō Dairy into three companies and the sale of three of its plants but by November 1949 had changed its recommendation to a two-firm reorganisation; the commission issued its final order to Hokkaidō Dairy on 22 January 1950. HCLC, "Findings of Fact for Rakuno", 27/6/1949, and Antitrust and Cartels Division and FTC, "Hokkaidō Rakuno Reorganization", 12/11/1949, in *The Occupation of Japan*, 4–115–1.49; Kimura, *Hokkaidō Rakunō Hyaku-nen Shi*, pp. 87–89.

59 Hadley, *Antitrust*, pp. 115–116, 118–120.
60 Kabushiki Kaisha Seiri Iinkai, ed., *Nihon Zaibatsu to Sono Kaitai*, Vol. 2, pp. 2–3.
61 Noda, *Zaibatsu Kaitai Shiki*, p. 210.
62 Ibid., p. 68.
63 Ibid., p. 151.
64 Ibid., pp. 150–151. For the June 1947 amendment of the HCLC ordinance to permit cash payments, see General Headquarters, Supreme Commander for the Allied Powers, *History of the Non-Military Activities of the Occupation of Japan*, Vol. 24, Chapter 4, "Surveillance of Zaibatsu Persons and Termination of Family Control", p. 126. Sumitomo came out of the Occupation with the most wealth of any zaibatsu family owing to its large holdings of forestland, which SCAP had left out of the land reform. Hadley, *Antitrust*, p. 60.
    In his memoir, Noda neglected to mention the impact on zaibatsu family wealth of runaway inflation: from 1945 to 1950, the total net assets of the designated persons fell by only 17 percent in nominal terms but by over 97 percent in actual value. HCLC, *Final Report*, p. 67.
65 Bisson, *Zaibatsu Dissolution*, p. 116.
66 Noda, *Zaibatsu Kaitai Shiki*, pp. 70, 198–199. Noda would later become president of Hotel Okura.
67 Ibid., p. 216.
68 Kabushiki Kaisha Seiri Iinkai, ed., *Nihon Zaibatsu to Sono Kaitai*, Vol. 1, p. 465. For a detailed discussion of the trade name and trademark controversy, see Hosoya, "Selected Aspects", pp. 186–243.
69 Hosoya, "Selected Aspects", pp. 199–200.
70 Ibid., pp. 211–213, 230, 242; Noda, *Zaibatsu Kaitai Shiki*, pp. 86–87, 215–219.
71 W. M. Tsutsui, *Banking Policy in Japan: American Efforts at Reform During the Occupation*, London: Routledge, 1988. SCAP did, however, require banks to divest of stockholdings in companies within their combine networks under the 1946 ordinance on intercorporate ties described below.
72 Wells, *Antitrust*, p. 153. The U.S. occupation in Germany placed a higher priority on financial reorganisation than did its counterpart in Japan, as Tsutsui points out; difference in timing was another factor: the German occupiers carried out the dissolution of banks before the full weight of Cold War concerns hit.
73 Noda, *Zaibatsu Kaitai Shiki*, pp. 145–146; Hosoya, "Selected Aspects", pp. 161–162; Bisson, *Zaibatsu Dissolution*, p. 145.
74 Hadley, *Antitrust*, p. 72; Bisson, *Zaibatsu Dissolution*, pp. 154–155.
75 Bisson, *Zaibatsu Dissolution*, pp. 256–261.
76 Hadley, *Antitrust*, p. 74.
77 Kabushiki Kaisha Seiri Iinkai, ed., *Nihon Zaibatsu to Sono Kaitai*, Vol. 2, pp. 24–88, 468–469.
78 Cited in James, *The Years of MacArthur*, p. 173.
79 M. Metzler, *Capital as Will and Imagination: Schumpeter's Guide to the Postwar Japanese Miracle*, Ithaca: Cornell University Press, 2013, p. 79.
80 Cohen, *Remaking Japan*, p. 358.
81 Bisson, *Zaibatsu Dissolution*, pp. 124–125. Confusingly, the 1,200 'restricted companies' were firms – including non-zaibatsu ones – whose assets the Japanese government

froze on SCAP orders in 1945 and were not identical to the 1,200 firms that the HCLC determined in 1946 to be subsidiaries of the top ten zaibatsu. Hadley, *Antitrust*, pp. 73–74.

82 Bisson, *Zaibatsu Dissolution*, pp. 125–126.

83 Hadley, *Antitrust*, p. 184, citing the law enacted in January 1947 establishing the Securities Coordinating Liquidation Committee, which coordinated the sale of securities by the HCLC, the Ministry of Finance, and the Closed Institutions Liquidation Commission. The chair of HCLC also headed the SCLC.

84 HCLC, *Final Report*, pp. 69–70.

85 Bisson, *Zaibatsu Dissolution*, pp. 114–115; Hadley, *Antitrust*, pp. 181–183; E. M. Hadley, with P. H. Kuwayama, *Memoir of a Trustbuster: A Lifelong Adventure With Japan*, Honolulu: University of Hawaii Press, 2003, p. 117.

86 HCLC, *Final Report*, p. 74. The commission was unable to sell about a third of the transferred shares; describing them as 'nothing but carcasses of the former Zaibatsus and in no way significant [for] control over enterprises', it returned those shares to their former owners between December 1950 and March 1951. Ibid., pp. 74–75.

87 Kabushiki Kaisha Seiri Iinkai, ed., *Nihon Zaibatsu to Sono Kaitai*, Vol. 2, pp. 506–507.

88 Bisson, *Zaibatsu Dissolution*, p. 119.

89 Ibid., pp. 118–119.

90 Hadley, *Antitrust*, pp. 193–194.

91 Noda, *Zaibatsu Kaitai Shiki*, p. 54.

2 Japan's postwar social metabolic crisis

Mark Metzler

Introduction

In the autumn of 1945, the people of Japan faced a multilevel calorific crisis. Under wartime restrictions, supplies of food, energy, and basic materials for civilian use had been contracting for five years or more. With the war's end, supplies were still further curtailed – energy supplies especially – reducing production of many basic goods to half or less of their pre-war levels. The country was returned to its island boundaries, and resource exchanges with other countries were largely cut off. This great contraction took place in one of the most surveilled and enumerated societies in the world, and the abundant statistics tell a story that is both detailed and stark. It was a kind of 'natural experiment', happening at some of the frontiers of human historical experience. The historical moment is doubly significant because this phase of radical constriction was followed, within a decade, by a tremendous ramping up of national material and energy usage, which would continue for another two decades at a pace that had not yet been seen in human industrial history.

This chapter outlines some aspects of postwar Japan's suddenly 'primitive state', as it was called by economic planner Ōkita Saburō, who perceived a calorific crisis happening simultaneously at the level of individual bodies, households, and entire industrial systems. Ōkita's energy-centred vision of economics brings these different levels into a single focus. The chapter also describes how Japan was poised, even before the war, at a number of resource frontiers. This situation was frequently interpreted in Malthus-type terms, whereby population pressure would induce social and economic calamities. It turned out instead to be a Boserup-type developmental frontier, with population pressure inducing organisational and technical intensification. This frontier position is more obvious in retrospect, making Japan's extreme postwar circumstances productive for thinking about other times, other places, and wider sets of industrial and ecological concerns. The chapter is intended as a step toward a larger ecological economic history of Japanese industrialisation. As a distinct field of research activity, ecological economic *history* does not yet exist under that name, although interest in the subject is arising from multiple directions. Ecological *economics* has already emerged as a new field, and part of its distinctiveness is a rejection of conventionally constructed boundaries between the 'social' and the 'environmental', or between the 'economic' and everything else.[1] As a method, ecological economics tends to focus on physical and biological indicators rather than on the monetary (or 'value') indicators that serve as the data for most economic analyses. Such a materially focused approach is especially necessary for thinking about late 1940s Japan, when basic material-supply problems were overwhelmingly salient (and when monetary conventions, in a time of record-high inflation, had become self-evidently arbitrary and unstable). Such an approach also reflects the thinking of the time itself.

Imagine an island world . . .

The situation of Japan being abruptly restricted to its island boundaries also connects to a thought experiment proposed in 1945 by the American natural resources geographer Edward A. Ackerman:

> Perhaps the best way to appreciate Japan's resources and their potential uses will be to consider a hypothetical situation. Suppose Japan were to continue a peacetime life sealed off economically from the rest of the world, very much in the manner of Tokugawa days.

During the war, Ackerman had conducted research on Japan's natural resources at Harvard University and taught at the School for Overseas Administration, established in 1943 to train cadres to govern prospective U.S.-occupied territories.[2] He came to Tokyo in October 1946 as Technical Advisor to the Natural Resources office of the Allied Occupation government (General Headquarters, hereafter GHQ); there, he directed a comprehensive national resource survey and authored a monumental report on the subject. He was later a top administrator in the Tennessee Valley Authority (TVA). Ackerman's work earned the respect of his Japanese collaborators, who were impressed by his ethic as an activist, politically neutral technical administrator and by his 'New Deal'-style developmental vision.[3]

As Ackerman suggested, a look back to Tokugawa times does indeed bring resource questions to the centre of the picture. The most fundamental question concerns the high ratio of population to farmable land. In the 80 years that had passed since the Tokugawa shogunate ended, this basic social-ecological challenge had not gone away. In fact, the monstrous continental land grabs conducted by the Japanese military had been justified especially after 1931 in population and resource terms – a line of argument that Ackerman was concerned to disprove. What would it mean if Japan's people now had to live within their own national calorific means? The recurring great famines of late Tokugawa times suggested one scenario. In that era, following the famine of the early 1730s, Japan's national population had levelled off for more than a century, at around 30 million people, as the country reached an apparent impasse in terms of the ratio of population to resources.[4] As of late 1945, the Japanese home islands would have to support twice that many, 72 million people. In 1946, they were joined by more than

four million Japanese who had returned from overseas. By 1949, the national population would reach 82 million.[5] Nonetheless, the message Ackerman delivered
in Tokyo concerning Japan's population/resource balance was an optimistic one.

Ackerman's message was particularly highly evaluated by the engineer-econo-
mist Ōkita Saburō. During the war, Ōkita, a power-systems engineer by training,
had been the official in charge of the electrical grid in Japanese-occupied north
China. Following that experience, he worked on resource surveys in Japan itself.
Beginning on 16 August 1945, the very day after Japan's surrender, Ōkita, then
just over 30 years old, became the de facto executive secretary for a series of governmental advisory councils that guided the planning of postwar economic recovery. In late 1946, when Ackerman arrived in Tokyo, Ōkita was working closely
with Arisawa Hiromi and others to design the 'Priority Production System', an
authoritative central plan intended to break the energy impasse by concentrating
scarce resources on coal mining. For several months beginning in January 1947,
Ōkita was temporarily a '*rōnin*' on leave from government service, and together
with a few colleagues he met almost weekly with Ackerman. It was, one can
imagine, an intensive research and practical seminar on both sides.[6] Ōkita went
on to become the top economic planning official in the Japanese government and
also later served as an influential development advisor to other Asian countries.
He finished his political career as the Japanese representative to the Trilateral
Commission and foreign minister in the Ōhira cabinet in 1979–1980.

Of special interest here are the themes and methods that Ōkita's approach
shares with recent analyses of what has been termed *industrial metabolism* or
social-economic metabolism, meaning people's material and energy exchanges
with their surrounding environments. Since the 1990s, analysts have begun to
systematically enumerate these material processes at the level of national economies according to the methods of *material flow accounting* (MFA; or *material and
energy flow accounting*, MEFA), constructing a parallel materially based system
of national accounts that counts economic activity in physical measures (tons,
gigajoules) rather than in monetary 'value' units.[7] As ecological economist Joan
Martinez-Alier and his co-authors write, physical, social, and 'economic' (meaning monetary) indicators are *non-equivalent* descriptions of economic activity.[8]
In fact, they may tell radically different stories. These energy and flow-based
conceptions of economic processes, recently inspired by ecological concerns, are
remarkably similar to the engineering inspired conceptions of national economy
developed by Ōkita and other Japanese government planners immediately after
the war. They also share some common intellectual lineages.[9] These linkages
appear clearly in their practical dimensions when one focuses on basic supplies of
food, fuel, fertilizer, basic materials, and transportation, and the remainder of this
chapter takes up each of these in turn.

Bodily level energy crisis

Central to Ōkita Saburō's method, which belongs to the larger stream that
would later be called systems theory, was an energy-based calorific vision that

brought the levels of human bodily energies, machine energies, and national or transnational systems of energy provision into a single quantitative framework. Bodily 'economic ecologies' are the most quickly and intuitively grasped. In 1946, questions of food supply and food rationing were understood as matters of life and death, and calorie counting was a basic technique of administrative allocation systems.

The numbers do indeed tell a story here. On the consumption side, family budget surveys show a picture of chronic hunger in urban areas. According to surveys in Tokyo, average calorific intake per person was at a level of 1,200 kcal per day during the hungry summer months of 1946. It improved to the level of 1,700 kcal at the end of 1946, but then fell back to around 1,200 kcal/day in the first half of 1947 – the classic 'spring hunger' characteristic of a year of dearth. In Tokyo and Osaka in late 1946 and 1947, price-controlled (rationed) food provided, at best, about 1,000 to 1,300 kcal per person per day. During the late spring and summer of 1947, the amount provided through officially sanctioned channels fell to 700 to 900 kcal per day. Tokyo and Osaka households were then spending two-thirds to three-quarters of their income on food. In Tokyo, price-controlled food provided about 60 to 75 percent of calories, costing on average about 20 percent of monthly household budgets. For the rest of their food, people turned to much more expensive black-market sources (providing roughly a third of calories, but taking 70 to 90 percent of household spending).[10]

Some ten million people also left the cities, causing Japan's population profile temporarily to revert to a more rural pattern. In February 1944, the urban population was recorded as 30.3 million people and the rural population as 42 million. By November 1945, the urban population was down to 19.5 million, while the rural population had risen to 52.5 million.[11] More people available for farm work meant more farm production, but with drastically diminishing returns per person working. It also meant more pressure on food supplies in the farm villages themselves.

On the production side of the national food picture, national rice harvests in the late 1930s ran at a level of around 65 million *koku*, or about nine million tons per year (one *koku*, a traditional per-person annual grain ration, equalled 180.4 litres, or about 150 kilograms of brown rice.). State authorities prioritised rice production over other crops during the war, and a good domestic rice harvest – over eight million tons – had been expected for 1945. This would have meant a national rice supply of more than one-tenth of a ton (100 kg) per person, not taking into account losses in storage and distribution (which were drastic in a year of heavy firebombing). However, in the autumn of 1945, poor weather reduced the actual harvest to only 6.45 million tons.[12]

At the beginning of the Pacific War, about 15 percent of the national food supply was provided by imports, mainly of rice, sugar, soybeans, and salt. Although 15 percent of the national food supply may sound relatively modest, in effect these imports equalled more than 40 percent of the urban food supply. To this extent, Japan's urban food supply networks had extended overseas. In the years before the war, total food imports ran at a level of more than four million tons annually, and in 1941, food imports peaked at 4.36 million tons. In 1945, only 1.85 million tons of food were imported. Rice alone had been imported at a rate of about 1.8 million tons per year in 1936-1942. Only 236,000 tons of rice were imported in 1945.[13]

The basically urban nature of this external dependency is reflected also in the distribution of postwar U.S. food aid. The worst point in the food crisis came in the first half of 1946. U.S. food shipments – more than 400,000 tons of wheat and wheat flour – covered a significant share of Japanese food needs.[14] In the summer of 1946, U.S. food aid actually covered the majority of Tokyo food needs. A good autumn harvest in 1946 improved things greatly, but the basic food deficit remained.

Dependency on external sources was especially high when it came to protein. Animal protein in the Japanese diet consisted almost entirely of fish, and Japan before the Pacific War was the largest fishing country in the world, systematically exploiting the natural biological production of vast oceanic regions. Here one can see a dimension in which Japan was at a kind of *developmental frontier* – at 'nature's edge', in a way of speaking. William Tsutsui's chapter in the present volume forcefully brings out some implications of this dependency.[15] It is also notable that large amounts of fishmeal and soybean cake had been used as fertilizers, mainly in rice farming. With the loss of colonial fishing areas and the destruction or immobilisation of much of Japan's fishing fleet, the national fisheries catch fell drastically (coastal fisheries from around two million tons to around one million tons; colonial fisheries from around two million tons to nothing).[16] The near disappearance of diesel fuel also meant that fishing for several years relied heavily on wooden sailing boats – a temporary reversion to an 'organic' (pre-fossil fuel) economy. Fishermen had begun to adopt diesel engines only in the past generation, so the knowledge of older methods fortunately remained, and a people farther in time from their pre-industrial traditions might have been less resilient. Simultaneously, the stoppage of soybean imports from Manchuria – previously more than 800,000 tons per year[17] – cut off Japan's main source of supply of vegetable protein.

Japan's position at a developmental frontier appears in agricultural production also, though this might not seem obvious on the surface of things. Farm work in Japan remained practically unmechanised – when it came to work in the fields, people's own bodily energies supplied the main motive force, meaning that the most important 'fuels' were rice, barley, and sweet potatoes. The employment of draft animals was also very low in comparison to agriculture in most other world regions. Therefore, as 'the first step toward the modernization of the nation's agriculture', Ōkita Saburō and collaborators argued in their 1946 *Plan for the Reconstruction of the Japanese Economy* for the greater use of animal power, meaning more horses and oxen. Needless to say, greater use of animals would not have struck an American agricultural expert as a form of modernisation. Moreover, as the 1946 report noted, most Japanese farms were too small even for the effective employment of animal power.[18] Draft animals also needed their own 'fuel' – rice straw, for instance – but in this era of maximum utilisation, use of straw for animal fodder competed with alternative uses of it as fertilizer, fuel for cooking, or as a raw material for making other products. Use of powered machinery in agriculture was largely limited to water pumps and to a modest number of trucks for transportation, most of which were in a poor state of repair.[19]

In fact, Japanese agriculture may well have been the most labour-intensive, in terms of hours of farmers' labour applied per unit of land, of any country in the world. Japanese farmers do though also appear to have produced the highest calorific yields per unit of land of any country, and Japan may also have had the highest national population density per unit of arable land of any large country. As a converter of solar energy into usable food grains, paddy rice produces some of the highest possible calorific yields per unit of land. Sweet potatoes, another staple, produce an even higher calorific yield per hectare.[20] Sweet potato production also held up quite well during these years, though compared to food grains, sweet potatoes had the disadvantage of being harder to transport and store.

Japan's agricultural position at this kind of per-hectare calorific frontier brings to mind Ester Boserup's macrohistorical schema wherein the increase of population drives the intensification of agricultural land use in a stepwise fashion. In these terms, the growing of multiple crops per year using wet-rice agriculture was historically the most intensive form of organic agriculture, requiring the highest labour inputs and yielding the highest calorific outputs per unit of land.[21] At the time, the very full exploitation of the possibilities of this type of agriculture seemed a potentially stark example of a Malthusian resource frontier. In Boserup's anti-Malthusian view, the approach to this kind of population/resource frontier could be taken not only as a danger but also as a stimulus and opportunity.

Postwar Japanese harvest shortfalls were further worsened by severe shortages of fertilizer. Japanese rice farming in the 1930s had already begun to depend heavily on chemical fertilizers, which also constituted farmers' single most expensive input.[22] 'Japan depends more on fertilizer than any other country in the world', in the words of GHQ economist Jerome Cohen.[23] The technologically advanced chemical complexes built during the 1920s and 1930s appeared to belong to a different era from the world of the rice fields, but in fact, looking at the two together, one sees another place where Japan, viewed in world-historical terms, was at a production frontier. During the war, fertilizer factories were converted to explosives production, and production of chemical fertilizer declined drastically. In 1945, production levels of the three major chemical fertilizers (ammonium sulphate, calcium cyanimide, and calcium superphosphate) had dropped, respectively, to one-fifth, one-third, and one-eighth of their former peak levels.[24]

Production of chemical fertilizer, in turn, required calorific inputs from hydropower or coal. As Ōkita Saburō put it, the electro-chemical industry 'us[es] electric power as a raw material'.[25] Calcium carbide, used to make calcium cyanamide fertilizer, was made by mixing lime and coke at very high temperature (2,200° C), which could be achieved only by using electric arc furnaces – so electrical power itself was an essential 'material' in the manufacturing process. During 1946 and 1947, when power generation relied almost entirely on hydropower, fertilizer production was thus lower during the drier winter months and higher during the June–July rainy season, so energy shortfalls also meant shortages of fertilizer.

One of the greatest savings of using commercial fertilizers was in terms of farmers' labour time, and the lack of commercial fertilizer therefore meant a further intensification of human labour. Simultaneously, the postwar increase in rural population made possible (and necessitated) a greater application of such labour. Organic methods of fertilisation had been developed to a very high degree in Japan, and they remained within farmers' field of experience. However, even the volume of green manure was estimated to have been drastically reduced during the postwar crisis, from a level of over five million tons in the years up to 1942 to less than half that in 1946 and 1947.[26] Despite these shortages, agricultural yields generally held up well. However, this was thought to represent a kind of eating into the 'capital' of existing soil fertility and to be unsustainable without renewed large inputs of nitrogen and other fertilizers in the medium term. The use of green fertilizer also created a further source of pressure on hillside vegetation.

In this context, it is interesting to consider Ōkita's reasoning in 1946 concerning the potential gains of introducing powered machinery into agriculture. 'When a person expends labour, he has to always consume calories and has to eat food to supplement the calories consumed', Ōkita wrote. He therefore estimated the fuel costs of work done by coal, petroleum, and electrical power compared to the fuel (rice and barley) costs of work done by human bodily power, as shown in Table 2.1.

On the basis of these calculations, Ōkita concluded that 'human power requires fuels that cost ten times as much as those required by other forms of power'. Thus, 'to use human power when mechanical power will do as well is the same as throwing rice, instead of coal, into [the firebox of] a boiler'. Reflecting the near-famine

Table 2.1 Ōkita Saburō's Calculations of the Fuel Costs of Human Labour Compared to those of Powered Machinery (1946)

Type of Fuel	Price	Price/10,000 kcal	Ratio of Calorific Energy Converted into Work	Cost of Fuel/Unit of Work*
Rice and barley	1 gō† = 500 kcal = ¥0.03	¥0.600	Human Power: 30%	100
Coal	1 kg = 6,000 kcal = ¥0.015	¥0.025	Steam Engine: 10%	13
Petroleum	1 kg = 11,000 kcal = ¥0.04	¥0.036	Petroleum Engine: 20%	9
Electric Power	1 kWh = 860 kcal = ¥0.02	¥0.230	Electric Motor: 90%	13

* With rice and barley set equal to 100. A conventional idea was that people in farming households ate a 70:30 rice-barley mix.
† One *gō* = 0.18 litres. 1,000 *gō* = 1 *koku*.

Source: Ōkita et al., *Postwar Reconstruction*, pp. 122–123; Nakamura and Ōmori, *Nihon Keizai Saiken*, pp. 218–219.

conditions of 1946, it is striking that Ōkita argued for the mechanisation of farm labour not because it saved people's time and labour but rather because the introduction of powered machinery might enable people 'to economize on food consumption by 500 [kilo]calories per farm worker' per day (that is, by one *go* of grain, a standard serving). Adding these small savings up at the national level, this would make it possible 'to economize on the consumption of rice and barley by five million *koku* per year' (meaning roughly a subsistence ration for five million people).[27] Ōkita was, of course, appealing to the overriding concerns of the time; his long term vision was one of technological improvement in order to increase social welfare. Nonetheless, the logic is revealing. This 'energetic' thinking is also a conceptual bridge between quantified food system analysis and national-level industrial analysis.

National-level energy crisis

'In the same way that human existence is based on the supply of calories . . . the activity level of a country is ruled by the supply of energy', as Ōkita put it.[28] Japan's total national throughput of energy (fuels, electric power) reached its highest point yet during the war years of 1938-1943, when the per capita energy supply reached the level of eight million kcal per person.[29] However, this 'average' number is not so informative socially, as at the time much of this energy was consumed by military agencies and used to destroy other people's lives and resources. Simply stopping this kind of energy usage was a gain.[30] Nonetheless, when the national supply of energy fell back to 3.7 million kcal per person in 1946, this reduction signified a great constriction of civilian energy use and also meant a general industrial crisis. National energy use did not regain the wartime level of eight million kcal/person until 1957 – at that time used almost entirely for civilian purposes and signifying the biggest economic boom yet seen in Japanese history.[31]

National energy use, as calculated in these estimates, does not include the flux of solar energy converted into agricultural crops, nor the animal power of horses or oxen (of which there were relatively few), nor the wind/sail power that helped drive small fishing vessels. These numbers do though include the biomass energy embodied in firewood and charcoal, which was sizable.

Breaking down estimates of Japan's total primary energy supply (TPES) by source gives the following picture for the years 1940 and 1946 (Table 2.2).

At the nationally aggregated level reflected by these numbers, coal and hydroelectric power were the bases of the national energy system. Socially, however, it is informative to start by considering the household level, meaning firewood and charcoal, which remained the main fuels for both cooking and home heating. Historically, of course, these were the oldest forms of fuel. Far from being displaced by other fuels, however, usage of firewood and charcoal had actually increased substantially in the 1930s in parallel with the increase in population. Use of biomass fuels thus reached an all-time peak in the decades from the 1930s through to the 1950s and then fell off rapidly in the 1960s.

Table 2.2 Japan's Total Primary Energy Supply (TPES) by Source, in Units of 10 Billion (10^{10}) Kcal and Percent of Total

Year	Total	Firewood and Charcoal	Coal	Hydroelectric	Petroleum
1940	634,000	66,000 (10%)	421,000 (66%)	101,000 (16%)	45,000 (7%)
1946	284,000	37,000 (13%)	127,000 (45%)	113,000 (40%)	6,000 (2%)

Source: *EDMC Handbook* (2007), pp. 226–229. Conversion factors: 1 gigajoule (GJ) = 10^9 joules $\approx 2.39 \times 10^5$ kcal. 1 kilowatt-hour (kWh) = 0.0036 GJ.

The most extreme moment of pressure on wood fuel resources doubtlessly came in 1945, when civilian need, combined with military fanaticism in the pursuit of fuel supplies, led to the stripping bare of many hillsides. Rural use of firewood and charcoal is difficult to quantify, though government agencies made an attempt at this. The numbers are more robust when it comes to urban use, as charcoal and firewood distribution were well-organised commercial industries. Fuel-wood production was also systematic. Coppicing was widely practiced for charcoal production, utilising hillside areas unsuited for more intensive forms of agriculture. For firewood and charcoal, there was though a postwar energy crisis; statistics suggest that available supplies fell by more than 40 percent from their former levels. Fuel production was one of several potentially competing uses of hillside areas. Other uses were the growing of trees for timber or pulp, the harvesting of green fertilizer, and, on less steep land, cultivation of upland crops like sweet potatoes. The use of upland areas to produce fuels for household use could thus be considered another kind of resource frontier (and as noted, hillsides were severely damaged by over-exploitation during the war). Conversely, in the same way that the use of commercial fertilizers freed a certain amount of human-appropriated biomass (green fertilizer) production for other purposes, so too did the use of coal and hydroelectric power.

In terms of total heat energy generated, coal was the biggest energy source. Thus, Ōkita Saburō could write, in an essay of November 1946, that as nutrition is the basic calorific source for people, so coal is for industry.[32] It is therefore instructive to think about the details of the country's monthly coal budget. From 1938 to 1944, average coal extraction within Japan was more than 50 million tons per year (more than four million tons per month). The net coal supply (including imports of coal) peaked in 1940 at over five million tons per month.[33] Miners had always worked under brutal conditions in Japan, and the peak production of the war years was achieved by the working to death of prisoners of war and slave labourers drafted from the Japanese-occupied territories. Imports of coal were almost cut off in 1944 and were practically nil in 1945, 1946, and 1947. In the early postwar years, from 1946 until September–October 1948, exports of coal actually exceeded imports of coal. Coal imports began to increase again from July 1948, though they were temporarily reduced during the Dodge Line retrenchment policy in 1949.

Coal extraction from mines inside Japan declined sharply in the early part of 1945, falling to 2.8 million tons in July 1945, and then to 1.7 million tons in August, the month of the surrender. By November 1945, the output of all Japanese coal mines had collapsed to a level of 554,000 tons, only one-eighth of the amounts extracted under conditions of slave labour during the war. Under freer working conditions, coal mining recovered more slowly, from 1.2 million tons in January 1946, to two million tons a year later, to 2.9 million tons in January 1948. The latter level constituted a visible, if partial, recovery.[34]

The crisis in mine productivity also directly involved the bodily energies of mine workers. From 1931 to 1940, the average extraction of coal per underground worker ran at a level of 20 to 25 tons per month.[35] By 1944, labour conscripts and foreign prisoners of war were being starved and worked to death in the mines. Extraction levels fell to 7.9 tons per underground worker per month in 1945. The number of coal miners declined greatly after the war, when foreign mine workers were liberated and Japanese workers resisted.[36] In January 1946, 250,000 people were employed in coal mining, and more than half of them worked underground. With the offer of better conditions, more than 100,000 additional workers were hired over the course of 1946. The amount of coal mined increased to an average of 9.7 tons per underground worker per month in 1946, and then to 10.5 tons in 1947.

The railways could be thought of as the country's basic materials-circulation system. Coal-fired steam locomotives supplied almost all of the motive power, and in 1946 coal production levels were barely enough to keep the railways running. The railways alone (together with the coal mines themselves) had most of their normal quota of coal. Manufacturing industries had only a modest fraction, at best a fourth or a fifth, of their normal coal requirements.[37] This was the problem addressed by the Japanese government's 'Coal Subcommittee', which directly succeeded the Ministry of Foreign Affairs Special Survey Committee, of which Ōkita Saburō had also been the executive secretary. Like the Special Survey Committee, this group was sponsored by Prime Minister Yoshida Shigeru, and it met in autumn 1946 at his out-of-the-way second office. The Coal Subcommittee's work is now a landmark in economic history. In these quietly conducted and intensive meetings, Ōkita argued, using the analogy of a person's basal metabolism, that as a person's minimum energy requirement, even when inactive and sleeping, is 1,400 kcal per day, so the current annual extraction target of 27 million tons of coal approximated the minimum energy requirement for a 'sleeping' Japanese economy. Just as a person requires additional energy in order to work, so too did the national economy; hence, he recommended the government's 1947 coal extraction target be raised to 30 million tons. Ōkita made this type of argument repeatedly (and successfully) and he later recalled it repeatedly as well.[38] Ōkita's argument was also connected to a successful request to GHQ to allow special shipments of heavy fuel oil from the United States, to be used for producing steel.[39]

The Coal Subcommittee also addressed the situation of the coal miners. The present chapter has set aside the dramatic politics of the postwar years in order to focus on other economic dimensions of the era, but in fact, these aspects are integrally connected. The revolt of the coal miners, which began practically as soon as the war ended, was a starting point for wider labour unrest, the most radical phase of which arguably came in 1946.[40] Ōkita's temporary departure from the government in early 1947 was itself caused by the Coal Subcommittee members' break with Prime Minister Yoshida, which was provoked by Yoshida's public denunciation of the labour unions.

Considering the monthly totals of coal mined per worker gives one a national-level manager's-eye view, useful for such things as planning the country's monthly coal budget, hiring the number of workers needed to mine the coal, and allocating the supplies needed by those workers. Indeed, planners like Arisawa and Ōkita were thinking about exactly these questions, as the subcommittee's meeting records reveal. How many extra calories did miners need in their rations compared to other people? How much extra sugar and how many extra cigarettes (at a time when both were scarce)? These were then national policy questions.[41] To gain a more personal sense of scale, one can consider the average output per working day per underground mine worker: 0.38 tons per day in 1946; 0.41 in 1947, and 0.44 in 1948. For this kind of heavy work, miners received the highest food ration levels allocated. Authorities also sought to feed the miners directly during their work time so that miners could not easily take food home from their own supplemented rations in order to share with their family members.

Aside from railway usage, coal in Japan was almost entirely for industrial use (including public utilities) rather than for home heating. Even before the war, less than ten percent of coal was for direct domestic usage. Coal was budgeted on a priority basis, with the prioritised users being the coal mines themselves, the railways, steel production, fertilizer production, and electric power.[42] Coal-fired electric power generation supplied a relatively small share of total electric power generation (though it was predominant in western Japan). In late 1945, it temporarily practically disappeared, and only three percent (600,000 tons) of coal was used for electric power generation by public utilities in 1946.

Thus, hydroelectric generation temporarily furnished nearly as much of the national energy supply as did coal. This 'fall-back' system, unlike other instances mentioned here, did not represent a revival of older methods but rather was the historically newest and most technologically advanced part of the national energy system. Moreover, hydroelectric power was 'almost the sole natural resource abundantly available in resource-poor Japan', according to Ōkita and his colleagues.[43] Despite the shortage of necessary materials and replacement parts, hydroelectric generation was the primary basis of the entire national energy system at this time.

Regarding electrification in general, one sees another kind of developmental frontier. In international comparison, Japan was early in having an interconnected nationwide electrical grid. The Overseas Consultants, Inc. (OCI) report of February 1948, commissioned by GHQ to study the question of postwar reparations, noted the prime importance of electricity in Japan. They also reported a remarkable fact: 'It is generally estimated that a higher proportion of Japanese industrial plants are electrified and a higher proportion of Japanese homes and farms are served with electricity than in any other country in the world'. Within this statement, the authors included the United States. In 1948, many of Japan's electrically networked homes and farms had only a few light bulbs installed (at best, as light bulbs, which had become a major Japanese export in the 1930s, were now among the goods in extremely short supply). It is of great significance, however, that a national power grid was in place. The OCI report noted that electric power was transmitted over great distances, and that there was a greater degree of national integration and coordination than in the United States.[44] In contrast to the other resource usage frontiers noted so far, electrification, as a universally recognised indicator of technological development, was also much easier to read as a sign of better things to come.

Hydroelectric power generation actually continued to increase during the war years, reaching a total of 30 billion kilowatt hours in 1944.[45] Japanese hydro-electric generation then relied heavily on small run-of-river plants rather than on large storage-reservoir plants. Run-of-river hydroelectric generation fluctuated seasonally, falling to its lowest levels in the drier winter months. In 1945, however, hydroelectric generation barely picked up in the summer. It then fell to an exceptionally low level (reaching a nadir of only one billion kWh per month) in the Autumn of the year, precisely the time when the coal crisis was at its worst. However, in 1946 hydropower again approached its prior levels and then maintained them – a bright spot in a generally bleak national energy picture.

On the consumption side, most electricity was also used for industrial purposes. Estimated residential consumption of electricity was less than a third of the total generated by public utilities: an estimated 500 million kWh per month in 1946 and 1947. These statistics for residential consumption include small shops and the estimated illicit consumption by people tapping into public utility power lines. Household usage of electricity also actually fell in 1948, to an estimated 470 million kWh per month.[46]

Last and least important among national energy sources was petroleum. In terms of its calorific value, petroleum counted for less of the national energy supply than did charcoal and firewood. Petroleum-derived fuels were essential, however, for powering ships, automobiles, and aircraft. Japan's oil refineries from the beginning had produced mainly for military purposes, and the refineries were mostly destroyed by American bombing in 1944 and 1945. In 1940, Japanese oil consumption had reached 22 million barrels. In 1945, consumption fell to a level of about two million barrels. Two million barrels was barely more than that which was extracted in a year in the Japanese home islands (2.5 million barrels in the year 1937, falling in 1945 to 1.5 million barrels, or 245,000 kilolitres).[47] The Occupation forces imported petroleum fuels for their own use, but GHQ did not permit any Japanese refineries to be rebuilt until 1949, and then only in partnership with American oil companies. Of the few Japanese automobiles that were running in 1945 and 1946, most ran on wood or charcoal burners (this was the case in many places during these years, especially in northern Europe). Thomas French's chapter in this volume describes the outsized place of the Willys jeep (fuelled by American gasoline) in this energy and transportation environment.

Producing basic materials

Production of textiles and many other consumer goods had been declining since the beginning of the China War in 1937, as the military effort bored more and more deeply into the Japanese civilian economy. Production of most basic materials – i.e. materials used to make other materials – peaked around 1941 and declined thereafter. During the first several years of the war, there was actually a large increase in the production of a few prioritised goods such as steel. Thus, steel production consumed resources that had formerly gone to other industries. Production in virtually all categories of materials declined steeply in 1944 and 1945. A few statistics of annual production levels can stand in for the larger picture here (see Table 2.3).

Metals, cement, chemicals, pulp, and paper were energy-intensive industries, and energy availability was a gating factor for production in all of them: if more coal was allocated to one industry, others had less. As noted above, coal allocations for each industry were administratively budgeted by state agencies rather than allocated by bidding up prices in a market.[48] This kind of state-mandated material budgeting across the entire national economy had begun during the war, and these methods were continued under the postwar 'Priority Production' strategy.

As Table 2.3 indicates, by 1952 or 1953, production of basic materials had largely regained the peak levels attained just before, or during, the war. Aggregated

Table 2.3 Annual Production of Selected Basic Materials (in Millions of Metric Tons)

Material	Peak Production Level (and Year)		Production in 1946 (and % of Peak Level)		Year when Production Regained Peak Level
Steel	7.84	(1943)	0.56	(7%)	1953
Cement	6.05	(1941)	0.93	(15%)	1953
Pulp	1.20	(1941)	0.21	(18%)	1952
Paper	1.54*	(1941)	0.21	(14%)	1952
Ammonium sulphate	1.24[†]	(1941)	0.47	(38%)	1949
Calcium cyanamide	0.26[†]	(1937)	0.14	(54%)	1949
Calcium superphosphate	1.70[†]	(1940)	0.20	(12%)	[n.a.]
Coal	57.36	(1941)	20.34	(35%)	never

* Including South Sakhalin production.
[†] Ammonium sulphate: the figure is for tons of 20 percent N_2 content; calcium cyanamide: tons of 16 percent N_2 content; calcium superphosphate: tons of 16 percent P_2O_5 content. Fertilizer production levels in 1945 were much lower than in 1946, as noted above.

Sources: *JES*, No. 34 Section 1 (6/1949), pp. 58, 76, 108, 113, 122, 133; *JES*, No. 36–37 Section 1 (8–9/1949), p. 98; Energy Data and Modeling Center, Institute of Energy Economics, Japan, *EDMC Handbook of Energy & Economic Statistics in Japan*, Tokyo: Energy Conservation Center, 2007, pp. 218–221.

economic statistics suggest that by 1955, the process of industrial recovery was largely complete.

It was also around 1955 that Japan entered onto the fastest and most intensive phase of industrial growth yet seen, not only in Japanese history, but also in the history of humanity's carbon-fired industrial revolution up to that point. By the early 1970s, when the period of 'high speed growth' ended, the production levels of the various materials listed in Table 2.3 would be roughly ten times greater than their level circa 1955. The exception to this statement was in coal mining, which largely ceased in Japan in the 1970s. Thus in 1966, looking back on Japan's situation of 20 years before, Ōkita called conditions at the time 'a kind of experiment on a living body', in the course of which national economic functions were first thrown back to an extremely primitive state, followed directly by the extremely rapid and concentrated development into a highly modern economy.[49]

Transporting basic materials

Japan had the world's third-largest merchant fleet before the war, and in 1939, Japanese merchant ships imported a total of 21.6 million tons of material of all kinds. They also exported 12.5 million tons of material. Most Japanese shipping was destroyed during the war by Allied submarine attacks, aerial bombing, and naval mines. In 1946, Japan imported only 511,000 tons and exported 953,000 tons of goods. Thus, by weight, only one-fortieth as much material was brought into the country in 1946 as in 1939. Only about one-thirteenth as much material was exported. The volume of imports actually declined further in 1947 to 407,000 tons, while export tonnage in 1947 increased modestly to 1.5 million tons.[50] External trade thus underwent one of the greatest contractions of all.

It was also remarkable that a greater tonnage of material was now being exported than imported. This was a reversal of the previous pattern. Japanese trade had, for several decades before the war, been characterised by a pattern of importing heavy raw materials and exporting lighter processed goods. Japan's physical balance of trade as measured in tons would quickly revert to this 'import-heavy' pattern after 1949. The pattern reversal of 1946-1948 was part of a temporary change in the composition of trade, which seemed like a throwback to the trade profile of early Meiji times when the country's staple exports were raw silk, tea, and coal. All three of these now appeared, momentarily, in the list of top exports.[51]

Inland transportation relied on the railways. The private railways were mainly urban commuter lines, and freight traffic was handled almost entirely by the national railways. The railways burned 500,000 to 600,000 tons of coal a month in order to run. Coal was also one of the main materials transported. In 1943-1945, the overloaded national railways handled a historically high level of 13 to 14 million metric tons per month. With the railways, as elsewhere, there was an eating into national capital in the form of over-usage and deferred maintenance. In 1946-1947, the volume of freight carried by the national railways fell to seven to eight million tons per month. By a more comprehensive measure, in ton-kilometres (tons loaded times distance carried), freight carried by rail fell from a peak of more than three billion ton-kilometres per year in 1944 and 1945, to less than half that, 1.4 billion ton-kilometres in 1947 (year ending March 31). At the same time, passenger traffic actually increased. Passenger trains were also greatly overloaded, and there was heavy usage of 'black-market trains' as city people travelled back and forth to the countryside to purchase food outside of official distribution channels.[52] Table 2.4 gives data for tons transported for both railways and coastal shipping.

It is apparent from Table 2.4 that much more cargo was carried by rail than by ship.[53] Also remarkable is the predominant role of wooden ships. Most of the steel ships had been sunk or confined to port by petroleum shortages, and in coastal shipping, wooden ships carried three times more cargo than did steel ships in 1946-1947. Moreover, these were mostly smaller wooden ships (under 100 gross

Table 2.4 Tons of Freight Carried by Rail and Coastal Shipping, 1946–1947

(Monthly Totals, in Thousands of Metric Tons)

Year/Month		National Railways	Coastwise Waterborne Shipments		
			Total	Wooden Ships	Steel Ships
1946	/ 1	6,230	884	677	207
	/ 2	6,870	968	720	248
	/ 3	7,196	1,106	801	305
	/ 4	8,094	1,313	954	359
	/ 5	8,539	1,396	1,020	376
	/ 6	8,140	1,380	1,011	369
	/ 7	8,070	1,511	1,152	359
	/ 8	8,237	1,591	1,223	368
	/ 9	9,083	1,734	1,370	364
	/ 10	9,048	1,903	1,478	425
	/ 11	8,521	2,016	1,580	436
	/ 12	7,814	1,789	1,367	422
1947	/ 1	7,397	1,744	1,312	432
	/ 2	7,568	1,709	1,314	395
	/ 3	9,434	2,158	1,638	520
	/ 4	9,289	2,234	1,633	601
	/ 5	9,653	2,521	1,922	599
	/ 6	9,405	2,671	1,945	726
	/ 7	9,514	2,659	1,969	690
	/ 8	9,272	2,530	1,860	670
	/ 9	9,044	2,627	1,937	690
	/ 10	9,872	2,748	2,061	687
	/ 11	9,408	2,773	1,960	813
	/ 12	8,925	2,806	2,070	736

Note: Numbers are for cargo carried on Japanese ships, not including the small number of tankers and the small amount of coastal trade carried by loaned U.S. ships.

Sources: Ministry of Transportation data, given in *JES*, No. 15 (11/1947), pp. 40–41; *JES*, No. 28 (12/1948), p. 59.

tons). As with the fishing fleet, it is a picture of an economy thrown back onto a smaller scale of operation and an older set of methods.

Coastal shipping also had a vital role when it came to transporting coal. Eighty percent of Japan's coal was mined on the islands of Kyūshū and Hokkaidō. Most of this coal went to Honshū and thus had to be carried by ship. The JES statistics for sea-borne cargo shipments did not give a breakdown by goods carried, but if one compares the monthly tonnage carried by coastal shipping to the monthly coal production of Kyūshū plus Hokkaidō (which rose from 950,000 tons in January 1946 to 1.7 million tons in December), it appears that the great bulk of this cargo actually consisted of coal.[54]

When it came to local transportation, including transportation to and from the railway stations, people were again thrown back onto their own bodily energies. Draft animals, never very numerous, were radically reduced in number during the war. Here as elsewhere, the government statistics provide a surprisingly detailed picture, although the present chapter can offer only a preliminary sketch. Bicycles, bicycle tires, bicycle trailers, and handcarts, which were transportation staples, were all in very short supply – not to mention trucks and cars.[55]

Conclusion: Japan at nature's edge/Japan at the edge of history

Thinking in 'systems' terms – of inputs and outputs, resources and energy conversions – brings life processes and power-machine processes into a single quantifiable framework. In the same way that one might analyse and measure our own bodily material exchanges with the rest of the world, so might one calculate the exchanges involving an individual farmstead, village, factory, or the entire national economy. Ideas that electrical engineers developed in order to understand the complex systems they were creating were in this way applied in the late 1940s to the analysis – and design – of human social systems or linked human-natural systems. Ōkita Saburō himself recognised the essentially technocratic nature of this approach.[56] His approach also has substantial points in common with recent ecologically oriented work on 'social metabolism'.

Several aspects of Japan's postwar 'experiment' now seem significant in different ways than they did to members of the generation who actually carried it out (or upon whom it was carried out). In the aftermath of the war, Ōkita and his colleagues strove to break an impasse characterised by a perceived surplus population, low wages, and low agricultural productivity. All of these problems were implicated, by both Japanese and foreign analysts, as reasons for the militaristic resource grabbing that had led the country into war. These problems were also intensified by postwar food shortages and energy famine. A solution was found in a great intensification of industrial development. In a form of counter movement, the ecological economic work that has emerged since the early 1970s has focused on the negative effects of economic growth, with an eye to 'de-materialization' or 'de-growth' as hopeful ways forward.

With these contrasts in mind, it is interesting to consider Japan's immediate postwar experience as an instance of unplanned and catastrophic material-economic contraction, of which we have an exceptionally detailed and quantified picture. The present chapter has suggested only a few of its basic outlines, but these are enough to suggest several questions for future research. On one hand, there was a forced reversion to organic methods. Japanese agriculture, formerly one of the world's heaviest users of chemical fertilizers, was temporarily thrown back on organic farming methods. The scarcity of fossil fuels intensified pressures on the use of biomass fuels. Reliance on small fishing boats powered by sails and on small wooden ships for coastal shipping forms another part of this picture. Damage to hillside areas intensified, while various forms of chemical pollution were reduced. It is also worth noting that estimated emissions of carbon dioxide, after having doubled through the 1930s to a then-record level in 1940, fell back to less than a third of that level in 1946. Estimated carbon dioxide emissions did not regain the 1940 level until 1957.[57] Such effects were in the nature of temporary reversals of the long-run direction of industrial development.

Fundamental questions are also raised by Japan's position, even before the war, at a developmental frontier, albeit not a frontier of a kind that would have been recognised by most economic analysts. Throughout the course of Japan's modern industrial revolution, at least until the 1980s, the 'follower' and 'catch-up' aspects of Japanese development were so salient that they tended to block perception of some of the most distinctive features of the Japanese economy's path. When analysts, Japanese or foreign, looked at what was distinctive about Japanese development, they tended to see *backwardness*.[58] The enforced primitivism of postwar circumstances intensified this perception. Knowing, with hindsight, that the country actually stood at the threshold of a modern 'economic miracle', things look different. The view of Japanese backwardness might thus be reversed. '*Japan at nature's edge*' is the evocative title of a book edited by Ian Miller, Julia Thomas, and Brett Walker,[59] and the phrase could also evoke the situation faced by the people of Japan in the mid-twentieth century. Under conditions of organic agriculture, Japanese farmers by the nineteenth century had achieved the highest yields per hectare of any farmers in the world – the methods may have been organic, but already in the late Tokugawa period, they were based on the production and sale of commercial fertilizers ('night soil', fishmeal, oil cake), transported over long distances.[60] The 'green revolution' that increased rice yields across Asia in the second half of the twentieth century has been widely publicised. It is much less known that this movement had already begun in Japan in the late nineteenth and early twentieth centuries, with the systematic development of new rice varieties responsive to heavy fertilizer applications.[61] From a planetary view, Japanese agriculture was thus at a sort of developmental frontier. With the world's largest deep-ocean fishing fleet and most intensive use of marine resources, Japan by the 1930s was also at a form of frontier. As noted, Japan also stood at a frontier position in the process of national electrification.

An additional evocative image of this transformation is provided by megacity Tokyo itself, whose population graph traces out a great fall and rise during these years. By 1940, the population of the Tokyo Metropolis (Tōkyō-to) had grown to 7.3 million. Following the March 1945 firebombing and evacuation, the population fell to less than half that, 3.5 million. The city did not regain its 1940 level until after 1952 – and by then, it was poised on the threshold of a new urban scale frontier in human history. By 1955, greater 'neo-Tokyo' surged to surpass the greater New York City metropolitan area to become the largest megacity yet seen in human history.

One might therefore also speak of Japan at the edge of history. One way to describe this situation would be to speak of national resource limits, or of a Malthusian frontier. In retrospect, it appears more as a Boserup-type developmental frontier. The postwar crisis, as an extremely sharp but temporary reversal at a time when Japan was entering into the fastest phase of its industrial transition, provides a unique microhistorical window into the workings of this macrohistorical process. As noted already, the Japanese material-processing system, from around 1955 to the early 1970s, was ramped up by about ten times per person in terms of material and energy usage. This systemic transformation was enabled by historically novel infrastructural elements connected to new systems of energy provision (supertankers, coastal petrochemical complexes [*konbinato*], and so on).[62] This great change of overall systemic scale, as described in material flow accounting terms by Fridolin Krausmann and colleagues, was followed by a levelling off since the 1970s. Japan's super-compressed 'metabolic transition' (as they call it) is now recognisable as the first instance of a series of such transitions across eastern Asia.[63] As the historical and environmental significance of this transition becomes clearer with time, we may benefit by looking back to these experiences in order to think about what may come next.

Notes

1   For an overall statement, see, among others: J. Martinez-Alier, with K. Schlupmann, *Ecological Economics: Energy, Environment, and Society*, Oxford: Basil Blackwell, 1987.
2   E. A. Ackerman, "Japan: Have or Have Not Nation?" in D. G. Harris, ed., *Japan's Prospect*, Cambridge, MA: Harvard University Press, 1946, pp. 25–41. There appear to be no scholarly studies of the School for Overseas Administration, despite its evident significance.
3   G. F. White, "Edward A. Ackerman, 1911–1973", *Annals of the Association of American Geographers*, Vol. 64, No. 2, 1974, pp. 297–309; General Headquarters (Supreme Commander for the Allied Powers), Natural Resources Section, *Japanese Natural Resources: A Comprehensive Survey*, Tokyo: Hosokawa Printing, 1949. Ōkita Saburō in his book *Gijutsu • Shigen • Keizai* (Technology, Resources, Economy), Tokyo: Hakuyōsha, 1949, devoted an entire section to Ackerman and to Japan's inter-agency Resource Committee which Ackerman helped inspire (pp. 126–152). See also J. Satō, *'Motazaru Kuni' no Shigenron: Jizoku Kanō na Kokudo o Meguru mō Hitotsu no Chi* (Resource Thinking of a 'Have-Not Country': An Alternative Vision of Sustainable National Land], Tokyo: Tōkyō Daigaku Shuppankai, 2011, and E. Dinmore, "Concrete Results? The TVA and the Appeal of Large Dams in Occupation-Era Japan", *Journal of Japanese Studies*, Vol. 39, No. 1, 2013, pp. 1–38.
4   See C. Totman, *Early Modern Japan*, Berkeley: University of California Press, 1993, and Totman, *Japan: An Environmental History*, London: I.B. Tauris, 2014, Ch. 6. This line of thought suggests also the arguments made by Kenneth Pomeranz (*The Great Divergence: Europe, China, and the Making of the Modern World Economy*, Princeton: Princeton University Press, 2000) and the discussion it has generated.

5 General Headquarters, Supreme Commander for the Allied Powers, Economic and Scientific Section, Research and Statistics Division (later, Research and Programs Division), *Japanese Economic Statistics* (hereafter, *JES*), No. 15, 11/1947, pp. 74–76; *JES*, No. 34, Section III, 6/1949.

6 Ōkita, *Gijutsu • Shigen • Keizai*; Satō, *'Motazaru Kuni'*. Further discussion of Ōkita's role is given in M. Metzler, *Capital as Will and Imagination: Schumpeter's Guide to the Postwar Japanese Miracle*, Ithaca: Cornell University Press, 2013; for a full biography, Y. Ono, *Waga Kokorozashi wa Senri ni Ari – Hyōden Ōkita Saburō* (My Aspiration is a Thousand Half-a-Leagues Distant – A Biography of Ōkita Saburō), Tokyo: Nihon Keizai Shinbunsha, 2004.

7 A team of Vienna-based scholars has taken a lead here; see, among much other work, H. Haberl, M. Fischer-Kowalski, F. Krausmann, H. Weisz, V. Winiwarter, "Progress Towards Sustainability? What the Conceptual Framework of Material and Energy Flow Accounting (MEFA) Can Offer", *Land Use Policy*, Vol. 21, No. 3, 2004, pp. 199–213. Material flow accounting has been adopted as a standard at the European level (Eurostat, "Statistics Explained – Material Flow Accounts", http://ec.europa.eu/euro stat/statistics-explained/index.php/Material_flow_accounts_-_flows_in_raw_mate rial_equivalents) and has been taken up by the United Nations Environment Program (UNEP) and Japanese Ministry of the Environment. This work is evidently the beginning of a bigger and fuller development of such ideas.

8 J. Martinez-Alier, L. Temper, and F. Demaria, "Social Metabolism and Environmental Conflicts in India", *Indi@logs*, Vol. 1, 2014, pp. 59–61.

9 M. Fischer-Kowalski, "Society's Metabolism: The Intellectual History of Materials Flow Analysis, Part I, 1860–1970", *Journal of Industrial Ecology*, Vol. 2, No. 1, 1998, pp. 61–78; M. Fischer-Kowalski and W. Hüttler, "Society's Metabolism: The Intellectual History of Materials Flow Analysis, Part II, 1970–1998", *Journal of Industrial Ecology*, Vol. 2, No. 4, 1999, pp. 107–136. See also J. B. Foster, B. Clark, and R. York, *The Ecological Rift: Capitalism's War on the Earth*, Monthly Review Press, 2011; and for wider thinking on the subject, J. W. Moore, *Capitalism in the Web of Life: Ecology and the Accumulation of Capital*, London: Verso, 2015. Ōkita was inspired by his professor at Tokyo Imperial University, Baba Keiji, who drew on the writings of North American and European energy theorists, including the writings of the U.S. Technocracy movement (Metzler, *Capital as Will and Imagination*, Ch. 4).

10 *JES*, No. 15, 11/1947, pp. 62–68.

11 J. B. Cohen, *Japan's Economy in War and Reconstruction*, Minneapolis: University of Minnesota Press, 1949, p. 408.

12 M. Umemura et al., *Nōringyō* (The Agriculture and Forestry Sector), Vol. 9 of *Chōki Keizai Tōkei, Suikei to Bunseki* (Estimates of Long Term Economic Statistics of Japan), Tokyo: Tōyō Keizai Shinpōsha, 1966, p. 168 (hereafter, *LTES*). The 1945 estimates given here were those of the Ministry of Agriculture and Forestry, which was appealing for massive food imports from the United States.

Estimated calorific value of 1 gram of brown rice was 3.37 kcal, and one gram of polished rice was 3.51 kcal (*JES*, No. 15, 11/1947, p. 2). *Tons* in this chapter means metric tons.

13 *JES*, No. 15, 11/1947, p. 42; S. J. Fuchs, "Feeding the Japanese: Food Policy, Land Reform, and Japan's Economic Recovery", in M. E. Caprio, and Y. Sugita, eds., *Democracy in Occupied Japan: The U.S. Occupation and Japanese Politics and Society*, Routledge, 2007, pp. 26–47; also C. Aldous, "Contesting Famine: Hunger and Nutrition in Occupied Japan, 1945–1952", *Journal of American-East Asian Relations*, Vol. 17, No. 3, 2010, pp. 230–256; and C. Aldous, "A Dearth of Animal Protein: Reforming Nutrition in Occupied Japan (1945–1952)", in K. J. Cwiertka, ed., *Food and War in Mid-Twentieth-Century East Asia*, London: Routledge, 2016.

14 *JES*, No. 15, 11/1947, p. 42; Fuchs, "Feeding the Japanese".

15 See William Tsutsui's chapter in this volume. See also W. Tsutsui, "The Pelagic Empire: Reconsidering Japanese Expansion", in I. J. Miller, J. A. Thomas, and B. L. Walker, eds., *Japan at Nature's Edge: The Environmental Context of a Global Power*, Honolulu: University of Hawaii Press, 2013, pp. 21–38.

16 Natural Resources Section, GHQ, *Japanese Natural Resources*, Tokyo: GHQ, 1949.

17 *JES*, No. 15, 11/1947, p. 42.

18 Special Survey Committee, Ministry of Foreign Affairs (Japan), *Postwar Reconstruction of the Japanese Economy*, compiled by S. Ōkita, Sept. 1946 (Tokyo: University of Tokyo Press, 1992), pp. 122–124; T. Nakamura, and T. Ōmori, eds., *Shiryō Sengo Nihon no Keizai Seisaku Kōsō, Vol. 1. Nihon Keizai Saiken no Kihon Mondai* (Basic Problems in the Reconstruction of the Japanese Economy), Tokyo: Tōkyō Daigaku Shuppankai, 1990.

19 See Thomas French's chapter in this volume.

20 Sweet potatoes had been popularised in Japan as an anti-famine food following the Kyōhō-era famine of the early 1730s. F. Marcon, *The Knowledge of Nature and the Nature of Knowledge in Early Modern Japan*, Chicago: University of Chicago Press, 2015, pp. 122–123.

21 E. Boserup, *The Conditions of Agricultural Growth*, London: George Allen and Unwin, 1965; in this connection see also O. Saito, "An Industrious Revolution in an East Asian Market Economy? Tokugawa Japan and Implications for the Great Divergence", *Australian Economic History Review*, Vol. 50, No. 3, 2010, pp. 240–261. Boserup's ideas provide one starting point for later ecological economic work; see M. Fischer-Kowalski, A. Reenberg, A. Schaffartzik, and A. Mayer, eds., *Ester Boserup's Legacy on Sustainability: Orientations for Contemporary Research*, Springer Open Access, 2014.

22 T. Ogura, ed., *Agricultural Development in Modern Japan*, Tokyo: Japan FAO Association, 1963, p. 222.

23 Cohen, *Japan's Economy*, p. 365; T. Higuchi, "Japan as an Organic Empire: Commercial Fertilizers, Nitrogen Supply, and Japan's Core-Peripheral Relationship", in B. Batten and P. C. Brown, eds., *Environment and Society in the Japanese Islands: From Prehistory to Present*, Corvallis: Oregon State University Press, 2015, pp. 139–157. The toxic aspects of this dependency have emerged more clearly since then.

24 *JES*, No. 15, 11/1947, p. 30; *JES*, No. 34, Section III, 6/1949, p. 122; also Table 2.3 above.

25 Ōkita et al., *Postwar Reconstruction*, p. 144.

26 *LTES*, Vol. 9, p. 209.

27 Ōkita et al., *Postwar Reconstruction*, pp. 122–123; Nakamura and Ōmori, *Nihon Keizai Saiken*, pp. 218–219. In the English translation of the report, the numbers for the calorific content of coal and for the price of electric power were given incorrectly.

28 Ōkita, *Gijutsu • Shigen • Keizai*, pp. 137–138.

29 Estimates from *EDMC Handbook*, 2007, pp. 209–211.

30 Here one sees illustrated a problem within orthodox ideas of economic calculation which would, by statistical implication, count this kind of production for destruction as an indicator of economic health.

31 In light of the distribution of actual energy usage, per capita calculations are not necessarily very informative socially, but they do give a measure of the total national energy system. To give a sense of the very different energetic scales involved, if one calculates a person's 'bodily economy' to run at a level of 2,500 kcal per day, that adds up to almost one million kcal per person per year. Of course, notwithstanding the reasoning of Ōkita and others, the logic of one scale-level is not necessarily translatable into the other.

32 Reprinted in Ōkita, *Gijutsu • Shigen • Keizai*, p. 294. One might compare the slogan of Chinese Communist Party chairman Mao Zedong that 'coal is the rice of industry', for which see Victor Seow's forthcoming study, *Coal Capital*.

33 *JES*, No. 15, p. 15 (export data: p. 47); *JES*, No. 34, Section 1, 6/1949, pp. 58–59.

34 Japan Coal Association (Nihon Sekitan Kōgyōkai) and other data, given in ibid. and in L. E. Hein, *Fueling Growth: The Energy Revolution and Economic Policy in Postwar Japan*, Cambridge, MA: Harvard University Press, 1990, p. 66.

35 *JES*, No. 15, 11/1947, p. 16; *JES*, No. 34, Section 1, 6/1949, p. 66.

36 See Juha Saunavaara's chapter in the current volume for more on labour unrest within the mining sector.

37 *JES*, No. 15, 11/1947, pp. 18–19.

38 H. Arisawa, and T. Nakamura, eds. *Shiryō, Sengo Nihon no Keizai Seisaku Kōsō. Vol. 2. Keisha Seisan Hōshiki to Sekitan Shōi'inkai* (The Priority Production Formula and the Coal Subcommittee), Tokyo: Tōkyō Daigaku Shuppankai, 1990, pp. 124, 151, 194–201, 222, 233–234; S. Ōkita, *Japan's Challenging Years: Reflections on My Lifetime*, transl. G. Bruce, Canberra: Australia-Japan Research Centre, Australian National University, 1983 (translation of *Tōhon Seisō – Watakushi no Rirekisho*, 1981), pp. 38–39.

39 Documented in Arisawa and Nakamura, *Shiryō, Keisha Seisan*. The original request appears to have been presented to the Japanese cabinet by the managing director of Nissan, who noted that because of higher calorific content and cleaner burning qualities, a ton of heavy fuel oil was equivalent to three tons of coal ("Nissan Sangyō Kabushikigaisha Torishimariyaku Shachō Nagai Kōtarō no Tōshinsho" (Nissan Industrial Holdings Board President Nagai Kōtarō's Report), 2 Oct. 1946, in *Shiryō, Keisha Seisan*, pp. 65–67).

40 Hein, *Fueling Growth*, gives a comprehensive political and policy history. For the revolt of the coalminers, see J. Moore, *Japanese Workers and the Struggle for Power, 1945–1947*, Madison: University of Wisconsin Press, 1983.

41 For example, see: "Sekitan Shōi'inkai Dai-ikkai Gijiroku", 11/1946, in Arisawa and Nakamura, *Shiryō, Keisha Seisan*, p. 160.

42 Statistics given in *JES*, No. 15, 11/1947, pp. 18–19; *JES*, No. 34, Section 1, 6/1949, pp. 67–70.

43 Ōkita et al., *Postwar Reconstruction*, p. 143.

44 OCI Report, 2/1948, p. 72–73, emphasis added.

45 R. Minami, *Tetsudō to Denryoku* (Railroads and Electric Power), *LTES*, Vol. 12, 1965, p. 197.

46 *JES*, No. 34, Section 1, 6/1949, p. 51.

47 Natural Resources Section, GHQ, *Japanese Natural Resources*, 1949, p. 209. By way of comparison, about 2.5 million barrels *per day* was then being pumped from the East Texas oil field.

48 Administrative price setting and market price setting were not simple 'opposites'. In this time of high price inflation, those best able to bid for resources were in any case those with the best access to new bank credit, and bank credit itself was subject to a kind of administrative allocation; see Metzler, *Capital as Will and Imagination*.

49 S. Ōkita Saburō, and H. Arisawa, "Keizai Saiken to Keisha Seisan' (Economic Recovery and Priority Production), in Y. Andō, ed., *Shōwa Keizaishi e no Shōgen* (Testimony on the Economic History of Shōwa), Vol. 2, Tokyo: Mainichi Shinbunsha, 1966, p. 293.

50 Statistics Bureau (Japan), *Nihon Chōki Tōkei Sōran – Historical Statistics of Japan*, New Edition, Vol. 3, Tokyo: Nihon Tōkei Kyōkai (Japan Statistical Association), 2006, pp. 116–117. These numbers do not include Allied forces' shipping of material into Japan. Given the greatly reduced volume of material circulation in Japan, and the significant 'leakage' of U.S. goods into Japanese consumption channels, this was significant.

51 Gaimushō Chōsakyoku Daisanka, "Waga Kuni no Bōeki Mondai" (Our Country's Foreign Trade Problem), 19/7/1946, in Arisawa and Nakamura, *Shiryō, Keisha Seisan*, p. 31.

52 For a vivid picture, see: O. Griffiths, "Need, Greed, and Protest in Japan's Black Market, 1938–1949", *Journal of Social History*, Vol. 35, No. 4, 2002, pp. 825–858.

53 According to data presented by Steven Ericson, rail freight first surpassed coastal freight around 1912, when measured in tons carried, and at some point after that in terms of ton-kilometres. S. Ericson, *The Sound of the Whistle: Railroads and the State in Meiji Japan*, Cambridge, MA: Harvard East Asian Monographs, 1996, p. 397.

54 *JES*, No. 15, 11/1947, pp. 14–15; *JES*, No. 34, Section 1, 6/1949, p. 58.

55 *JES*, No. 34, Section 1, 6/1949, pp. 94–95; See Thomas French's chapter in this volume.

56 'I was operating rather technocratically' (*yaya tekunokrāto-teki ni yatte ita*), as Ōkita said in a 1984 interview (in Arisawa and Nakamura, *Shiryō, Keisha Seisan*, p. 222).

57 *EDMC Handbook*, 2007, pp. 226–229.

58 See: A. E. Barshay, *The Social Sciences in Modern Japan: The Marxian and Modernist Traditions*, Berkeley: University of California Press, 2004. This distinctiveness, more positively evaluated, is highlighted in Kaoru Sugihara's analyses of an East Asian labour-intensive developmental path, e.g., K. Sugihara, "The East Asian Path of Economic Development: A Long-Term Perspective", in G. Arrighi, T. Hamashita, and M. Selden, eds., *The Resurgence of East Asia: 500, 150 and 50 Year Perspectives*, London: Routledge, 2003, pp. 78–123.

59 Miller, Thomas, and Walker, *Japan at Nature's Edge*. See also the companion volume by Batten and Brown, *Environment and Society*. Bruce Batten's chapter includes a wide-ranging introduction to Japanese-language literature on the subject.

60 D. L. Howell, *Capitalism From Within: Economy, Society, and the State in a Japanese Fishery*, Berkeley: University of California Press, 1995.

61 Ogura, *Agricultural Development*, pp. 223, 367–374.

62 See also: S. G. Bunker and P. S. Ciccantell, *Globalization and the Race for Resources*, Baltimore, MD: Johns Hopkins Press, 2005; and S. Bunker and P. Ciccantell, *East Asia and the Global Economy: Japan's Ascent, With Implications for China's Future*, Baltimore, MD: Johns Hopkins University Press, 2007.

63 See: F. Krausmann, S. Gingrich, and R. Nourbakhch-Sabet, "The Metabolic Transition in Japan: A Material Flow Account for the Period 1878 to 2005", *Journal of Industrial Ecology*, Vol. 15, 2011, pp. 877–892; also H. Schandl, M. Fischer-Kowalski, C. Grunbuhel, F. Krausmann, "Socio-Metabolic Transitions in Developing Asia", *Technological Forecasting & Social Change*, Vol. 76, 2009, pp. 267–281.

3 The role of the frontier

GHQ's economic policies and Hokkaidō

Juha Saunavaara

Introduction

The general interest in Hokkaidō's economic potential and its untapped natural resources peaked during the Occupation period, not least because Japan had lost Karafuto (its territory on Sakhalin) and its important colonies and conquests in continental Asia. Besides the Japanese central government and local actors, the future of Hokkaidō's economy was inevitably also in the hands of the occupiers – who in policy papers referred to Hokkaidō as the last economic frontier of Japan.[1]

Based on a hypothesis that the Occupation authorities and their policies had both direct and indirect influences on the economic development of Hokkaidō at the beginning of the postwar era, this chapter concentrates on the following questions: who defined the aims of the economic development of Hokkaidō under the Occupation, what were these aims, through which kinds of policies were these aims striven for, and how were these policies implemented? These questions, however, cannot be analysed without proper contextualisation, i.e. placing them within the framework of the changing overall objectives of the Occupation. To enable an analysis of the changes occurring during the Occupation period, a short introduction of Hokkaidō's pre-war economic and industrial development is also included. While this chapter focuses on the development of economic activity in Hokkaidō and occasionally pays attention to the behaviour of its local government, for example, it does not touch on the development of public sector finance in detail.[2]

The early stages of Hokkaidō's modern development and industrialisation

The origin of Hokkaidō's post-Meiji development policies can be found in the Bureau of Colonial Affairs (*Kaitakushi*) established in 1869. This organisation was the first step in a process that aimed to bind Hokkaidō more closely to the rest of Japan not only due to reasons of security and foreign policy, but also in order to better utilise the rich natural resources of the island. The years between the establishment of the Kaitakushi and the establishment of the Hokkaidō Agency (*Hokkaidō-chō*) in 1886 can be generalised as a period when the colonisation of

Hokkaidō came under the direct control of the central Meiji government and the island's modern industrial development was launched. This progressed through the selling of government-owned land, and early industry utilising local natural resources was expanded, focusing on government-controlled factories. However, the government's nurturing attitude toward Hokkaidō, which still lacked sufficient private capital and suffered from poor infrastructure, was revised around the turn of the century. Although the establishment of the Hokkaidō Colonial Bank (*Hokkaidō Takushoku Ginkō*) by the government in 1900 played a role in this development, the major change took place among private sector actors.[3]

The advancement of the Japanese economy and the accumulation of capital took place during a time when the country fought victorious wars against China (1894-1895) and Russia (1904-1905). During these years, the previously government-managed factories were sold to the private sector for far less than the cost originally required for their construction. Meanwhile, major investments were made in Hokkaidō in the fields of iron and paper manufacturing, and the wood pulp industry. Furthermore, small and middle-sized foodstuffs and timber manufacturing industries began to develop. The changes in agricultural reclamation regulations paved the way for the increase in the cultivated land in possession of wealthy landlords and for the emergence of the tenant farming system. Furthermore, agriculture surpassed the fishing industry – fish being Hokkaidō's traditional export product – as the largest industrial sector, but this position was itself soon also challenged by the growing mining industry.[4]

These years of economic expansion were soon followed by the World War One boom. Thus, the first two decades of the twentieth century witnessed a great development of Hokkaidō based industry that penetrated into the world market. This was also a time when the First Hokkaidō Reclamation Plan (1910-1926), suffering from budgetary trouble and gradually shifting away from projects establishing the foundations of the economy and industry to more direct assistance for enterprises and immigrants, was implemented. Although the new colonies were now taking their share of immigrants, the population of Hokkaidō still increased. New legislation sped up the sale of state-owned land, stimulated reclamation, and also enabled private ownership and control over Hokkaidō's mines. The zaibatsu also advanced into Hokkaidō and expanded into various parts of the heavy chemical industry growing on the island. The endeavours to increase Hokkaidō's production and population were also supported by various infrastructure projects ranging from hydroelectric plants and harbour improvements, to railroad, road, and bridge construction. In general, the transportation system was developed to answer the need to export raw materials from the island. Overall, while significant development took place, for example in the dairy industry and in fields utilising Hokkaidō timber, the 1920s were to introduce challenges that resulted from Hokkaidō's deepened integration into the world economy.[5]

Following the end of the Great War boom, Japan fell into recession and the demand for agricultural products coming from Hokkaidō dropped. In an attempt to adapt to the new international situation, and influenced by the crisis caused by the Great Kantō earthquake of 1923, consecutive poor harvests, and the outbreak of the Shōwa crisis that started from the monetary circulation crisis in 1927, the economy of Hokkaidō underwent a major reorganisation. Meanwhile, the second Hokkaidō Reclamation Plan (1927-1946) was prepared at a time of both nation-wide rural depression and increased unemployment among the urban popula-tion. This ambitious plan envisioned a Hokkaidō with a population of six million people and urged great changes in agriculture through the promotion of animal husbandry, the dairy industry, and paddy rice agriculture. Nevertheless, it soon became evident that the planned budget was not available for these initiatives.[6]

Rationalisation and reorganisation also advanced in the manufacturing indus-try. While the fields of spinning and ceramics suffered, the relative importance of the capital-intensive heavy chemical, machine, and metals industries increased. The agricultural sector also invested in the dairy and sugar industries, and the timber and wood products industries also tried to escape the recession through a higher degree of mechanisation that led to the development of the furniture, veneer and plywood industries.[7]

The path of militarism, aggression and expansion in the 1930s, leading first to the war against China and then to the Pacific War, had huge effects on Hokkaidō's economy. The island's special position as a 'domestic colonisation area' lapsed somewhat due to the overseas colonisation project, which was mainly directed to Manchuria. Nevertheless, Hokkaidō continued to have an important role in the wartime economic structure because it possessed a great variety of resources necessary for the munitions industry. In agricultural production, the development of the livestock industry was replaced by an official emphasis on the cultivation of rice, barley, and potatoes to secure a reasonable level of food production. The implementation of labour mobilisation plans also meant that the workforce was re-allocated to serve the needs of coal mining, munitions production, and other fields considered especially important.[8]

Although the northernmost main island of Japan did not witness the kind of widespread devastation that was typical of the Japanese heartland during the war, the importance of Hokkaidō's natural resources and its industrial and agri-cultural products was understood by the enemy. The U.S. Navy began to dis-rupt shipping from Hokkaidō and coal production in certain areas had to be stopped because of problems regarding transportation to Honshū. However, direct attacks on Hokkaidō were rare – with the most famous being the cam-paign against key port cities involved in transportation of coal in mid-July 1945. Repatriation became a major issue after the surrender, but the Japanese gov-ernment had already decided in the spring of 1945 on large-scale immigration and resettlement of evacuees from Tokyo to Hokkaidō. Although only small groups of those moving to Hokkaidō arrived before the war was over, even they faced serious hardship. The only land available for reclamation was uninhab-ited wasteland, which previous immigrants and pioneers had ignored. Soon the arrival of evacuees from Karafuto and the return of demobilised soldiers made the situation even more difficult.[9]

Hokkaidō's crucial role in the policy concerning agricultural production and the coal industry

A Natural Resource Section (NRS) report concluded in August 1946 that the production of coal ranked next to the production of food as the most urgent problem in postwar Japan.[10] Therefore, it is not surprising that the questions concerning agricultural production and the coal industry dominated the discussion of Hokkaidō, both within the Japanese government and General Headquarters of the Supreme Commander for the Allied Powers (GHQ). When the Occupation authorities strove to solve these fundamental national problems, they planned and executed acts that focused heavily on Hokkaidō.

As the wartime planners had failed to agree on the desired land reform policy, GHQ was without clear instructions at the beginning of the Occupation. During the Autumn of 1945, the Shidehara Cabinet discarded a progressive reform proposal put forward by the Ministry of Agriculture and Forestry. Meanwhile, GHQ ordered the government to submit a plan for long term food production goals and instructed the government to develop a comprehensive land reform program. When the Japanese Diet promulgated the Agricultural Land Adjustment Law that still favoured big landlords at the expense of the tenant farmers in December, it faced strong opposition from GHQ.[11]

At the same time, a policy concerning land reclamation was put together in great haste. The Ministry of Agriculture and Forestry established its own Reclamation Bureau[12] in mid-October 1945, and the Japanese government approved the land reclamation plan in November. The plan aimed at bringing an additional 1,550,000 chōbu (one chōbu is approximately 0.9917 hectares or 2,471 acres) of land into cultivation nationwide in the coming five years. Nearly half of this new land was to be reclaimed in Hokkaidō. In October, the Hokkaidō Agency had also activated a plan for the enforcement of postwar land reclamation in Hokkaidō. These preparations were made for the sake of resettling immigrants from Honshū and from the lost colonies. The newcomers were expected to derive their livelihoods from agriculture and help solve the national food shortage by contributing to the increase in domestic food production.[13]

The land reform law was finally enacted in October 1946. The law placed Hokkaidō in an exceptional position. While the maximum area of land ownership in other areas was set at three chōbu, the limit was 12 chōbu in Hokkaidō. The same multiplier was also applied in the case of pastoral land where the Hokkaidō maximum was set at 20 chōbu.[14] The cultivated land reform program was nearly completed by the end of 1948 under the surveillance of NRS. However, the progress of the pasture land reform and the development of the livestock industry were slower. Livestock farms in Hokkaidō were described as inefficient, and the fact that many of them had been temporarily exempted from land reform caused dissatisfaction.[15] Furthermore, problems around land reform in Hokkaidō received some publicity when its constitutionality was challenged in the Asahikawa District Court. While NRS tried to persuade the reluctant Government Section (GS) on the necessity of GHQ intervention, similar cases began to appear in other parts of Japan. Finally, the Occupation authorities intervened in the legal proceedings and effectively declared that the land reform program did not violate the constitution.[16] Another peculiarity in the advancement of land reform in Hokkaidō was bound into the endeavour to exempt Ainu lands from the land reform laws, as described in detail by Richard Siddle.[17]

The ambitious land reclamation plan which accompanied land reform eventually failed both at the national level and in Hokkaidō,[18] but the Ministry of Agriculture and Forestry announced new policies concerning the development and management of reclamation area agriculture in August 1947. An outline for the enforcement of reclamation projects, aimed at increasing farm village populations, was enacted in October. Nevertheless, the cost efficiency of land reclamation as a method in order to increase food production, in comparison, for example, with the improvement of the fertility of the land already cultivated, was gradually questioned by the Occupation and the Japanese government.[19]

Coal production and the industries related to it played a crucial role at the beginning of the Occupation. The importance of coal became visible, for example, in the Priority Production Plan launched at the end of 1946. According to the plan, available capital, natural resources, labour, and direct government subsidies were allocated to key industrial sectors such as coal, electric power, steel and iron, shipbuilding, fertilisers, and textiles.[20] However, despite all the effort, the shortage of coal restricted the early postwar production of even the Hokkaidō iron manufacturers that were not far from the coalfields.[21]

The coal industry was also at the centre of many economic and political disputes. The workers in the Hokkaidō mines – especially the Chinese and Korean labourers who had kept them operating during the war – formed the forefront of the workers' movement. When violent struggles broke out in late September 1945, the Occupation authorities intervened. GHQ supported the establishment of a democratic labour movement and issued a proclamation concerning the maintenance of order in the mines. Another proclamation was issued in November that prohibited strikes in mining and other areas vital to the Occupation's mission and, effectively, forced the Chinese and Korean workers to dig coal for the Occupation forces. However, these orders did not solve the problem, and GHQ decided to repatriate the remaining foreign labourers in mid-November. This caused an immediate shortage of labour in the Hokkaidō coal mines and within the iron and steel industries.[22]

The first actions by the Japanese miners were influenced by the example set by the Chinese and Koreans, but they also owed much to the pre-war labour movement in Hokkaidō. Nevertheless, the Hokkaidō miners also departed from the pre-war system and formed a trade union that was not confined to one mine or enterprise, but encompassed all the island's mines. Thus, the unionisation in other regions and sectors not only lagged behind Hokkaidō, but also took a different form. The fact that the All-Japan Federation of Coal Miners' Unions (*Zentan*) replaced the enterprise unions in Hokkaidō and gave a particular strength to the coal miners' demands. For example, the strike that began on 10 October 1946 as a part of the so-called 'October Offensive' turned out to be a victory for the

Hokkaidō miners, while the pre-war style enterprise based unions in Kyūshū were unable to match the regional management federations.[23] This strong local position also caused confusion later when the Hokkaidō miners were unwilling to accept the production bonuses stipulated by national agreements as their previously negotiated bonuses were already better.[24]

NRS was very interested in Hokkaidō at the beginning of the Occupation. The section wrote dozens of reports concerning Japan's natural resources, and many of these studies paid special attention to Hokkaidō. Besides the issues of land reclamation, land tenancy, agricultural production and coal mines, NRS was also active in questions concerning the structure of the Hokkaidō's development administration and local government. Although these issues seem to be quite far from the section's regular field of interest, it did not hesitate to pressure GS and the Ministry of Agriculture and Forestry to win support for its ideas concerning Hokkaidō.[25]

NRS described the future of the Ishikari coalfield, which accounted for about one-fourth of Japanese coal production, in a positive light in late November 1947.[26] Soon after, on 1 December 1947, the 'Plan for the Acceleration of Coal Production' was approved by GHQ. This aimed for the consistent production of coal, and a total of 36,000,000 tons for 1948, an amount considered the minimum requirement to support a functioning economy and provide for some export production. At the same time, the Labour Division of Economic and Scientific Section (ESS) conducted a field trip with the Hokkaidō coal team (consisting of both Japanese experts and Occupation officials) to learn about the reasons behind the unsatisfactorily low production of coal.[27]

As the vigorous activities instituted for the sake of increased production seemed to bear immediate fruit, the coal production teams in Hokkaidō and Kyūshū that had been established in December 1947 were terminated in February 1948. However, they were re-established by April. This was because the desired rate of production was maintained only in the early weeks of 1948. A mission under the command of Major Charles S. Merriam, leader of the coal production team in Hokkaidō, was also dispatched to stop the decline of coal production in May. Merriam's report stated that there was no single group that could be blamed but argued that there was a pronounced lack of spirit on the part of everyone concerned. The passiveness of the management with regards to increasing production was explained through the fact that they were constantly losing money because of the low price of coal, that they were constantly facing new demands for wage increases, and that their own positions with respect to the decentralisation program were insecure. In addition to this, the government's plans to nationalise the coal mines also caused further insecurity.[28]

ESS concluded in June 1948 that the Japanese had to be assisted and advised by GHQ and a certain amount of continuous surveillance would have to be exercised for the sake of achieving the coal production targets. In the case of Hokkaidō, the need for education and supervision was argued to be based on the isolation of the Hokkaidō coal mining sector and to its distance from the central government. This surveillance was to be executed by Eighth Army Military Government teams and the Japanese teams working in conjunction with local Coal Board authorities.

Thus, ESS repeated the recommendation it had already given in April that NRS and other sections should limit their activity to periodic contact in the field with the Military Government teams. Relations with the Japanese government were to be handled by the personal representative of the Chief of ESS.[29]

These initiatives were effective and the production targets were even exceeded in September 1948. Yet, when the representative of ESS reported to the press about this production increase and the GHQ cooperation with the coal industry, he also warned the managers of unprofitable Japanese mines that government subsidies to offset their mounting deficits could not last forever. This was clearly a reaction against the early policy where the price of coal was kept low and the highly sought after increase in coal production was pursued through the increase of the number of miners and their working hours, while serious attempts to increase efficiency through rationalisation and mechanisation were delayed. These changes, combined with radical revisions to government subsidies and deficit loans to coal companies, were connected to a major policy shift that redefined the objectives of the Occupation.[30]

The announcement of the nine principles of economic stabilisation that were to be adopted in Japan was a sign of a shift that made economic recovery the top priority within Occupation policy. Here, the Occupation took a step away from the spirit of the Joint Chiefs of Staff's 'Basic Initial Post-Surrender Directive' (JCS 1380/15), which had stated that the Supreme Commander would not assume any responsibility for the economic rehabilitation of Japan or the strengthening of the Japanese economy. This shift materialised when the Economic Stabilization Program was launched under the guidance of Joseph M. Dodge. The program sought to cut the costs of the Occupation, revive the economy, and enable Japanese companies to return to international markets. It also emphasised a balanced budget, a strengthened tax system, the promotion of exports, and increased industrial output. It was therefore not surprising that GHQ demanded a rapid increase in efficiency in the coal sector as well. The endeavours to balance the budget also changed the instruments through which the public sector supported the coal companies.[31]

Although coal, iron, and steel producing enterprises suffered from decreased government subsidies, the Hokkaidō coal mines were not neglected by GHQ.[32] The instrumental steps toward mechanised coal mining were taken only in the 1950s, but some improvements were made in Hokkaidō with the assistance of U.S. Aid Counterpart Fund loans after this new instrument replaced the Reconstruction Finance Bank that had awarded policy-guided loans to priority production sectors. The same funding instrument was also utilised in the construction of hydroelectric power plants in Hokkaidō.[33]

Observing industrial development and working through transportation problems

The lack of Hokkaidō-specific initiatives did not mean that the Occupation authorities were disinterested in the development of other fields of industry and suggested their reform. The occupiers observed, for example, the conditions and problems within Hokkaidō's fishing industry. An NRS report in January 1946 highlighted the need for fuel, extra food allowances, and fishing equipment to secure Hokkaidō's capability to produce its normal amount of fish.[34] Nonetheless, GHQ did not show genuine willingness to intervene in the development of the fishing industry in Hokkaidō.[35] While many interest groups in Hokkaidō and around Japan eagerly expressed their opinions concerning reform, the new Fishing Industry Law that finally passed the Diet in the spring of 1950 was drawn up by the government under instructions from GHQ.[36]

The role of observer, similar to that exercised over the fishing industry, was adopted in the case of forestry and its related industries. NRS completed a positive analysis of the forestry situation in Hokkaidō by December 1945, and it seemed to them that the forests in Hokkaidō were in good condition and that logging activities could be increased. However, the related industries of lumber, veneer, and plywood production were described as suffering from outdated machinery and a shortage of labour, lubricants, chemicals, and glue. Furthermore, the poor condition of the transportation infrastructure was noted. In April 1946, another report emphasised the great need for lumber industry products and the problems regarding their production. The lack of transportation was considered a critical problem, both in terms of rail and water-based shipments. The report describing the veneer and plywood manufacturing followed the same pattern. Hokkaidō, one of the major production areas, but with limited consumption of its own, could not ship out all of the plywood it manufactured.[37]

These troubles in relation to transportation, labour, supplies, and materials were also recognised through the observation of the iron and steel industries.[38] The importance of Hokkaidō-based facilities was increasing because Japan's pre-war role as an eminent steel producer had been based on imported raw materials. The Kuchan limonite mine in Hokkaidō and Kamaishi in Iwate accounted for approximately 70 percent of the production of domestic iron mines. Furthermore, only two major iron and steel plants, Muroran (in Hokkaidō) and Kamaishi (in Iwate), were situated near iron mines, with the rest suffering from the wider transportation issues Japanese industry was struggling under at this time.[39]

The Occupation authorities did not, however, turn a blind eye to problems. The Civil Transportation Section (CTS) sent a representative to Hokkaidō at the beginning of 1948 when serious problems in transporting timber from the railway stations to coal mines were discovered.[40] The administration of Hokkaidō's road development projects had already been criticised earlier, but no traces of direct action by GHQ have been found.[41] Yet, it was the question of Hokkaidō's harbours that drew the greatest attention. The fact that the bulk of freight cargo shipment was shifting from Otaru, which had suffered from the loss of Karafuto, to the southern shore of Hokkaidō made the question of the development and requisite capacity of the island's harbours a rather complex matter.[42] This discussion culminated in the enactment of the Harbour Law in May 1950. The new law was objected to in Hokkaidō as it was to shift part of the funding responsibilities for harbour development from the central government to Hokkaidō. Governor Tanaka

Toshifumi and representatives of the Hokkaidō Prefectural Assembly appealed to various ministers in an attempt to get the central government more involved in the construction and maintenance of ports and harbours in Hokkaidō. Hokkaidō-based groups emphasised the importance of these activities but underlined the financial inability of the local government to bear the heavy cost of such work. They stated that the volume of coal, timber, and other raw materials shipped out of Hokkaidō amounted to 70 percent of the aggregate volume of the cargo shipped in and out of Hokkaidō. Therefore, it was argued, the state should consider the service of Hokkaidō to the rest of the country as a supplier of the raw materials and help develop and maintain its ports and harbours.[43]

These appeals were heard in the Diet, which approved the enactment of a special law covering the costs of the construction of harbours in Hokkaidō. However, this was not unanimously approved of within GHQ. CTS was opposed and urged GS not to accept the passing of the bill at the end of July 1950. According to CTS, the continuation of virtually all subsidies from the central government for port construction or improvement work in Hokkaidō was not desirable because it would reduce the local governments to their former position of 'petitioners' for the favours of the central government. CTS believed that if the central government was to cover all the costs of construction it would also decide on everything. Therefore, the proposed legislation was directly against GHQ policy of encouraging local autonomy and the responsibility of local governments. Moreover, the chief of CTS argued that there was already an oversupply of port and harbour facilities in Hokkaidō.[44]

While the delegation from Hokkaidō could not change the opinion of CTS in September, Legal Section (LS) informed GS that it had no legal objections concerning the bill in November. Although the position of LS was a bit more circumspect, when the bill was presented to the House of Representatives at the end of January 1951,[45] GHQ did not intervene, and the law concerning harbour construction for the development of Hokkaidō was approved in March.[46]

Reparations and the effects of economic deconcentration on Hokkaidō-based enterprises

Both the Potsdam Declaration and JCS 1380/15 demanded compensation for the countries Japan had ravaged, and the Occupation authorities promptly began to survey, inventory and protect all industrial machinery and plants which could potentially be used as reparations. This task was headed by Reparations Commissioner Edwin W. Pauley. The Pauley Mission presented its recommendations in mid-December 1945 and proposed the reorientation of Japanese industry toward agriculture and light industry. Following the spirit of divesting Japan of its heavy industrial capacity, GHQ began to draw up lists of plants and factories earmarked for removal.[47]

However, these lists were ripped up when the general objectives of the Occupation changed. Clifford S. Strike completed a review of the reparations program in March 1948. His conclusions differed from those of the Pauley Mission and called for dramatic cuts in the reparations targets. Furthermore, these proposals, paving the way for the elimination of reparations in May 1949, recommended that industries such as pig iron, steel, and machine tools be exempted from the reparations program in order to jump-start domestic production.[48] Although the program vanished without major long term effects, the re-starts of many Hokkaidō industries were at least partly delayed because of it. Namely, many of the Hokkaidō-based production facilities that had suffered hardly any war damage – especially in the field of heavy chemical industry – were designated as reparations material and thus remained inactive for years.[49]

The activities aiming at the dissolution of the large industrial and banking combines which had exercised control over a great part of Japan's trade and industry are discussed elsewhere in this volume, but the effects and the implementation of the program in Hokkaidō itself can be studied through the cases of three enterprises: the Japanese-Russian Fishing Company (*Nichirō Gyogyō*), Ōji Paper Manufacturing Company (*Ōji Seishi*), and the Hokkaidō Cooperative Dairy Association (*Hokkaidō Rakunō Kyōdō*), all of which played a major role in Hokkaidō industry. However, these cases do not cover all the fields of industry affected by the economic deconcentration program. The Hokkaidō Colliery and Steamship Company (*Hokkaidō Tankō Kisen, Hokutan*), for example, as a subsidiary of the Mitsui zaibatsu and the Muroran-based iron and steel companies, encountered their share of the turbulence that was felt throughout the coal and metal mining industries.[50]

Nichirō Gyogyō, established in 1914, had grown during the pre-war period through purchases of, and amalgamations with, other companies involved in fishing and the production of canned fish. This had been followed by a complete amalgamation in 1943 under the terms of the Enterprise Reconstruction Act. In practice, the remaining interests engaged in fishing operations in northern waters were ordered to join with Nichirō Gyogyō. The level of the company's operations was drastically cut during the last years of the war as the northern waters became increasingly unsafe. After the surrender, the company lost all of its operations and large capital investments that were widely distributed on Kamchatka, the Kuriles, and Karafuto. The company was, however, able to overcome these financial difficulties through the utilisation of its reserves and continued to be involved in various fishing and crabbing operations, mainly in Hokkaidō.[51]

When GHQ compiled a list of private companies whose executives should be removed as a part of the economic purge, NRS's Fisheries Division recommended Nichirō be included. The Japanese government requested the company be removed from the list in March and April of 1947, but GS went along with the view of NRS.[52] Eventually the company lost, if only temporarily, five of its leaders in the purge, including its politically active President Hiratsuka Tsunejirō and Vice-President Kōno Ichirō.[53] ESS became interested in Nichirō Gyogyō in September 1947 and again in May 1948, but did not recommend any actions against the company. The Holding Company Liquidation Commission (HCLC) cancelled the designation of the Nichirō Gyogyō as 'a company subject to operation in accordance with the elimination of excessive concentration of economic power' in December 1948.[54] There are no sources directly validating such an argument, but it is worth considering whether the treatment of Nichirō Gyogyō here was connected to the promotion of the Japanese export-oriented fishing industry.[55]

The Ōji Paper Manufacturing Company, which was closely associated with the Mitsui zaibatsu, achieved a virtual paper production monopoly in 1933 when two rivals facing economic difficulties were pressured to amalgamate with it. The company remained in a dominant position during the war but the amount of its production decreased. At the end of the war, Ōji Paper suffered a major blow through the loss of production facilities and pulpwood resources, especially in Karafuto, but also on the Asian mainland. Moreover, the company soon caught the eye of GHQ and, from early 1946 onwards, it began to submit pre-emptive reorganisation plans to ESS suggesting the idea of splitting into two operating companies, although ESS rejected these. By May, ESS expressed its preference for a three-company plan, suggesting that the facilities in Hokkaidō would form one company, but this was only the first step of an ongoing and complex process.[56]

After rejecting another reorganisation plan in the spring of 1947, the representatives of ESS verbally informed Ōji Paper that it should be broken up into nine units by the end of June. M. E. Foley, the officer studying the reorganisation of Ōji Paper, accepted that the combination of the three paper mills in Kyūshū under one company that could then compete with the Tomakomai mill in Hokkaidō, which had a virtual monopoly in the production of newsprint paper. The company provided a seven-company counter proposal in July 1947, ESS again demanded a plan based on nine companies in December.[57]

Ōji Paper then submitted a new five company reorganisation plan to the HCLC in June 1948. In this plan, the Tomakomai and Kushiro mills were again within the same company. Yet, these facilities were separated in a six-company plan discussed in a conference with the representatives of ESS and the HCLC in mid-July. ESS was satisfied with the outcome of these negotiations, but NRS then disagreed. It pointed out that the company had overcut forest resources in every area serving their mills with the exception of Hokkaidō, and over 90 percent of the forest area and the stock stands of timber owned by the company were located in Hokkaidō. It was therefore assumed that the two mills in Hokkaidō would have a great advantage over the others, which might fail and thereby recreate a monopoly, albeit for the Hokkaidō mills.[58]

After ESS and NRS reached an agreement, this issue was forwarded to the HCLC in October 1948. Here the basic scheme for the reorganisation was changed once more. When the HCLC finally gave its order for the reorganisation of Ōji Paper in January 1949, the company was to be dismantled into three independent companies. Company A was to include the Tomakomai Mill, whereas the Kushiro Mill was included in Company B. Whether it was due to the HCLC's activities aimed at scaling back economic reforms and the containment of business deconcentration is hard to tell, but the HCLC's order here resembled the company's original proposals.[59] While failing to make a distinction between GHQ and the HCLC, the official history of Ōji Paper describes this result as the best conceivable one.[60]

Although the economic deconcentration program caused changes to Ōji Paper's structure, the effectiveness in reality of these changes can be questioned. Namely, it had already been argued already in November 1947 that Fujiwara Ginjirō, the purged former president of the company, was still controlling the company through his subordinates.[61] Furthermore, several new facilities were constructed to correspond with the rising demand for paper in the early 1950s and Tomakomai Seishi expanded into Honshū. The company renamed itself in June 1952 and resurrected the old name of Ōji Seishi Kabushiki Kaisha (that had been banned by the Occupation authorities) in December 1960.[62]

The wartime reconstruction of the Japanese economy also touched on the Hokkaidō dairy industry when the Hokkaidō Agricultural Cooperation Corporation (*Hokkaidō Kōnō Kōsha*) was established in April 1941. This was a scheme to unify all dairy plants in Hokkaidō and, among other things, promote the manufacture of new agricultural products, and contribute to agricultural land improvement projects. The organisation changed its name and structure following the defeat and became the Hokkaidō Cooperative Dairy Association (HCDA) in December 1947.[63] Through this process, thousands of dairy farmers became shareholders, and the non-milk-related branches were separated from the mother company. Nevertheless, the new company was responsible for almost 60 percent of all the milk produced in Japan, and the share was even larger in the case of butter. Although the HCDA's relative postwar strength also owed something to decreased production in Honshū, it was still designated an applicable company under the elimination of excessive economic concentration order in February 1948.[64]

The company repeated its unsuccessful appeals against the designation but its travails increased when it ran into trouble with the purge program in May 1949. The leadership of the HCDA consisted of many well-known and politically active figures who had been purged during the first years of the Occupation. However, the demand for their immediate resignation in 1949 came as a surprise. According to the Minister of Justice, this stipulation originated from GHQ. Eventually, the resignation of seven top executives and heated debate within GHQ itself on the future of the company did not prevent its dissolution. The main points of argument in the clash between NRS and ESS were the selection of appropriate recipients for the assets of the HCDA once it was split and the actual physical division of these assets. The HCLC decided, in consultation with ESS, to return the three facilities that had been absorbed into the Kōnō Kōsha back to Meiji and Morinaga, while the remaining 45 facilities were to be divided between three new companies. This decision reflected the wishes of Meiji and Morinaga, which argued that their facilities had been forcefully amalgamated into the Kōnō Kōsha in 1941.[65]

Following the announcement of this decision, the HCDA submitted data indicating that only one of the new companies could survive. Therefore, the decision was revised to favour the establishment of a single company comprising all the 45 facilities not scheduled for delivery to Meiji and Morinaga. However, the HCLC did not favour any revision in the decision, as it affected the two major dairy companies. According to a representative of the Ministry of Agriculture and Forestry, this was because ESS had initiated the proposal. Meanwhile, neither the Agricultural Administration Bureau of the Ministry of Agriculture nor NRS, which were the agencies of the Japanese government and GHQ responsible for agricultural cooperatives, were consulted.[66]

NRS, which claimed to represent the majority opinion within the Ministry of Agriculture and Forestry, thus objected to the reorganisation plan. It argued that the proposal was against the formally adopted policy of encouragement of cooperatives. While it demanded a new plan which would comply with GHQ policy on agricultural cooperatives, NRS also reminded ESS that it had the primary responsibility for maximising domestic agricultural production and insuring the implementation of directives and laws related to that.[67] Eventually, in 1950, Meiji and Morinaga received the facilities which NRS described as the 'crown jewels' of the HCDA, and the remaining company and its assets were split in two. Following this reorganisation, Snow Brand Milk Company (*Yuki Jirushi Nyūgyō*) and Hokkaidō Butter (*Hokkaidō Batā*) were established. Nevertheless, this enforced arrangement was not long lasting, as these companies re-unified in 1958.[68]

GHQ and the planning of the future of Hokkaidō's economy

The future of Hokkaidō's economy was widely discussed towards the end of the Occupation when the First Comprehensive Hokkaidō Development Plan was formulated. While connected with the questions of by whom, how, and why Hokkaidō's economy should be developed, this debate revealed the differences in the reasoning about such development between the Hokkaidō and the central government sides. The latter approached the development of Hokkaidō as a method of solving overpopulation and repatriation problems, and as a means of locating and activating resources needed during the postwar economic recovery.[69] The former, however, argued that development should contribute to the improvement of the quality of life in Hokkaidō.[70]

The course that led to the establishment of the postwar Hokkaidō development system did not lack twists and turns.[71] In summary, GHQ did not accept the establishment of the Hokkaidō Development Agency (*Hokkaidō Kaihatsu-chō*) in the spring of 1947, but allowed the establishment of a Regional Committee (*Chiiki Iinkai*) in March 1948 and a Regional Development Conference (*Chihō Kaihatsu Kyōgikai*) within the Economic Stabilization Board (ESB) in May 1948. At the time when the Hokkaidō Comprehensive Development Plan was discussed in the Regional Development Conference, the general aims of Occupation policy had changed. The Hokkaidō Comprehensive Development Council (*Hokkaidō Sōgō Kaihatsu Shingikai*) was then established as an advisory organ to the Prime Minister. This new organisation, which met for the first time in May 1949, took over a substantial amount of the work of the Regional Development Conference. The differences in reasoning concerning Hokkaidō's development between Hokkaidō and the central government were also visible in this new organisation. However, even though the 'ultra-balanced budget' severely restricted the funds available to the development of Hokkaidō, an agreement concerning the establishment of the

Hokkaidō Development Agency (located within the Prime Minister's Office) and the enactment of the Hokkaidō Development Law was reached.

After the opposition of various ministries led to significant revisions and the elimination of some of the proposed powers of the Agency, the Japanese Cabinet approved the Hokkaidō Development Bill, and it was submitted to GHQ in February 1950. The bill was studied and revised by LS, accepted by GS, and sent back to the Japanese government. The Law passed the Diet but was revised again just a year later when the Hokkaidō Development Bureau was established. This revision reallocated various administrative and executive functions from prefectural to national jurisdiction. Although this contradicted earlier Occupation policy, GHQ followed its announced 'hands-off' policy and did not veto the new legislation.[72]

The Hokkaidō Development Agency produced an ambitious comprehensive development plan that covered the period of 1952-1961. An initial Five Year Plan, for the years 1952-1956, was intended to lay the foundations for the rapid expansion of industry, agriculture, and, consequently, population. It therefore concentrated upon the improvement and expansion of electric power and an increase in coal and iron production. While the emphasis was on transport and industry, agriculture was not neglected, and the plan envisioned a great increase in overall food production in Hokkaidō. The development of roads, bridges, harbours, and water management was to help both industry and the people living in Hokkaidō. This grand plan had great aims, but it lacked a realistic funding scheme. Nevertheless, the Occupation authorities did not prevent the execution of the plan, the achievements of which were criticised among policy-makers and in public debate during the second half of the 1950s. It should not, however, be forgotten that some of the planned projects were actually carried out, and some of these received funding from the World Bank.[73]

Conclusion

It is often argued that three different roles were allocated to Hokkaidō at the beginning of the postwar period. These were: roles as a region where repatriates from the lost colonies, demobilised soldiers, and war-displaced persons could immigrate into; a food supply centre that could help the country facing a serious shortage of food; and a supply centre of the raw materials and energy needed for the reconstruction of Japan's economy.[74] While these conclusions are accurate, they do not clarify the role played by the Occupation authorities in pursuing them and the numerous economic reforms initiated by GHQ.

GHQ was clearly committed to, and involved in, two Hokkaidō-specific economic policies. GHQ did its utmost to maximise the coal and food production in Hokkaidō. Thus, it contributed to the process of cementing Hokkaidō's dependence on these two sectors. Furthermore, early Occupation policy continued the wartime policy of emphasising increases in production and the low pricing of coal. This caused an accumulated deficit and a great weight of debts that later constrained the competitiveness of the coal companies.[75] It would, however, be an overstatement to argue that GHQ initiated the future troubles of Hokkaidō's economy that followed in the second half of the 1950s when imported oil gradually began to overtake domestic coal as a major source of energy.

The continuity between the pre-1945 to the postwar periods is a distinctive feature of the structure of Hokkaidō's economy and development. However, it is also obvious that the circumstances and operational preconditions for many economic activities changed drastically. This had great effects on individuals, individual companies, and fields of industry. Yet, the conceptualisation of the broader structure of Hokkaidō's economy remained. The ideas concerning the rapid population increase, the existence of new land suitable for reclamation, and the importance of coal had existed as the basis for economic policies concerning Hokkaidō for decades before the Occupation. At the same time, it can be concluded that the Occupation authorities did not initiate any significant attempts to diversify Hokkaidō's economy and industry. They did not interfere in the pattern where Hokkaidō mainly exported primary sector products to Japan's industrial heartland and imported manufactured goods with a higher degree of processing.[76] This 'semi-colonial' form of internal exchange reflected Hokkaidō's reinforced importance as an internal resource frontier after the loss of the Empire.

Yet, one should not forget that the development of Hokkaidō's economy and the profitability of Hokkaidō-based enterprises were not solely dependent on governmental and GHQ policies. For example, the outbreak of the Korean War in the summer of 1950 increased the demand for, and price of, lumber industry products and caused a lumber boom in Hokkaidō.[77] The early postwar development of various private companies in Hokkaidō was affected by reforms initiated by GHQ; however, there is no indication that the business community of Hokkaidō was a special target for GHQ. Furthermore, it seems that many of the forced adjustments made by GHQ were reversed soon after the Occupation ceased.

Finally, despite the arguments suggesting that GHQ supported the idea of comprehensive development and the claim that the proximity of the Soviet Union increased interest in strengthening Hokkaidō, the Occupation authorities did not have a comprehensive policy concerning the development of Hokkaidō. In other words, there is no evidence to be found in Hokkaidō to support Dinmore's claim that the Occupation authorities played an important role in promoting the ideas of comprehensive development, especially one related to the Tennessee Valley Authority (TVA) model.[78] For example, although Governor Tanaka Toshifumi talked about the TVA as a model for the development of Hokkaidō, GHQ handled the issues concerning Hokkaidō's economy across various bureaucratic sections and did not find it necessary to coordinate the handling of these in a way that would have created a special overall policy for a given geographical region.[79]

Notes

1 Hokkaidō: Japan's Last Economic Frontier, 5/1950. National Diet Library, Tokyo (hereafter NDL), CHS(B) 00757.

2 For more about the taxation and the national government's financial assistance to local governments to carry out the minimum standard of local government services, see: Hokkaidō, *Shin Hokkaidō Shi: Dai 6 Kan, Tsūsetsu 5* (New History of Hokkaidō,

Volume 6, General view 5), Sapporo, 1977, pp. 121–133; E. Takemae, *The Allied Occupation of Japan*, New York: The Continuum International Publishing Group, 2003, pp. 301–304.

3 M. Ōnuma, "Sōron" (General Remarks), *Hokkaidō Sangyōshi* (Industrial History of Hokkaidō), Sapporo: Hokkaidō Daigaku Tosho Kankōkai, 2004, pp. 13–15; A. B. Irish, *Hokkaidō: A History of Ethnic Transition and Development on Japan's Northern Island*, Jefferson, NC and London: McFarland & Company, 2009, p. 223.

4 Ōnuma, "Sōron", pp. 10–12, 15–16. See William Tsutsui's chapter in the current volume for more on the fishing industry.

5 Ibid., pp. 15–16; H. Okuda, "Kensetsugyō" (Construction Industry), *Hokkaidō Sangyōshi* (Industrial History of Hokkaidō), Sapporo: Hokkaidō Daigaku Tosho Kankōkai, 2004, p. 163; Y. Ōba, "Seijuku to Sensō no Jidai" (Maturity and Wartime Period), *Hokkaidō no Rekishi (Ge): Kindai – Gendai Hen* (History of Hokkaidō (Second half). Modern – Contemporary Volume), Sapporo: Hokkaidō Shimbunsha, 2006, pp. 213, 216, 223–224, 230; Irish, *Hokkaidō*, pp. 223–224.

6 Ōnuma, "Sōron", pp. 16–17; Ōba, "Seijuku to Sensō no Jidai", pp. 215–217; A. Banno, *Hokkaidō Kaihatsu Kyoku to ha Nanika: GHQ Senryōka ni Okeru Nijū Gyōsei no Hajimari* (What is the Hokkaidō Development Bureau? The Beginning of the Double Administration under the GHQ Occupation), Yūgen Kaisha Jurōsha, Sapporo 2003, pp. 30–31.

7 Ōnuma, "Sōron", pp. 17–18.

8 Ibid.; Ōba, "Seijuku to Sensō no Jidai", pp. 240–244.

9 Banno, *Hokkaidō Kaihatsu Kyoku*, p. 73; Irish, *Hokkaidō*, pp. 245–248, 251, 253; J. Bull, "Occupation-era Hokkaidō and the Emergence of the Karafuto Repatriate: The Role of Repatriate Leaders", in S. Paichadze and P. A. Seaton, eds., *Voices From the Shifting Russo-Japanese Border – Karafuto/Sakhalin*, London and New York: Routledge, 2015, p. 70. See also Steven Ivings's chapter in this volume.

10 GHQ, SCAP, NRS, Report Number 52, 21/8/1946. NDL, NRS 02083. See Mark Metzler's chapter in the current volume for more on Japan's energy/food crisis.

11 Takemae, *The Allied Occupation of Japan*, pp. 340–341.

12 The Home Ministry that was dissolved at the end of 1947 already consisted of a Reclamation Bureau.

13 F. C. Jones, *Hokkaidō: Its Present State of Development and Future Prospects*, London: Oxford University Press, 1958, p. 42; Banno, *Hokkaidō Kaihatsu Kyoku*, p. 73. See Steven Ivings's chapter in the current volume for more on repatriates' employment in agriculture.

14 Yuki Jirushi Nyūgyōshi Hensan Iinkai, *Yuki Jirushi Nyūgyōshi, Dai 1-Kan* (History of Snow Brand Milk Products, Volume 1), Sapporo: Yuki Jirushi Nyūgyō Kabushiki Kaisha, 1960, pp. 529–530; Takemae, *The Allied Occupation of Japan*, pp. 342–344.

15 L. A. Brown, GHQ, SCAP, NRS, Memorandum for Record, 16/6/1947. The United States National Archives, College Park, Maryland (hereafter NARA), RG 331, Entry1812, Box 8782, Folder 2; GHQ, SCAP, NRS, Memorandum for Record, 12/11/1946. NARA, RG 331, Entry 1815, Box 8854, Folder 5; GHQ, SCAP, NRS, Memorandum for Record, 29/7/1948. NARA, RG 331, Entry 1424, Box 2383, Folder 7; L. I. Hewes, Jr., GHQ, SCAP, NRS, Memorandum for Record, 14/10/1948. NARA, RG 331, Entry 1815, Box 8854, Folder 5; R. R. Richie, GHQ, SCAP, NRS, Memorandum for Record, 2/2/1949. NARA, RG 331, Entry 1815, Box 8858, Folder 16; W. I. Ladejinsky, GHQ, SCAP, NRS, Memorandum for Chief of Section, 9/8/1948. NARA, RG 331, Entry 1815, Box 8858, Folder 24. See also: Hokkaidō, *Shin Hokkaidō Shi*, pp. 212–230.

16 For documentation concerning the court case against the constitutionality of the land reform, see: NARA, RG 331, Entry 1815, Box 8854, Folder 3.

17 See R. Siddle, *Race, Resistance and the Ainu of Japan*, Abingdon: Routledge, 1996.

18 By March 1950, less than a quarter of the original allotment had been reclaimed and only a quarter of this land was in Hokkaidō. Jones, *Hokkaidō*, p. 42.

19 GHQ, SCAP, NRS, Memorandum for Record, 22/10/1948. NARA, RG 331, Entry 1812, Box 8781, Folder 13; Banno, *Hokkaidō Kaihatsu Kyoku*, pp. 74, 146.

20 J. W. Dower, *Embracing Defeat: Japan in the Wake of World War II*, New York: W.W. Norton & Company and The New Press, 2000, pp. 118, 534–535; Takemae, *The Allied Occupation of Japan*, pp. 310, 486; S. Sugiyama, "'Keisha Seisan' Kōsō to Shizai Rōdōryoku Shikin Mondai" ('Priority Production' Plan and Material, Labour Power, Funding Problems), *Nihon Sekitan Sangyō no Suitai. Sengo Hokkaidō ni Okeru Kigyō to Chiiki* (The Decline of Japan's Coal Industry, Business and Region in Postwar Hokkaidō), Tokyo: Keiō Gijuku Daigaku Shuppan, 2012, pp. 58–62.

21 K. Koda, "Kiso Sozai Kōgyō" (Basic Material Industry), *Hokkaidō Sangyōshi* (Industrial History of Hokkaidō), Sapporo: Hokkaidō Daigaku Tosho Kankōkai, 2004, p. 188. See Mark Metzler's chapter in the current volume.

22 J. Moore, *Japanese Workers and the Struggle for Power 1945–1947*, Madison: The University of Wisconsin Press, 1983, pp. 33–40, 44, 46; M. Itabashi, *Kussetsu Shita no Hokkaidō no Kōgyō Kaihatsu: Senzen no Mitsui Bussan to Hokutan Nikkō* (Twisted Hokkaidō Industrial Development: The Prewar Mitsui Bussan Nikkō), Sapporo: Hokkaidō Shimbunsha, 1992, pp. 162, 166; Sugiyama, "'Keisha Seisan' Kōsō to Shizai", p. 79.

23 Moore, *Japanese Workers*, pp. 33–40, 44, 46, 213–216; Takemae, *The Allied Occupation of Japan*, p. 312.

24 ESS, Industrial Division, Daily Conference Report, 18/2/1948. NDL, NRS 09395; Progress Report No. 9, 20/3/1948. NDL, CIE(D) 00579.

25 J. Saunavaara, "Postwar Development of Hokkaidō: The U.S. Occupation Authorities' Local Government Reform in Japan", *The Journal of American-East Asian Relations*, Vol. 21, 2014, pp. 140–144, 147.

26 GHQ, SCAP, NRS, Report Number 99, 28/11/1947. NDL, NRS 02166 – NRS 02117.

27 GHQ, SCAP, ESS, Labor Division, Report on Field Trip with Hokkaidō Coal Team, 5/1/1948. NARA, RG 331, Entry 1469, Box 2616, Folder 20; Banno, *Hokkaidō Kaihatsu Kyoku*, pp. 118–119; Sugiyama, "'Keisha Seisan' Kōsō to Shizai", p. 70.

28 R. W. Beasley, GHQ, SCAP, ESS, Memorandum to the Chief of Staff, 30/4/1948. NARA, RG 331, Entry 1469, Box 2616, Folder 20; C. S. Merriam, Memorandum for record, 4/6/1948. NDL, NRS 09395.

29 W. F. Marquat, GHQ, SCAP, ESS, Memorandum for the Chief of Staff, 30/4/1948. NDL, NRS 09395; W. F. Marquat, GHQ, SCAP, ESS, Memorandum to the Chief of Staff, 21/6/1948. NARA, RG 331, Entry 1469, Box 2616, Folder 20; F. P. Jecusco, ESS, Industry Division, To: Coal Coordinator, Chief of Industry Division. Chief of Price & Distribution Division of ESS, 3/6/1948. NARA, RG 331, Entry 1835, Box 9163, Folder 3.

30 Banno, *Hokkaidō Kaihatsu Kyoku*, p. 120; H. Miyashita, "Sekitangyō" (Coal Industry), *Hokkaidō Sangyōshi* (Industrial History of Hokkaidō), Sapporo: Hokkaidō Daigaku Tosho Kankōkai, 2004, pp. 145–148.

31 R. B. Finn, *Winners in Peace: MacArthur, Yoshida, and Postwar Japan*, Berkeley: University of California Press, 1992, pp. 195–204; Dower, *Embracing Defeat*, pp. 540–541; Takemae, *The Allied Occupation of Japan*, pp. 143, 173, 468–469; Miyashita, "Sekitangyō", pp. 145–148.

32 Itabashi, "Kussetsu Shita no Hokkaidō", pp. 168–169.

33 GHQ, SCAP, NRS, Technical Examination of Coal Mines in the Ishikari Coal Field, Hokkaidō, 15/11/1949. NARA, RG 331, Entry 1469, Box 2616, Folder 20; Jones, *Hokkaidō*, p. 50; Takemae, *The Allied Occupation of Japan*, p. 469; Miyashita, "Sekitangyō", p. 149. See Mark Metzler's chapter in the current volume for more on hydropower.

34 According to the report Hokkaidō produced one-third of the total fishery output of Japan proper and exported approximately 61 percent of its marine products, mainly to Honshū. GHQ, SCAP, NRS, Report Number 14, 20/1/1946. NDL, NRS 02061.

35 See William Tsutsui's chapter in this volume for more on the fishing industry.

36 Hokkaidō, *Shin Hokkaidō Shi*, pp. 238–239; H. Ikeda, "Gyogyō" (Fishery), *Hokkaidō Sangyōshi* (Industrial History of Hokkaidō), Sapporo: Hokkaidō Daigaku Tosho Kankōkai, 2004, p. 101.

37 GHQ, SCAP, NRS, Report Number 11, 22/12/1945. NDL, NRS 02060; GHQ, SCAP, NRS, Report Number 32, 26/4/1946. NDL, NRS 02069; GHQ, SCAP, NRS, Report Number 34, 8/5/1946. NDL, NRS 02069.

38 See Mark Metzler's chapter in this volume for more on the crisis of material and energy flows at this time.

39 GHQ, SCAP, NRS, Report Number 50, 31/10/1946. NDL, NRS 02081 – NRS 02082; GHQ, SCAP, NRS, Report Number 69, 26/2/1947. NRS 02096 – NRS 02097; GHQ, SCAP, NRS, Report Number 64, 15/1/1947. NDL, NRS 02090; Monthly Military Occupational Activities Report Apr. 47. NDL, *Senryōki Todōfuken Gunsei Shiryō, Dai 2 Kan, Hokkaidō* 2. See also Thomas French's chapter in this volume.

40 ESS, Industrial Division, Daily Conference Report, 18/2/1948. NDL, NRS 09395.

41 A. T. M., Memo for File, ESB-Hokkaidō Road and Street Improvement and Development, 29/5/1947. NARA, RG 331, Entry 1812, Box 8781, Folder 19. See Thomas French's chapter in this volume for more on the poor state of Japan's roads in this era.

42 Newspaper Translation, News, Asahi Shimbun, 31/8/1950. NDL, CAS(A) 02077.

43 Memo Routing Clip, From Mr. Osmond + re Enactment of Law Regarding Harbor Construction for the Purpose of Development of Hokkaidō, n.d. NDL, CTS 02192; Petition, Governor Tanaka et al. to Prime Minister et al. NDL, CTS 02192.

44 Check Sheet, From CTS to GS, 28/7/1950. NDL, CTS 02192. The CTS had also opposed a proposal that would have allowed special treatment for ports of Yokohama and Kōbe in April 1950. See: NARA, RG 331, Entry 1805, Box 8720, Folder 31.

45 Memo Routing Clip, From Mr. Osmond NDL, CTS 02192; From LS to GS, 11/1950. NDL, 11791; House of Representatives, Bill for the Port Construction for the Development of Hokkaidō, Presented by Tamaki, S, 30/1/1951. NDL, LS 11791; F. C. Goodman, from LS to GS, 5/2/1951. NDL, LS 11791.

46 The law can be found at, http://law.e-gov.go.jp/htmldata/S26/S26HO073.html, accessed 11/11/2015.

47 M. Schaller, *The American Occupation of Japan: the Origins of Cold War in Asia*, New York: Oxford University Press, 1985, pp. 33–38, 120; T. Cohen, *Remaking Japan: the American Occupation as New Deal*, New York: The Free Press, 1987, pp. 146–150.

48 Ibid.

49 Itabashi, "Kussetsu Shita no Hokkaidō", p. 165; Koda, "Kiso Sozai Kōgyō", pp. 188, 190. In some cases, the Occupation army used reparation plant materials in Hokkaidō. Nevertheless, the scale of this utilisation of Japanese privately owned assets seems to have been so small that it should not be over-emphasised when the development of Hokkaidō's economy is considered. See, for example: NDL, CPC 31469; 31521; CPC 33809; CPC 33810.

50 See, for example: Hokkaidō, *Shin Hokkaidō Shi*, p. 255; Itabashi, "Kussetsu Shita no Hokkaidō", pp. 165–167; Koda, "Kiso Sozai Kōgyō", p. 190.

51 C. V. Duval, ESS, A&C, Memorandum for Chief, Antitrust and Cartels Division, 30/9/1947. NDL, ESS(A) 12575; C. V. Duval, ESS, A&C, Memorandum for Chief, Antitrust and Cartels Division, 4/5/1948. NDL, ESS(A) 12570. See William Tsutsui's chapter in this volume for more on the fishing industry.

52 T. Kanamori, Memorandum for General Whitney, Chief of GS, 31/3/1947. NDL, GS(B) 00355 – GS(B) 00356; B. Sirota, Memorandum to Major Napier, Chief Purge Officer, 17/4/1947. NDL, GS(B) 00356; R. W. Snow, Jr., GHQ, SCAP, GS, Memorandum for Record, 15/5/1947. NDL, GS(B) 00355.

53 Hiratsuka Kiju Kinen Kankōkai Hen, *Kiju Hiratsuka Tsunejirō Ryakufu* (A Simple Genealogy of Hiratsuka Tsunejirō on his Seventy-Seventh Birthday), Tokyo: Nichiro Gyogyō, 1957, p. 42; J. Saunavaara, "Multilevel Relations in Japanese Political Parties at the Beginning of the Post-war Period: Hokkaidō as a Case Study", *Contemporary Japan*, Vol. 27, No. 2, 2015, pp. 154–155, 158, 162.

54 C. V. Duval, ESS, A&C, Memorandum for Chief, Antitrust and Cartels Division, 30/9/1947. NDL, ESS(A) 12575; C. V. Duval, ESS, A&C, Memorandum for Chief, Antitrust and Cartels Division, 4/5/1948. NDL, ESS(A) 12570; HCLC, Order of Cancellation of Designation, 17/12/1948. NDL, ESS(A) 12570. See Steven Ericson's chapter in the current volume for more on the HCLC.

55 See William Tsutsui's chapter in this volume for more on the export of fish.

56 The Oji Paper Manufacturing Co. LTD. To J. M. Henderson, 7/3/1946. NDL, ESS(H) 02047; M. E. Foley, Memorandum to Chief, Zaibatsu Branch, 5/4/1946. NDL, ESS(H) 02047; M. E. Foley, Memorandum to Chief, Zaibatsu Branch, 10/4/1946. NDL, ESS(H) 02047; M. E. Foley, Oji Paper Company, Conference on 20 May 1946, 20/5/1946. NDL, ESS(H) 02046; M. E. Foley, Memorandum to Chief of Antitrust and Cartels Section, Mr. Henderson, 31/5/1946; M. E. Foley, GHQ, SCAP, ESS, Memorandum to Chief, Antitrust and Cartels Division, 18/4/1947. NDL, ESS(H) 02047. See also, Ōji Seishi Kabushikigaisha, *Ōji Seishi Shashi, Honpen* (Ōji Paper Company History, Main Volume), Tokyo: Ōji Seishi Kabushikigaisha, 2001, pp. 66, 71–75; Y. Ishii, "Ringyō" (Forestry), *Hokkaidō Sangyōshi* (Industrial History of Hokkaidō), Sapporo: Hokkaidō Daigaku Tosho Kankōkai, 2004, p. 116.

57 M. E. Foley, GHQ, SCAP, ESS, Memorandum to Chief, Antitrust and Cartels Division, 18/4/1947. NDL, ESS(H) 02047; The Oji Paper Manufacturing Co. LTD. to G. R. Lunn, Jr., Antitrust and Cartels Division, 22/4/1946. NDL, ESS(H) 02046; M. E. Foley, ESS, Antitrust and Cartels Division, Memorandum for Chief, Antitrust and Cartels Division, 6/5/1947. NDL, ESS(H) 02046; The Oji Paper Manufacturing Co. LTD. to G. R. Lunn, Jr., Antitrust and Cartels Division, 9/7/1947. NDL, ESS(H) 02046; M. E. Foley, ESS, Antitrust and Cartels Division, Memorandum for Chief, Antitrust and Cartels Division, 22/7/1947. NDL, ESS(H) 02046; The Oji Paper Manufacturing Co. LTD. to G. R. Lunn, Jr., Antitrust and Cartels Division, 23/7/1947. NDL, ESS(H) 02055; M. E. Foley, Recommendations, 3/12/1947. NDL, ESS(H) 02055; M. E. Foley, Memorandum for Chief, Antitrust and Cartels Division, 9/12/1947. NDL, ESS(H) 02055.

58 M. E. Foley, ESS, Antitrust and Cartels Division, Memorandum for Chief, Antitrust and Cartels Division, 5/6/1948. NDL, ESS(H) 02054.; M. E. Foley, ESS, Antitrust and Cartels Division, Memorandum for Chief, Antitrust and Cartels Division, 16/7/1948. NDL, ESS(H) 02054; E. C. Welsh, ESS, Antitrust and Cartels Division, Memo for file, 2/8/1948. NDL, ESS(H)02054; Check sheets between the NRS and ESS in August 1948, 8/1948. NDL, ESS(H) 02053; M. E. Foley, ESS, Antitrust and Cartels Division, Memorandum for Chief, Antitrust and Cartels Division, 10/9/1948. NDL, ESS(H)02053; The Future of Japan's Paper Industry, H. R. Murdock, Head, Pulp and Paper Branch, Forestry Division, NRS. NDL, ESS(H) 02053; M. E. Foley, ESS, Antitrust and Cartels Division, Conference between Natural Resources and ESS/AC, 22/9/1948. NDL, ESS(H) 02053; E. C. Welsh, Memo for file, 23/9/1948. NDL, ESS(H) 02053.

59 See Steven Ericson's chapter in this volume.

60 H. H. Scheier, ESS, Antirust and Cartels Division, Memorandum for Deconcentration Review Board, 10/10/1948. NDL, ESS(H) 02052; HCLC, In the Matter of Oji Seishi Kabushiki Kaisha, Final Order of Reorganization, 1/1949. NDL, ESS(H) 02051; Ōji Seishi Kabushikigaisha, *Ōji Seishi Shashi,* pp. 75–76.

61 GHQ, SCAP, ATIS, Letter from Tanaka Kishiichi to General MacArthur, 15/11/1947. NDL, ESS(H) 02055. Many of the company's top executives and managers reacted to the increasing risk of being purged by resigning willingly from late 1946 onwards. Ōji Seishi Kabushikigaisha, *Ōji Seishi Shashi,* p. 73.

62 Koda, "Kiso Sozai Kōgyō", pp. 189–190.

63 Referred often as the Hokkaidō Cooperative Dairy Company (HCDC) in the GHQ/SCAP documents.

64 Yuki Jirushi Nyūgyōshi Hensan Iinkai, *Yuki Jirushi Nyūgyōshi*, pp. 522–523, 578, 683–684; 688; Hokkaidō, *Shin Hokkaidō Shi*, pp. 256–259; J. Nakahara, "Rakunō" (Dairy Farming), *Hokkaidō Sangyōshi* (Industrial History of Hokkaidō), Sapporo: Hokkaidō Daigaku Tosho Kankōkai, 2004, pp. 65–67; Megmilk Snow Band Co., Ltd Homepage, History, www.meg-snow.com/corporate/history/, accessed on 9/12/2015.

65 GHQ, SCAP, NRS, Memorandum for Record, 28/1/1949. NARA, RG 331, Entry 1815, Box 8858, Folder 16; R. R. Richie, GHQ, SCAP, NRS, Memorandum for Record (Initial), 22/5/1949. NARA, RG 331, Entry 1815, Box 8858, Folder 16; D. C. Goodwin, GHQ, SCAP, NRS, Memorandum for Record, 9/8. NARA, RG 331, Entry 1815, Box 8858, Folder 23. See also: Yuki Jirushi Nyūgyōshi Hensan Iinkai, *Yuki Jirushi Nyūgyōshi*, pp. 685, 687–694, 699–700.

66 Ibid.

67 H. G. S., NR to ESS, Reorganization Plan for Properties Belonging to Hokkaidō Cooperative Dairy Company, n.d. NARA, RG 331, Entry 1815, Box 8858, Folder 23.

68 Hokkaidō, *Shin Hokkaidō Shi*, pp. 256, 259; Nakahara, 2004, p. 67; Megmilk Snow Brand Co., Ltd Homepage.

69 See Steven Ivings's chapter in the current volume.

70 A. Takahashi, *Shōgen: Hokkaidō Sengoshi – Tanaka Dōsei to Sono Jidai* (Testimony: The Postwar History of Hokkaidō – Period of Tanaka in Hokkaidō Politics), Sapporo: Hokkaidō Shimbunsha, 1982, pp. 222–225; Banno, *Hokkaidō Kaihatsu Kyoku*, pp. 139, 149–150.

71 For detailed descriptions, see: Banno, *Hokkaidō Kaihatsu Kyoku*; S. Koiso, *Hokkaidō Kaihatsu no Kiseki: Sengo Hokkaidō Kaihatsu Gyōsei Shisutemu no Keisei Katei* (The Path of Hokkaidō Development: The Formation Process of Postwar Hokkaidō Development Administration System), Sapporo: Hokkaidō Kaihatsu Kyōkai, 2003; S. Koiso, and M. Yamazaki, *Sengo Hokkaidō Kaihatsu no Kiseki 1945–2006* (The Path of Hokkaidō Development in the Postwar Period, 1945–2006), Sapporo: Hokkaidō Kaihatsu Kyōkai, 2007; Saunavaara, "Postwar Development of Hokkaidō", 2014.

72 After General Matthew B. Ridgway replaced General Douglas MacArthur as the Supreme Commander for the Allied Powers, he authorised the Japanese government to review existing laws and ordinances. Thereafter, GHQ did not veto any legislation that did not directly violate explicit GHQ orders or directives. Saunavaara, "Postwar Development of Hokkaidō", p. 150.

73 Jones, *Hokkaidō*, pp. v, 43–46, 74; Ōnuma, "Sōron", p. 24; M. Yamazaki, *Kokudo Kaihatsu ni Jidai – Sengo Hokkaidō wo Meguru Jichi to Tōchi* (The Period of Land Development – Autonomy and Rule around Postwar Hokkaidō), Tokyo: Tokyo Daigaku Shuppankai, 2006, pp. 71–74; Koiso and Yamazaki, *Sengo Hokkaidō Kaihatsu*, pp. 111–112, 118.

74 Banno, *Hokkaidō Kaihatsu Kyoku*, pp. 146–147, 165; Ōnuma, "Sōron", pp. 18, 23–24; Y. Kobayashi, *Hokkaidō no Keizai to Kaihatsu: Ronten to Kadai* (Hokkaidō Economy and Development: The Point of Argument and Issues), Sapporo: Hokkaidō Daigaku Shuppankai, 2010, pp. 27, 38, 46.

75 For more, see: Miyashita, "Sekitangyō", p. 148.

76 For more details, see: Ōnuma, "Sōron", p. 23.

77 Newspaper Translation, News, Yomiuri Shimbun, 3/9/1950. NDL, CAS(A) 02077; Newspaper Translation, News, Mainichi Shimbun, 6/12/1950. NDL, CAS(A) 02078.

78 According to Dinmore GHQ officers, many of whom had backgrounds in the New Deal program, acted through and in close cooperation with the ESB. E. Dinmore, "Concrete Results? The TVA and the Appeal of Large Dams in Occupation-Era Japan", *The Journal of Japanese Studies*, Vol. 39, No. 1, Winter 2013, pp. 1, 19, 21, 25–27.

79 A similar kind of conclusion can be drawn through the study of GHQ policy concerning the Hokkaidō development administration. See: Saunavaara, "Postwar Development of Hokkaidō".

Part 2

Industries under the Occupation

4   An empire reborn

The Japanese fishing industry during
the Occupation

William M. Tsutsui

Introduction

This chapter on the experience of Japanese fisheries during the Allied Occupation is a concise overview of a neglected period in the history of a neglected industry in the historiography of modern Japan. Despite the tremendous importance of commercial fishing to the history of Japanese industrialisation and the expansion of the Japanese empire before World War Two, not to mention its contributions to Japan's high-growth, export-oriented economy after the Occupation, the fishing industry has received little attention from business and economic historians. Even those who have written extensively about Japan's fisheries have frequently glossed over the experience of Japanese fishermen and fishing enterprises during World War Two and the Occupation, often overlooking this time as almost an aberration, a period of disruption and discontinuity separating two eras of Japanese global dominance in fisheries production. What literature is available on this period tends to focus on fishing as an issue in international relations, and specifically in the making of postwar ocean management regimes, or as a component of food security policy, rather than as an industry of fundamental significance to Japan's economic growth and international trade.[1] In other words, the history of Japan's fisheries after World War Two, at least in the English-language literature, has been told almost exclusively as a political story (and generally one of only tangential significance to larger superpower rivalries) rather than as an economic narrative of central importance to Japan's postwar recovery and the emergence of an export-driven 'miracle' economy.

This chapter is based on an argument that, while seemingly modest in ambition, advances our understanding of Japan's fisheries from economic, environmental, and transwar perspectives. Put simply, the assertion here is that the Occupation was a critical period of revitalisation for the Japanese fishing industry after the dislocations and devastation of war. Even though, as in so many areas of political, social, and economic life touched by the Supreme Commander for the Allied Powers (SCAP), the Americans brought with them strong reformist ideas regarding Japanese fisheries, the Occupation authorities ended up affirming (rather than transforming) existing practices and strategies originally developed in Japan during the drive for empire and the mobilisation for war. Occupation policy thus served as a bridge, almost seamlessly connecting what has elsewhere been dubbed Japan's 'pelagic empire' of the early twentieth century to the sprawling, global, informal empire of fisheries that Japanese firms and the state built from the 1950s to the 1970s.[2]

This chapter will begin with a brief outline of the political economy of Japan's pelagic empire prior to World War Two, before surveying the state of Japanese fisheries during total war in the early 1940s. It will then describe the Occupation's initial efforts to rebuild the fishing industry in the wake of the war, a rapid reconstruction that led quickly to excess capacity, acute competition, and the depletion of marine resources. Despite an outspoken commitment among Occupation personnel to conservation-based fisheries practices, and constant pressure from American and other international fishing interests to limit the growth of Japanese operations, SCAP ultimately endorsed many of the aggressive strategies that had characterised Japan's pre-war drive for pelagic empire. This Occupation sponsorship of the regional and global resurgence of the Japanese fishing industry set the stage for Japan's return after 1952 to a dominant position among the world's fishing nations.[3]

The legacy of the pelagic empire

Japanese fishermen and whalers had long worked the nation's coasts, but a modern offshore fishing industry only began to develop in the late nineteenth century as Japan was increasingly integrated into the world economy. From the 1870s, Japanese fishermen first gained rights in Russian waters and assertively started operations in Sakhalin and along the coast of the Sea of Okhotsk.[4] After victory in the Russo-Japanese War (1904-1905), additional concessions were won off Kamchatka, and Japanese concerns were soon exploiting them aggressively. Advanced gear and techniques introduced from the West also contributed to the growing reach and productivity of the Japanese fleet. Japan's first modern otter trawler was purchased from Great Britain in 1908 and Japanese shipbuilders soon learned to replicate it quickly and inexpensively; within just a few years, over a hundred new vessels were operating from Japanese ports.[5] Japan's first motor-powered tuna boat was launched in 1906, and they soon were being used to pursue skipjack through the Ogasawara Islands.[6] Importantly, Japan's initial efforts to establish offshore fisheries closely paralleled the earliest growth of Japan's terrestrial empire. With new possessions acquired in the Sino-Japanese (1894-1895) and Russo-Japanese (1904-1905) Wars, and with the 1910 annexation of Korea, Japanese fishermen ventured quickly and enthusiastically beyond the coastal waters of home and into the neighbouring seas of northeast Asia.

The geographical and economic expansion of Japanese fisheries in the first decades of the twentieth century was unprecedented in Japan's (and, quite possibly, the world's) history. Motor-powered fishing boats, for instance, increased in number from less than three dozen in 1908 to almost 6,000 in 1920. Over the same span of just over a decade, Japanese fishermen could boast five-fold growth in their offshore catches. By the early 1930s, Japan could justifiably claim to be the world's leading fishing nation, with fisheries production at home and in the empire exceeding five million tonnes a year.[7] The bulk of this burgeoning growth came in offshore and deep-sea fisheries, even though the yield from coastal waters continued to rise steadily in the pre-war decades.[8] Japanese trawlers first swept the East China and Yellow Seas in 1921, the South China Sea in 1927, and the Gulf of Tonkin in 1928. Japanese fishermen chased tuna through the southwestern Pacific, especially after Germany's scattered island possessions in Micronesia passed to Japan as the spoils of World War One. Even as Japanese boats ventured ever further south and east, in rich northern seas, the Japanese were pioneers in developing the crab fishery and came to dominate it: Japanese crabbers began to venture into the Kuriles in 1909 and Japanese factory ships started working the Siberian coast in 1922. The bounty from crabbing, as from Japan's other new fisheries, was remarkable: by the start of the 1930s, Japanese interests were producing over 400,000 cases of canned crab annually, more than 80 times the output of just a decade earlier.[9]

After the onset of the Great Depression, Japan's push to increase fisheries production only accelerated. Although scholars have commonly assumed that feeding a hungry Japanese populace and provisioning a swelling Asian empire were driving the intensification in fisheries, Japanese policymakers do not appear to have been motivated primarily by concerns over food security.[10] Similarly, even as fisheries provided jobs for hundreds of thousands of Japanese, including many along the economically hard-hit northeastern coast, maintaining employment during a time of global distress seems not to have been pivotal in Japanese government planning either.[11] Instead, Japan's fishing industry was mobilised in the years after the Manchurian Incident of 1931 as part of the nation's increasingly all-consuming imperial project. Thus, what Tokyo demanded from Japanese fishermen and whalers was less marine protein for domestic consumers or employment opportunities for idle workers than the foreign exchange essential for keeping Japan's empire growing and its armed services amply supplied with imports of oil, ore, rubber, and other strategic raw materials. Thus, more than ever before, Japanese fisheries were expected to deliver ever more export goods and hard currency, to find, catch, and process ever more of the oceans' fish, and to market their products ever more aggressively throughout Asia, in Europe and America, and around the world.

The diversity of marine goods offered to global consumers by Japan's eager exporters was impressive. Canned seafood, which was originally promoted in Japan to support military demand, was a focus of the export drive, with over 80 percent of the goods bound for overseas markets. Japanese canned salmon and crab production went largely to Britain and the United States, while Japanese canned tuna became dominant in the American market, undercutting domestic producers on price. Japanese fishermen sold prawns caught off Mexico's coast and frozen albacore from the central Pacific to Californian wholesalers, supplied dried and salted fish to buyers in China and Southeast Asia, and dominated local seafood distribution channels in Singapore and other outposts of the European empires. Meanwhile, Japanese trawlers and factory ships relentlessly worked the

Sea of Japan, the Sea of Okhotsk, and the Bering Sea, manufacturing other marine commodities like fishmeal and liver oil, much of it sold to consumers in Germany.[12] The advantages of fisheries as a critical export industry for resource-poor Japan were apparent: as one observer noted in 1940, at the height of the pre-war export drive:

> The fishing industry serves Japan as an important source of foreign exchange. Her exports of marine products amount annually in value to between ¥150,000,000 and ¥160,000,000 and thus rank third after raw silk, and cotton yarn and piece-goods exports. Also, the fish cost practically nothing, whereas raw cotton must be imported for the textile industry and vast mulberry plantations must be maintained by silk-growers.[13]

From the beginning of Japan's modern fisheries, the state played a central role in the progress of the fishing industry, and especially its growth into distant-water, export-oriented operations. 'Fisheries build up the nation' (*suisan rikkoku*) became a frequently repeated slogan from the 1890s as political leaders and fishermen alike acknowledged a shared interest in building the industry and extending the reach of the Japanese fleet. Echoing the aspirations of Meiji modernisation and nation (as well as empire) building, one 1900 fisheries textbook proclaimed that 'fishery development is the basis of a rich nation, as well as the basis of a strong army'.[14] Japan's Foreign Ministry, for instance, consistently promoted fishing interests, pushing assertively for expanded fishing rights in treaty negotiations, especially with the Russians. The Japanese military and the fishing industry enjoyed particularly close ties: the technology for the canning of seafood was encouraged by the armed forces, seeking rations rich in protein for soldiers and sailors; naval vessels often found new life as fishing boats after being decommissioned and, in turn, ships from the fishing fleet were mobilized for military use during war; and, most notably, Japanese fishermen could count on assistance from the Imperial Navy when venturing into disputed (or, in some cases, indisputably Russian or Chinese) fishing grounds.[15] The government was also a dependable source of monetary support for the fishing industry as it sought to boost production and develop ever more distant waters. From 1897 and the passage of the Pelagic Fisheries Encouragement Law, Tokyo provided subsidies to spur the construction of new, technologically advanced ships designed for offshore and deep-sea operations. Subsequent state initiatives helped private fishing interests invest in high-capacity factory ships, build state-of-the-art refrigeration and ice-making facilities, and develop new enterprises overseas, particularly in Southeast Asia.[16] In addition, the central authorities took the lead in establishing quality standards and enforcing inspection regulations designed to enhance the reputation and appeal of critical export commodities (like canned salmon) in markets abroad.[17]

Japan's government, in short, understood that fishing (and especially the high-technology, high-investment, high-returns offshore and pelagic fisheries) was an industry and, as such, required encouragement, guidance, and management every bit as much as Japan's other strategic industries like steel, textiles, or machine tools.[18] In fact, it seems apparent in retrospect that Japan's famed 'industrial policy', traced by Chalmers Johnson back to the interwar period, was applied as early and as effectively to fisheries as it was to other important economic sectors.[19] Officials in the Fisheries Bureau of the Ministry of Agriculture and Forestry were actively involved in charting the growth of the fishing industry, enjoying particularly close relations with the handful of large enterprises that dominated Japan's export-oriented, deep-sea fisheries. As one bureaucrat described the state's role in 1939, 'the Government controls and supervises the high seas fisheries in a prudent manner [so that] demand and supply of aquatic products [may be] perfectly adjusted'.[20] To minimise conflicts and prevent 'excessive competition' (a fixation of Japan's interwar economic planners) in the rapidly expanding industry, the authorities created an elaborate licensing system for deep-sea operations and established a wide range of trade organisations, from cooperatives to producers' federations. When private interests clashed on the fishing grounds, the state was generally quick to intervene, encouraging cooperation, strong-arming consolidation of operations or restricting licenses in waters with declining yields.[21]

Significantly, the Fisheries Bureau was also focused on the strategic goals of extending the reach and growing the production of the industry. Thus, the state was often at the fore of efforts to explore and develop new grounds and new markets for Japanese fishermen. Tokyo promoted and financed a series of exploratory expeditions, dispatching government research ships or small groups of private fishing vessels to assess the potential of unexploited, often quite distant, waters. These reconnaissance missions paved the way for intensive Japanese trawling in the South China Sea, in the northern Sea of Japan, and into the Bering Sea in the 1920s; by the 1930s, state-organised prospecting for fish stocks took place through the peripheral waters of the Pacific, into the Indian Ocean and the Bay of Bengal, and even as far afield as the Arabian Sea.[22] Nomura Masuzō, president of the influential Imperial Fisheries Association, proudly declared in 1939 that 'As a result of aggressive measures taken by the Government to promote the industry, coupled with application of scientific provisions, both the scale and technical skill of the industry have made marked progress in official and public undertakings'.[23]

A critical element in Japan's swift ascent as the world's leading fishing nation was an elaborate infrastructure of educational and research institutions created and funded by the central and local governments. At the apex stood the Imperial Fisheries Institute (*Suisan Kōshūjo*), founded by industry leaders in the 1880s and absorbed by the Ministry of Agriculture and Commerce in 1897, which gained an international reputation for its research activities and coordinated nationwide training programs. Coastal prefectures and municipalities began establishing fisheries experiment stations and local high schools focused on marine science and vocational education for fishermen from the 1890s. These public institutions, many of which deployed state-of-the-art research and training ships, not only produced skilled workers for the growing fishing industry but also were responsible for important technological advances (including in commercially important areas like the canning of crab and tuna). In addition, Tokyo developed and administered a sprawling web of oceanographic laboratories and marine observation stations ringing Japan and later extending throughout the empire.[24] This comprehensive institutional framework was dedicated to applying scientific knowledge and the power of education to further the productivity and profitability of Japanese fisheries. Thus, 'just as pre-war Japanese fishermen were mobilized for the needs of the state and the demands of empire, so oceanography and fisheries education were mobilized in the support of ever-greater catches and ever-growing export returns'.[25]

The swelling catches of Japan's fishing industry came with environmental consequences, however. Even as growth may have boosted the nation's food supply, employment rate, and (above all) its export statistics, the wide-ranging and notoriously efficient Japanese fishing fleet put ever-increasing pressure on fish stocks and marine ecosystems across the Pacific and even beyond. Japan's push into offshore and distant-water operations from the start of the twentieth century was at least partially motivated by increasingly apparent signs of stress on heavily exploited coastal fishing grounds. One expert concluded that 'At present we are often told of the devastation of the coastal fisheries or of the scarcity of fish along the coast. We are unable to prove the patent facts of these reports, due to the imperfection of statistics, but the decrease of fish and the deterioration of their breeding rate are felt everywhere'.[26] As Japan's fleets of modern trawlers and factory ships moved progressively further in search of untapped stocks, the same legacy of environmental strain seemed to follow in their wakes. The yield of valuable commercial species (notably bream and croaker) dipped during the 1920s in the East China and Yellow Seas, leading Japanese fishermen to new trawling grounds. A collapse in the sardine and herring fisheries in the 1930s similarly forced Japanese interests to look to different waters and seek out more plentiful species for exploitation. Moreover, through the decades prior to World War Two, Japanese crab, tuna, and salmon producers were almost constantly challenged to open more distant resource frontiers in order to grow (and, increasingly, even just maintain) production levels.[27]

As Japan's fishing fleet pushed relentlessly into new waters and landed ever-greater catches, Japanese fishermen gained a reputation as unapologetic international outlaws and ruthlessly efficient exploiters of the oceans, unimpeded by concern for either regulations or conservation. The Russians and the Chinese had long experience of intrusions by Japanese trawlers and factory ships and, as a result, were outspoken (and ever vigilant) critics of Japan's fishing practices.[28] Across the Pacific, American awareness of the threat posed by Japan's marine ambitions first stirred in 1906, after a party of Japanese poachers raided the fur seal rookery on St. Paul Island in the Bering Sea.[29] Three decades later, when Japanese ships made an exploratory sweep through the rich salmon waters of Bristol Bay, Alaskan politicians and fishing interests, as well as media commentators across the United States, angrily branded Japan's actions 'a damaging invasion' and an 'attack'.[30] The *New York Times* warned that 'just as the Nipponese military juggernaut rolls across China without regard for the amenities of civilization, so do these fishing vessels from Tokyo completely overlook conservation rules and principles in their quest for the finny wealth of the ocean'.[31] John Steinbeck, who travelled the coastline of Baja California in 1940 in an American sardine boat, left a chilling account of Japanese shrimpers in *The Log from the Sea of Cortez*:

> In about an hour we came to the Japanese fishing fleet. There were six ships doing the actual dredging while a large mother ship of at least 10,000 tons stood farther offshore at anchor . . . There were twelve boats in the combined fleet including the mother ship, and they were doing a very systematic job, not only of taking every shrimp from the bottom, but every other living thing as well . . . The sea bottom must have been scraped completely clean. The moment the net dropped open and spilled this mass of living things on the deck, the crew of Japanese went to work. Fish were thrown overboard immediately, and only the shrimps kept. The sea was littered with dead fish . . . The waste of this good food supply was appalling, and it was strange that the Japanese, who are usually so saving, should have done it . . . We liked the people on this boat very much. They were good men, but they were caught in a large destructive machine, good men doing a bad thing. With their many and large boats, with their industry and efficiency, but most of all with their intense energy, these Japanese will obviously soon clean out all the shrimps of the region. . .[T]hey were committing a true crime against nature and against . . . the eventual welfare of the whole human species.[32]

Japanese whaling, like the nation's commercial fisheries, also grew rapidly in the early twentieth century. Although the Japanese had long practiced small-scale coastal whaling using basic and relatively inefficient pre-industrial technology, Japan's whalers began to modernise in the last decades of the Meiji period. Motivated by falling catches in coastal waters and with encouragement from the state, whaling interests began operating larger ships, embraced the latest European technologies, and moved well beyond Japan's home waters.[33] Japanese vessels only arrived in the seas off Antarctica, the world's most productive and competitive whaling area, in 1934, but they quickly made their presence felt. Within only a few years, six Japanese fleets were working the Antarctic and Japan could claim to be third among the world's top whaling nations, lagging behind only Great Britain and Norway in production. Japan's slice of the global catch soared from only one percent in 1930 to 12 percent in 1938.[34] Significantly, although many scholars have simply assumed that Japanese whaling has historically been driven solely by food security concerns, the expansion of the 1930s was very much focused on producing exports and delivering hard currency for Japan's economic and imperial needs. While the whale meat produced in the Antarctic was consumed in Japan's home market, policymakers and operators considered it secondary to the production of whale oil, the majority of which was exported to Europe for the manufacture of margarine and soap.[35]

By 1941, the Japanese fishing industry could boast a sprawling, virtually global reach, stretching from the Arctic Circle to the Antarctic Ocean, from the North Pacific to the South Atlantic, and from the Bay of Bengal to the Gulf of California. Japan's fisheries, by far the largest in the world, constituted a veritable pelagic empire of trawling grounds and rich tuna waters, purse seiners and factory ships, state-of-the-art processing facilities, advanced oceanographic laboratories, and sophisticated distribution networks. Fishing was a thoroughly modern industry, an important and dependable source of foreign exchange earnings, a major employer, a supplier of valuable protein, and an intrinsic part of Japan's imperial vision.[36] Japan exploited the seas with the same determination that it did the soy and sorghum fields of Manchuria, the coal mines and rice paddies of Korea, and the camphor forests on Taiwan.[37] Moreover, while Japan's marine imperium would collapse as quickly and as thoroughly as its terrestrial one would in the months after Pearl Harbor, Japan's pre-war experience in fishing would leave critical legacies for the postwar rebuilding and resurgence of the industry. Foremost among these were:

(1) A history of exploiting the 'freedom of the seas' for Japan's economic benefit and venturing far from home waters to tap the riches of the world's oceans.
(2) A worldwide reputation for aggressive, predatory fishing practices and a lack of respect for international norms.
(3) A legacy of distant-water fisheries that contributed to domestic food needs, but were often oriented primarily toward export markets.
(4) A pervasive government influence over all aspects of the fishing industry.
(5) An infrastructure of research and educational institutions designed to support the commercial advance of Japanese fisheries.
(6) An economic model based on highly mechanised, large-scale deep-sea fishing operations using low-wage crews to assure competitiveness in international markets.
(7) A pattern of continuously expanding fishing grounds and enhancing fishing technology as existing waters were overfished and depleted.[38]

Rehabilitating the fishing industry in occupied Japan

Ironically, just as Japan's imperial reach grew to its greatest extent in the first months of the Pacific War, its empire of fisheries began to retreat and fade. Deep-sea and offshore operations, including pelagic whaling, ground to a halt as Japan's large fishing vessels were drafted into the war effort. Hundreds of thousands of Japan's experienced fishermen were also called into service by the Imperial Navy. In any case, dwindling supplies of critical resources and the dangers posed by American submarines meant that venturing into distant waters was a wartime impossibility. Indeed, even Japan's coastal fisheries contracted significantly as endemic shortages of cotton yarn, ramie, manila hemp, and, most critically, petroleum depressed wartime production. The statistics show the story of wartime decline: the total value of Japanese fisheries production peaked in 1940 and decreased rapidly, especially with the suspension of Antarctic whaling after the 1941 season and salmon and crab factory ship operations in 1942. Production by weight declined by almost 60 percent between 1940 and 1945, with the catch from offshore waters declining even more steeply. Ice-making capacity fell by more than half over the same time period.[39] The number of Japanese employed in fishing and processing also plummeted, from more than 1.4 million in 1940 to less than a million at the end of the war.[40] In any case, as Japan embarked on an autonomous course in 1941, the primary impetus that had driven the growth of the pelagic empire – generating trade surpluses to fuel Japanese expansion – lost all momentum.

By the time of Japan's surrender in 1945, the fishing industry was, like the economy as a whole, shattered and reeling. Japan's fishing fleet had declined by almost 35 percent in number of vessels and 60 percent in tonnage since 1940.[41] Virtually all of Japan's large, modern trawlers and factory ships were destroyed during the war. Nets, lines, and other fishing gear were ragged from the years of deprivation. Japan's offshore fishing and whaling companies, which the government had pushed to amalgamate from the 1930s, had been rationalized down to four struggling enterprises (*Nippon Suisan, Nichiro Gyogyō, Taiyō Gyogyō*, and *Kyokuyō Hogei*). Port facilities were also in desperate need of repair and ice-making capacity had fallen by well over half. Networks of subsidiaries, joint-ventures, and investments through Asia and around the world were in a shambles. Many of Japan's most productive offshore and deep-sea fishing grounds were also lost with the empire. Meanwhile, per capita fish consumption in the home islands, which was a lean 42 grams per day in 1937 (at the pre-war peak), slumped to just 26 grams per day after the surrender.[42] As one American official later described it, Japan's 'fishery industry [was] in a demoralized condition' and 'virtually at a standstill' when the Occupation forces arrived.[43]

Japan's American occupiers, however, were quick to realise the critical importance of fisheries, and not simply to the urgent, immediate priorities of feeding the malnourished Japanese people and providing employment to the hundreds of thousands of fishermen demobilised from the defeated armed forces. The initial mandate to the Supreme Commander for the Allied Powers from Washington in August 1945 was modest in scope and focused on the perceived humanitarian crisis in food supply in Japan: 'coastal fisheries and fish culture should be utilized as the primary sources for domestic consumption. To the extent that [they] are unable to meet the minimum domestic requirements, deep sea fisheries and other fisheries in water open to Japanese operations may be utilized'.[44] Yet, Occupation staff almost immediately recognised the broader significance of fisheries, appreciating the role of the fishing industry in the pre-war Japanese economy and, above all, in the nation's overseas trade. As a result, American officials in Tokyo prioritised the rapid rebuilding of Japanese fisheries as essential to restoring the nation's economic self-sufficiency, stimulating the growth of other industries (including shipbuilding), serving as a key sector for the revitalisation of the moribund economy, and restarting Japanese exports.[45] As early as November 1945, even Washington had come to similar conclusions, as the Joint Chiefs of Staff pointedly advised SCAP that 'the Japanese authorities will have to make the *utmost effort to maximize* production of agricultural and fisheries products' (emphasis in the original).[46] At the very least, as one American expert declared, 'rehabilitation of the fishery industry . . . was important to American citizens, for every ton of food produced locally by the Japanese themselves relieved the United States from shipping that amount of food to Japan'.[47]

Although Japanese fishermen were severely restricted at first out of Occupation security concerns, within weeks of defeat the American forces authorized the return of Japanese boats to coastal waters and, in a series of rapid incremental moves, to ever-larger areas of the seas surrounding Japan.[48] At the same time, scarce raw materials were targeted to the rebuilding of the nation's fishing capacity. SCAP instructed the Japanese government to 'expedite the rehabilitation' of the industry and soon financing was flowing from Tokyo for the repair and rebuilding of fishing boats, the reconstruction of port infrastructure, and the rejuvenation of ice-making and cold storage equipment.[49] In a four-stage plan executed in 1946 and 1947, for example, over 1,000 new fishing vessels, including trawlers, bonito and tuna boats, and transport ships, were constructed with state assistance.[50] Noting chronic bottlenecks in basic supplies, such as cotton for nets, the Occupation authorities allocated special shipments of materials – above all, petroleum – for dedicated use in fisheries.[51] The resulting revival was rapid and strong: by 1947, Japan had more fishing vessels than at the pre-war peak, and the fleet was made up of larger boats and had a higher proportion of powered ships. Even in 1946, Japanese fisheries production was almost equal to landings in the United States and by the following year, the catch exceeded two-thirds of what had been achieved in the 1930s.[52] By 1950, price and distribution controls on fish (first established by the 1 April 1946 Marine Products Control Order) were abolished, reflecting a plentiful supply of seafood in the domestic market.[53] By 1952, the Japanese people were consuming almost 25 percent more fish per capita than they had at the pre-war peak.[54]

Perhaps not surprisingly, the immediate postwar resurgence of the fishing industry soon showed signs of overheating. With so many fishermen demobilised from the Navy and repatriated from the far outposts of empire, with former naval shipyards enthusiastically retooling to produce new, high-capacity fishing vessels, with the four large fisheries companies eager to resume their offshore and deep-sea fishing and whaling operations, and with capital and raw materials showered on the industry by SCAP and the Japanese authorities, excess capacity became a very real concern. Coastal and near-water fish stocks (especially in the East China and Yellow Seas) rapidly began to show signs of stress from overfishing as more Japanese fishermen, in more and larger vessels, with improved supplies and technology, intensively worked the strictly delineated areas permitted by the Occupation.[55] With yields plateauing, productivity declining, and the incomes of fishermen suffering, a developing crisis was apparent to Japanese and SCAP officials as early as 1947. As one Occupation report described the situation, the industry was 'in a chaotic condition featured [sic] by too many fishermen, overfishing, contradictory and ambiguous laws and regulations, widespread law evasion, and inadequate law enforcement, accompanied by a general lack of appreciation for the serious nature of the situation'.[56]

Confronted by a hungry Japanese populace, a Japanese fishing industry eager to expand, and a government in Washington growing weary of providing food aid to Japan, the Occupation responded to signs of depletion in the existing fishing grounds just as the pre-war Japanese state consistently had, by encouraging Japan's growing fleet to tap less heavily exploited stocks of fish even further from home.[57] Although virtually all of America's wartime allies with interests in the Pacific – the Soviet Union, China, Australia, Canada, the Philippines – vigorously opposed the return of Japanese trawlers and factory ships to their coastlines (not to mention increased competition from the Japanese on the high seas), SCAP progressively relaxed its restrictions on the grounds open to Japanese fishing. The so-called MacArthur Line, which delineated areas authorised for Japanese fishing operations, was repeatedly extended, eventually stretching from the East China Sea to the southern tip of Sakhalin, east to the 180th meridian and south to the former Japanese Mandate in the South Seas (*Nan'yo*), including the Caroline, Marshall, and Mariana Islands. Japanese fishermen were already allowed back into the waters which had yielded 80 percent of the pre-war catch by 1946 and, by 1950, had returned in force to the richest tuna grounds of the Western and Central Pacific.[58] Moreover, since enforcement of the MacArthur Line by the American and Japanese authorities was generally passive, incursions by Japanese fishing boats into waters claimed by the Chinese, Koreans, and Soviets were common.[59]

SCAP officials paid generous lip-service to conservation-minded fisheries practices, excoriating the Japanese government for lax regulation, Japanese fishermen for ignoring licences and catch restrictions, and the industry for pressing 'strongly on exploitation [and giving] very little thought or effort . . . to conservation'.[60] The American authorities also bemoaned the postwar proliferation of high-efficiency, high-capacity fishing boats and Japan's history of relentlessly expanding distant-water operations, even as they continued to approve new shipbuilding programs and facilitated the return of Japanese ships to the very same offshore grounds worked intensively before the war.[61] Moreover, despite stout protestations from Occupation headquarters that it was not caving in to Japanese pressure – 'There was no stampeding of SCAP authorities as a result of the numerous petitions from the fishing industry and requests from the Japanese government',[62] one American staffer insisted – rumours persisted that personal entreaties from the Japanese Emperor to the Supreme Commander had hastened the extension of the MacArthur Line.[63] Douglas MacArthur did, it seems, take a strong personal interest in the success of Japanese fishing under his stewardship: he bristled at intervention from Washington and American fisheries interests, regarded foreign intervention as narrow self-interest, and stubbornly defended the Potsdam Declaration's promise that the defeated Japan would be permitted 'access to, as distinguished from control of, raw materials' (in this case, fish).[64] The evolving Cold War context also had some impact on SCAP fisheries policy, with increased American concern for Japan's economic growth (including the contributions of a key industry like fishing) and a heightened interest in utilising Japanese fishermen to check Soviet and Chinese maritime expansion.[65]

Not surprisingly, as Japanese fishermen were allowed to venture further afield and the acuteness of Japan's immediate postwar food crisis abated, Occupation officials increasingly emphasised the exports of Japanese fisheries products. As early as April 1946, SCAP officials were discussing fisheries exports as a means of generating foreign exchange and reducing Japan's dependence on American aid.[66] As one observer from Washington insightfully put it in 1948, 'From this point on, further increments in the Japanese fisheries are primarily for the purpose of *fishing for dollars* rather than *fishing for food*' (emphasis in the original).[67] American and other overseas fisheries interests stridently opposed the return of Japanese exports to their home markets, but the Occupation, acknowledging the importance of fishing to Japan's economic self-sufficiency, energetically supported Japan's resurgence in the global trade in seafood. SCAP opened an office in New York City to promote Japanese exports in 1947, and the following year, Japanese canned tuna was again on American supermarket shelves. Despite efforts by American tuna producers to raise tariffs (a move opposed by the U.S. Department of State on behalf of SCAP), the inexpensive Japanese product soon flooded the market, leading to the mothballing of American canneries and the docking of much of the West Coast fleet.[68] By 1950, Japan's annual exports (by weight) of both canned and frozen tuna were more than three times the average in the late 1930s.[69] As Nippon Suisan's official history later declared, 'Tuna canning for export was particularly robust given growing demand in the United States. In fact, tuna canning was so strong that it was known as the "axis of exports" '.[70]

Export promotion was also an important element motivating Occupation sponsorship of a series of trial expeditions reintroducing Japanese ships to whaling in the Antarctic Ocean (starting in 1946) and mothership-based tuna fishing (from 1950) beyond the MacArthur Line in the Western Pacific. The resumption of large-scale Japanese whaling beyond home waters proved particularly controversial, especially as Japan had not signed the International Agreement for the Regulation of Whaling prior to World War Two. Despite trenchant opposition from the Far Eastern Commission, a multilateral body nominally charged with recommending policy for the Occupation, SCAP permitted two Japanese whaling fleets to work the Antarctic for the 1946-1947 season, arguing for the acute need for marine protein in Japan.[71] The fleets, operated by Nippon Suisan and Taiyō Gyogyō and comprising mother ships (converted from wartime oil tankers) as well as 19 catcher and carrier boats, produced 21,000 metric tonnes of meat for domestic consumption. However, the expedition also yielded 11 tonnes of valuable liver oil, most of which went to the British and American zones of occupied Germany, and over 12,000 metric tonnes of whale oil, all of which was sold in Europe for margarine production, with the bulk of the returns (totalling some $6,000,000) accruing to SCAP.[72] As David McCracken, an official American observer serving on the Nippon Suisan mother ship, observed, 'Since the only expense to the United States [from the whaling expedition] was some $800,000 worth of fuel oil, the project has been about the sole source of income found yet in Japan to help offset the value of imports to her'.[73] Subsequent annual expeditions proved even more successful in the provision of food products and, above all, in the efficient production of whale oil for export. As a result of applying American managerial and technical expertise, one Occupation report bragged, oil production 'per blue whale unit from Antarctic whaling . . . increased almost 200 percent over prewar averages [sic]'.[74]

In many respects, SCAP stepped directly into the role of the interventionist pre-war and wartime Japanese state, providing support and guidance for Japanese fisheries, enhancing programs and institutions that served fishing interests, and championing the industry in overseas disputes. In addition to its promotion of distant-water whaling and fishing expeditions, the Occupation sponsored foreign study trips for Japanese experts, brought American fishery specialists to Japan as consultants, and facilitated technology transfer.[75] SCAP officials worked to bolster marine research programs in Japan and revitalise fisheries schools and institutes neglected during wartime mobilisation. The American authorities also sought to increase the influence of their counterparts in the Japanese bureaucracy: the Fisheries Bureau in the Ministry of Agriculture and Forestry was upgraded to Agency status and, in the landmark 1949 Fishery Law, state regulatory authority over both coastal and offshore operations was strengthened and extended.[76] Perhaps most remarkably, SCAP rallied U.S. Navy ships (much as the Imperial Navy had once been used) in the East China Sea and off Hokkaidō to protect Japanese trawlers from Chinese, Korean, and especially Soviet patrols.[77]

The Occupation had long been sensitive to the fact that no industry 'impinges upon international relations so directly as does that of fisheries' and that, in the decades prior to 1941, 'the Japanese aroused international antagonisms by their ruthless methods of exploitation and contempt for the rights and interests of others'.[78] SCAP had hoped, through the restrictions under the MacArthur Line, 'to give the Japanese fishermen an opportunity to demonstrate that they had changed some of their attitudes and activities, which had made the Japanese pre-war fishing objectionable to the people of other nations'.[79] However, international antagonism was persistent, and, perhaps not surprisingly, fishing became a critical and sometimes contentious topic in the making of a peace treaty between Japan and the United States, to the extent that John Foster Dulles worried that the negotiations had degenerated into an 'international fisheries convention'.[80] Bowing to political pressure from fisheries interests in the Pacific Northwest, who feared a reprise of Japan's 1937 'invasion' of Bristol Bay, Occupation authorities and Washington diplomats did extract some voluntary concessions from Japan. Under the 1950 Law for the Prevention of the Exhaustion of Marine Resources, the Japanese government made token gestures toward more conservation-minded fisheries regulation and moderation in the growth of Japanese fishing capacity.[81] Japan hesitantly joined the International Whaling Convention in April 1951. Most significantly, in the International Convention for the High Seas Fisheries of the North Pacific Ocean, hammered out in the final months before Japan regained its independence in 1952, Japan agreed to an 'abstention' from harvesting salmon, halibut, and herring from a broad swathe of ocean worked by American and Canadian fishermen. At the same time, however, Washington supported Japan's efforts to secure 'freedom of the seas' for its fishing fleet elsewhere in the Pacific and around the world.[82] As one scholar described it, by the time of the signing of the

San Francisco Treaty, 'the United States had positioned Japan to recapture its position as the world's leading marine fishing power'.[83]

The Occupation and the making of Japan's informal empire of fisheries

Japan was, of course, remarkably quick to re-establish its pre-war dominance in global fisheries. Even well before the San Francisco Treaty and the departure of Japan's American occupiers, the Japanese fishing industry could boast annual catches larger than any prior to World War Two, and Japan could convincingly lay claim to again being the world's premier fishing nation. Over the course of the 1950s, Japan's already impressive fisheries production doubled; between 1960 and 1973, production doubled once more.[84] Japan, a relative latecomer to pelagic whaling, would be the world's pacesetter by 1960 and recorded its record annual harvest (some 226,000 tonnes of whale meat) in 1962.[85] Only a decade after the surrender, when the Japanese fishing industry had been shattered and dispirited by war and defeat, Japan's trawlers, tuna boats, and factory ships were again plying most of the waters they had worked so efficiently in the 1930s and were, indeed, eagerly seeking out new resource frontiers to exploit.[86] Agreeing to an 'abstention' in sensitive North Pacific waters may have calmed American fishing interests and their political backers in 1952, but this unconventional diplomatic gesture had little (if, in fact, any) impact on the resurgence of Japan's fisheries in oceans around the world or in seafood markets globally.

Although the fishing industry has almost never been recognised by scholars as a significant contributor to Japan's 'miraculous' postwar growth, fisheries and whaling played an important role – just like shipbuilding, automobiles, and con- sumer electronics – in Japan's celebrated and unprecedented economic expan- sion in the decades after World War Two. Marine products were a pillar of the Japanese export economy from the Occupation era through the 1960s and, in fact, were even more significant drivers of growth and engines of foreign exchange earnings after the war than they had been during the intense export drive of the 1930s. From 1948, when Japanese canned salmon and tuna once more became available to European and American consumers, Japan's high-quality, low-cost seafood products rapidly captured international markets, and Japan was soon the world's top fisheries exporter once again. Many factors contributed to the over- seas success of the Japanese fishing industry, from a worldwide shortage of food (especially protein) after World War Two, to the liberalisation of trade in canned goods in the United Kingdom, to a growing global appetite for frozen fish.[87] In the mid-1950s, for instance, fish (canned, frozen, and dried) constituted just under six percent of Japan's total exports, a substantially higher share than the pre-war peak of 3.9 percent achieved in 1936. Seafood products ranked fourth among all Japanese export goods at the time (after ships, cotton textiles, and artificial fibres) and were America's second largest import from Japan by value, trailing only silk. By 1960, in the glory days of Japan's high-growth economy, Japanese fisheries grossed almost $200 million a year in exports.[88]

Although advances in technology – from radar and fish finders to massive, highly mechanised new motherships – certainly were a substantial factor in the postwar achievements of Japan's fisheries, the industry's strong resurgence after 1945 can be traced, in no small part, to the legacies left by Japan's pre-war pelagic empire.[89] As the Japanese fishing industry pivoted from being an instrument of Japan's imperial ambitions to being a critical component in a new national drive for prosperity and economic power, it drew upon a longstanding repertoire of practices and strategies originally developed between the Meiji period and the 1930s. In this almost seamless transition from pelagic empire prior to 1941 to a more informal realm of global presence and market leadership in fisheries after the war, the Occupation played a critical role. Just as Chalmers Johnson and others have argued that SCAP sustained and indeed furthered Japan's nascent industrial policy, in spite of its guiding ideology of democratisation, so the American authorities appear to have affirmed, embraced, and strengthened the fundamental principles that had defined and built the pre-war pelagic empire. Thus despite a nagging conscience of conservation-minded fisheries management, outraged complaints from Allied nations, and persistent opposition from American fishing interests, MacArthur's Occupation found itself embracing virtually the full range of fisheries policies pursued by Japan's imperial state, from an orientation toward exports and the generation of foreign currency, to the promotion of distant-water fisheries exploiting high technology and low-wage crews, to a generous system of state subsidisation and pervasive diplomatic, institutional, and even military support for the relentless expansion of fishing grounds. In short, the postwar flourishing of Japan's fishing industry, what has elsewhere been described as an informal empire of fisheries, would have been impossible without the bridge to pre-war imperial practices provided by the Occupation.[90]

Significantly, the historical record reveals that the Occupation was not simply a passive presence in the reconstruction of the Japanese fishing industry, but was in fact an active force supporting, encouraging, and leading the resurgence of fisheries in an otherwise bleak economic landscape and a generally hostile international environment. The officials of SCAP did not simply cede the initiative to Japanese bureaucrats, business associations, and private fishing enterprises (as Johnson and others have suggested was the case in other critical industries); instead, the American authorities quickly and thoroughly embraced the rebuilding of Japan's fisheries, targeting generous financing and scarce commodities to the industry, progressively granting access to rich fishing grounds over the strident objections of other nations, nurturing seafood exports as a key contributor to Japanese economic recovery and self-sufficiency, and driving technological change, improvements in fisheries education and research, and a renewed commitment to pelagic whaling.

Notably, SCAP policy toward fisheries did not follow the standard narrative of Occupation historiography, with a short but intense period of democratising reformism giving way to a 'reverse course' driven by Cold War anxieties and economic worries.[91] The recovery of Japanese fisheries was an explicit priority from the start of the Occupation, American efforts at systemic reform (and specifically the establishment of a more conservation-minded ethos in the fishing industry) were late-coming and half-hearted, and most of the international tensions over fisheries involved conflicts with the Allied powers rather than with the Soviet and Chinese communist regimes. Indeed, throughout SCAP's tenure in Tokyo, American stewardship of the fishing industry tracked more closely with the established logic of Japan's pelagic empire – characterised by a high-efficiency, low-cost production model, an activist state, a pattern of resource depletion and inexorable expansion, and the dogged pursuit of exports – rather than with the standard Occupation historiography of early reformist fervour and later 'reverse course' backtracking. As such, the experience of the fishing industry suggests that historians would do well to reconsider the role of the Occupation more broadly in the postwar revival of Japanese business and the making of Japan's export-oriented, high-growth 'miracle' economy.

Notes

1 The two most recent and important additions to this limited literature are C. Finley, *All the Fish in the Sea: Maximum Sustainable Yield and the Failure of Fisheries Management*, Chicago: University of Chicago Press, 2011, and R. D. Smith, *Japan's International Fisheries Policy: Law, Diplomacy and Policy Governing Resource Security*, Abingdon, Oxon: Routledge, 2015.

2 W. M. Tsutsui, "The Pelagic Empire: Reconsidering Japanese Expansion", in B. Walker, J. Thomas, and I. Miller, eds., *Japan at Nature's Edge*, Honolulu: University of Hawai'i Press, 2013, pp. 21–38.

3 This chapter draws extensively on Tsutsui, "The Pelagic Empire" and W. M. Tsutsui and T. Vuorisalo, "Japanese Imperialism and Marine Resources", in S. Laakkonen, R. P. Tucker and T. Vuorisalo, eds., *The Long Shadows: A Global Environmental History of the Second World War*, Corvallis: Oregon State University Press, 2017, pp. 251–274. See also T. Vuorisalo and J. Lahdenperä, "Japanin Valloituspolitiikka, Luonnonvarat Ja Ympäristö" (Japan's Conquest Policy: Natural Resources and the Environment), in S. Laakkonen and T. Vuorisalo eds., *Sodan Ekologia: Nykyaikaisen Sodankäynnin Ympäristöhistoriaa* (Ecology of War: The Environmental History of Warfare), Helsinki: Suomalaisen Kirjallisuuden Seura, 2007, pp. 403–432.

4 J. Stephan, *Sakhalin: A History*, Oxford: Clarendon Press, 1971, p. 76.

5 *Japanese Offshore Trawling*, Tokyo: Supreme Commander for the Allied Powers, Natural Resources Section Report 138, 1950, p. 7.

6 *The Japanese Tuna Fisheries*, Tokyo: Supreme Commander for the Allied Powers, Natural Resources Section Report 104, 1948, p. 6. On technological change in the Japanese fisheries, see T. Ninohei, *Nihon Gyogyō Kindaishi* (A Modern History of Japanese Fisheries), Tokyo: Heibonsha, 1999.

7 *Japanese Fisheries Production 1908–46 (A Statistical Report)*, Tokyo: Supreme Commander for the Allied Powers, Natural Resources Section Report 95, 1947, pp. 8, 31.

8 *The Economic Development of the Japanese Fishing Industry*, Tokyo: Association for Liberty of Trading, 1933, p. 5.

9 Ibid., p. 9.

10 Even two of the most knowledgeable experts on Japan's modern fisheries, Carmel Finley and Roger Smith, mistakenly focus on food security as the major impetus behind the rapid growth of the Japanese industry in the mid-twentieth century. See Finley, *All the Fish in the Sea*; Smith, *Japan's International Fisheries Policy*; R. Smith, "Japan's High Seas Fisheries in the North Pacific Ocean: Food Security and Foreign Policy",

in D. Edgington, ed., *Japan at the Millennium: Joining Past and Future*, Vancouver: UBC Press, 2003, pp. 67–90; R. Smith, "Food Security and International Fisheries Policy in Japan's Postwar Planning", *Social Sciences Japan Journal*, Vol. 11, No. 2, 10/2008, pp. 259–276.

11 S. Shozui, "Our Fishing Industry", *Contemporary Japan*, Vol. IX, No. 6, 6/1940, p. 701; J. Stephan, *The Kuril Islands*, Oxford: Oxford University Press, 1974, p. 122; *The Economic Development of the Japanese Fishing Industry*, p. 13.

12 *Marine Foods Canning Industry in Japan*, Tokyo: Nichiro Gyogyō Kaisha, Ltd., 1934; *Japan's Fisheries Industry 1939*, Tokyo: The Japan Times and Mail, 1939, pp. 74–75; T. Haraguchi, "Japan's Contributions in the South Seas", *Contemporary Japan*, Vol. VIII, No. 2, 4/1939, pp. 261–262.

13 Shozui, "Our Fishing Industry", p. 701.

14 Quoted in M. Muscolino, "Fisheries Build Up the Nation: Marine Environmental Encounters between Japan and China", in B. Walker, J. Thomas, and I. Miller, eds., *Japan at Nature's Edge*, Honolulu: University of Hawai'i Press, 2013, pp. 59.

15 *Japan's Fisheries Industry 1939*, p. 144; Stephan, *Kuril Islands*, p. 130.

16 *Japan, Special Catalogue, Fisheries*, Tokyo: Imperial Fisheries Bureau, 1915, pp. 101–104; *Japanese Fisheries: Their Development and Present Status*, Tokyo: Asia Kyokai, 1957, p. 2; H. Shimizu and H. Hirakawa, *Japan and Singapore in the World Economy: Japan's Economic Advance into Singapore, 1870–1965*, London: Routledge, 1999, pp. 96–97.

17 *Marine Foods Canning Industry in Japan*, pp. 33–35, 50–54.

18 Tsutsui and Vuorisalo, "Japanese Imperialism and Marine Resources", p. 255; Muscolino, "Fisheries Build Up the Nation", pp. 56–59.

19 C. Johnson, *MITI and the Japanese Miracle: The Growth of Industrial Policy, 1925–1975*, Stanford: Stanford University Press, 1982.

20 Fujita Iwao quoted in *Japan's Fisheries Industry 1939*, p. 10.

21 *Japanese Offshore Trawling*, Tokyo: Supreme Commander for the Allied Powers, Natural Resources Section Report 138, 1950, pp. 26–29; G. Borgstrom, *Japan's World Success in Fishing*, London: Fishing News Books, 1964, pp. 23, 247; Finley, *All the Fish in the Sea*, pp. 22–31.

22 Borgstrom, *Japan's World Success*, pp. 252–255.

23 *Japan's Fisheries Industry 1939*, p. 6.

24 M. Uda, *The Fisheries of Japan*, Nanaimo, British Columbia: Fisheries Research Board of Canada, 1959, p. 8; *Japan, Special Catalogue, Fisheries*, pp. 105–139; *Japan's Fisheries Industry 1939*, pp. 16–17.

25 Tsutsui and Vuorisalo, "Japanese Imperialism and Marine Resources", p. 256; see also "Fisheries Education and Research in Japan", Chicago: U.S. Department of the Interior, Fish and Wildlife Service, Fisheries Leaflet 236, 5/1947.

26 *The Economic Development of the Japanese Fishing Industry*, p. 21.

27 *Japanese Fisheries Production 1908–46*, pp. 32–35; Borgstrom, *Japan's World Success*, pp. 44–45; Muscolino, "Fisheries Build Up the Nation", p. 65.

28 See M. Muscolino, "The Yellow Croaker War: Fishery Disputes Between China and Japan, 1925–1935", *Environmental History*, Vol. 13, No. 2, 4/2008, pp. 306–324.

29 Finley, *All the Fish in the Sea*, p. 30.

30 Joseph Bingham (1938) quoted in J. Minghi, "The Conflict of Salmon Fishing Policies in the North Pacific", *Pacific Viewpoint*, Vol. 2, No. 1, 3/1961, p. 77; Anthony Dimond quoted in L. Leonard, *International Regulation of Fisheries*, Washington, DC: Carnegie Endowment for International Peace, 1944, p. 134.

31 Richard Neuberger quoted in Finley, *All the Fish in the Sea*, p. 34.

32 J. Steinbeck, *The Log From the Sea of Cortez*, New York: Penguin Books, 1995, pp. 204–207.

33 "Small-Type Coastal Whaling in Japan", http://luna.pos.to/whale/gen_coast.html, accessed 19/4/2005.

34 W. M. Tsutsui, "Landscapes in the Dark Valley: Toward an Environmental History of Wartime Japan", *Environmental History*, Vol. 8, No. 2, 4/2003, p. 298.

35 "A History of the Traditional Diet: Japanese and the Whale", http:/luna.pos.to/whale/jwa_trad.html; accessed 27/9/2006. Japan was not a signatory of the first international whaling convention in 1931, with its modest attempts at catch limits, but Tokyo did later did impose some limited restrictions on the Japanese harvest. See S. Lyster, *International Wildlife Law: An Analysis of International Treaties Concerned with the Conservation of Wildlife*, Cambridge: Cambridge University Press, 1993, p. 18.

36 On fisheries and Japan's 'imperial imaginary', see Tsutsui, "The Pelagic Empire", pp. 28–30.

37 Finley, *All the Fish in the Sea*, pp. 3, 20.

38 Tsutsui and Vuorisalo, "Japanese Imperialism and Marine Resources", p. 259.

39 *A History of Hundred Years of Nippon Suisan Kaisha, Ltd.*, Tokyo: Nippon Suisan Kaisha, Ltd., 2012, p. 132.

40 *Japanese Fisheries Production 1908–46*, pp. 8, 20–21, 28, 30.

41 *Japanese Fisheries: Their Development and Present Status*, p. 2.

42 Ibid., pp. 2–3.

43 R. Fiedler, *Operation Fisheries in Japan*, Chicago: U.S. Department of the Interior Fish and Wildlife Service, Fishery Leaflet 229, 4/1947, p. 2.

44 Quoted in H. Scheiber, *Inter-Allied Conflicts and Ocean Law, 1945–53: The Occupation Command's Revival of Japanese Whaling and Marine Fisheries*, Taipei: Academia Sinica, 2001, p. 53.

45 See, for example, H. Esterly, "Overseas Fisheries and International Politics in the Occupation of Japan, 1945–1952", in L. Redford, ed., *The Occupation of Japan: Economic Policy and Reform*, Norfolk, Virginia: The MacArthur Memorial, 1980, pp. 92–123 and Fiedler, "Operation Fisheries", p. 6.

46 Quoted in H. Esterly, "Japanese High Seas Fisheries and the International Politics of the Occupation, 1945–1951", Ph.D dissertation, Columbia University, 1965, p. 25.

47 Fiedler, "Operation Fisheries", p. 2.

48 Useful summaries of the relaxation of Occupation restrictions are provided in Scheiber, *Inter-Allied Conflicts*, pp. 214–215; Esterly, *Japanese High Seas Fisheries*, p. 30ff; and *A History of Hundred Years of Nippon Suisan Kaisha*, pp. 137–138.

49 Fiedler, "Operation Fisheries", p. 3.

50 *A History of Hundred Years of Nippon Suisan Kaisha*, p. 136.

51 Fiedler, "Operation Fisheries", p. 3; *Japanese Fisheries: Their Development and Present Status*, pp. 3–4; *Fisheries Programs in Japan, 1945–51*, Tokyo: Supreme Commander for the Allied Powers, Natural Resources Section Report 152, 1951, pp. 10–15. The U.S. Congress provided 'emergency allocations' of $15 million in 1947 and $45 million in 1948 for fishing supplies in more acute need in Japan. Esterly, *Japanese High Seas Fisheries*, p. 310.

52 "The Present Condition of the Tuna Fisheries", in *The Japanese Tuna Fishing Industry*, trans. W. Van Campen, Washington, DC: U.S. Department of the Interior, Special Scientific Report: Fisheries, No. 79, 7/1952, p. 1; *Fisheries Programs in Japan, 1945–51*, pp. 7, 11; Scheiber, *Inter-Allied Conflicts*, p. 62; Fiedler, "Operation Fisheries", p. 3. See also *Suisan Nenkan* (Fisheries Yearbook), Tokyo: Suisansha, 1954.

53 *A History of Hundred Years of Nippon Suisan Kaisha*, pp. 135–136, 152.

54 *Japanese Fisheries: Their Development and Present Status*, p. 5; *Japanese Offshore Trawling*, pp. 6, 54.

55 *A History of Hundred Years of Nippon Suisan Kaisha*, pp. 140, 166.

56 W. C. Herrington, *A Program for Japanese Coastal Fisheries*, Tokyo: Supreme Commander for the Allied Powers, Natural Resources Section Preliminary Study No. 48, 5/1951, p. 44. Carmel Finley estimates a 70 percent increase in Japanese fishing capacity by the end of the Occupation compared to the 1939 level. C. Finley, "The Tragedy of Enclosure: Fish, Fisheries Science, and U.S. Foreign Policy, 1920–1960", PhD dissertation, University of California, San Diego, 2007, pp. 352–354.

57 Finley, *All the Fish in the Sea*, pp. 73–75, 106–107.

58 H. Scheiber, "Postwar Fishery Regimes of the Pacific: Ocean Law, International Rivalry, and Japanese Economic Expansion after 1945", in H. Scheiber, ed., *Ocean Resources: Industries and Rivalries Since 1800*, Berkeley: University of California Intercampus Economic History Program, 1990, p. 5. On the 'MacArthur Line' and its extensions, see Y. Matsuda, "Postwar Development and Expansion of Japan's Tuna Fishery", in D. Doulman, ed., *Tuna Issues and Perspectives in the Pacific Islands Region*, Honolulu: East-West Center, 1987, pp. 72–73.

59 Esterly, *Japanese High Seas Fisheries*, pp. 168ff, 220ff; U. Granados, "Chinese Ocean Policies Towards the South China Sea in a Transitional Period, 1946–1952", *The China Review*, Vol. 6, No. 1, Spring 2006, p. 168; *A History of Hundred Years of Nippon Suisan Kaisha*, pp. 157–165. Patrols to enforce the MacArthur Line were only instituted by the Japanese government in 1949, at the insistence of SCAP. Esterly, *Japanese High Seas Fisheries*, p. 273ff. Thomas French has created an enlightening online visualisation of seizures of Japanese fishing boats by the Soviets, Chinese, and Koreans during the Occupation, https://occupiedjapan.cartodb.com/viz/0c7531c8-cea8-11e3-86a5-0edbca4b5057/public_map, accessed 3/6/2016. See also T. French, "Using Geospatial Data to Study the Origins of Japan's Post-Occupation Maritime Boundaries", *Asia Pacific Perspectives*, Vol. 13, No. 1, Spring/Summer 2015, pp. 28–56.

60 Herrington, *A Program for Japanese Coastal Fisheries*, p. 19.

61 See, for instance, *Fisheries Programs in Japan, 1945–51*, esp. pp. 33–36, 43–45 and Finley, *The Tragedy of Enclosure*, esp. Chapter 6. In 1949, for instance, a group of U.S. experts surveying fisheries programs in Japan concluded that 'immediately after the war there was such pressure to increase the food supply that the trawling fleet . . . was rebuilt rapidly, and to a level beyond that necessary to fish the authorized areas. This overconstruction was unwisely approved by SCAP'. "U.S. Special Mission Reviews Japanese Fisheries Situation", Washington: U.S. Department of the Interior, Fish and Wildlife Service, Fishery Leaflet, No. 346, 6/1949, p. 6.

62 Esterly, "Overseas Fisheries", p. 99.

63 Scheiber, *Inter-Allied Conflicts*, p. 91.

64 Ibid., pp. 35, 134ff, 159; Finley, *The Tragedy of Enclosure*, p. 254.

65 Harry Scheiber has stressed the role of 'geopolitics' in motivating 'a carefully designed and vigorously pursued U.S. policy to rebuild as quickly as possible this segment [fisheries] of the Japanese economy'. Scheiber, "Postwar Fishery Regimes of the Pacific", p. 5. See also Finley, *The Tragedy of Enclosure*, p. 255.

66 Esterly, *Japanese High Seas Fisheries*, pp. 49–50, 59.

67 Quoted in Scheiber, *Inter-Allied Conflicts*, p. 63.

68 Finley, *The Tragedy of Enclosure*, pp. 257, 355ff; R. Smith, "Japanese Distant Water Fisheries in the Early Post-war Period", *Social Science Japan*, Vol. 26, 5/2003, p. 11.

69 *The Japanese Tuna Fishing Industry*, p. 6.

70 *A History of Hundred Years of Nippon Suisan Kaisha*, p. 174.

71 Scheiber, *Inter-Allied Conflicts*, Chapter 3; Esterly, *Japanese High Seas Fisheries*, Chapter 4; *Fisheries Programs in Japan, 1945–51*, pp. 16–18; *A History of Hundred Years of Nippon Suisan Kaisha*, p. 147ff.

72 K. Brandt, *Whaling and Whale Oil During and After World War II*, Stanford: Food Research Institute, Stanford University, 1948, p. 28. The impact of whale meat on Japanese nutrition during the Occupation was an issue of contention. While SCAP claimed (somewhat dubiously) that over 40 percent of animal protein in the Japanese diet in 1947 came from whale meat, representatives from nations opposed to the reopening of Japanese pelagic whaling argued that, when considered as a part of consumption of *total* protein, whale meat only contributed one percent. Scheiber, *Inter-Allied Conflicts*, p. 131.

73 D. R. McCracken, *Four Months on a Jap Whaler*, New York: Robert M. McBride & Company, 1948, p. vi.

74 *Fisheries Programs in Japan, 1945–51*, p. 18.

75 Ibid., pp. 14–15, 26ff.
76 Scheiber, *Inter-Allied Conflicts*, p. 65ff; *Fisheries Programs in Japan, 1945–51*, pp. 23–26, 35.
77 Ibid., p. 79.
78 "U.S. Special Mission Reviews Japanese Fisheries Situation", pp. 2, 6.
79 *Fisheries Programs in Japan, 1945–51*, p. 20.
80 Quoted in Smith, "Japanese Distant Water Fisheries", p. 9.
81 Smith, "Food Security and International Fisheries Policy", p. 271.
82 See Scheiber, *Inter-Allied Conflicts* and Finley, *All the Fish in the Sea*, esp. Chapter 6.
83 Scheiber, *Inter-Allied Conflicts*, p. 195.
84 FAOSTAT (UN Food and Agriculture Organization, Statistics Division), http://faostat. fao.org/, accessed 15/7/2012.
85 See: "A History of the Traditional Diet".
86 On the postwar expansion of Japanese fisheries, see Borgstrom, *Japan's World Success*, esp. Chapters 10–20; Uda, *Fisheries of Japan*; *Japanese Fisheries: Their Development and Present Status*.
87 Borgstrom, *Japan's World Success*, pp. 97–102, Chapters 10–20; *Japanese Fisheries: Their Development and Present Status*, p. 112ff.
88 Finley, *All the Fish in the Sea*, p. 125; *Japanese Fisheries: Their Development and Present Status*, pp. 90, 112ff.
89 See, for example, Uda, *Fisheries of Japan*, pp. 3–5.
90 Tsutsui and Vuorisalo, "Japanese Imperialism and Marine Resources", pp. 266–271.
91 A number of authors have assumed, often without explicit analysis, that there was a clear 'reverse course' in Occupation policy toward Japanese fisheries. See Esterley, *Japanese High Seas Fisheries*, p. 307ff; Smith, *Japan's International Fisheries Policy*, pp. 35–36; *Suisanchō 50-nen Shi* (A 50-Year History of the Fisheries Agency), Tokyo: Dai-Nihon Suisankai, 1998, p. 46.

5 Fiats and jeeps

The Occupation, jeeps, and the postwar automotive industry

Thomas French

Introduction

The importance of the Occupation within Japanese economic history is beyond doubt, as the various chapters of this volume testify; however, there still remain various partially explored regions within the scholarly landscape of the period. One subject which falls into this category is the impact of small four-wheel-drive passenger vehicles, or jeeps, during the Occupation. This subject can be considered 'partially explored', as within the scholarship its cultural impact is clearly mapped out, and often linked in the process to the power of the Occupation itself, but within the economic sphere, the jeep remains all but invisible, somewhat akin to the censorship of the jeep (and all other visible symbols of the Occupation) from Japanese films produced at the time.[1]

The reasons for this curious partial absence of perhaps the most visible symbol of the Occupation vary, as detailed below. Indeed, the jeep could be said to be in some ways a mechanical embodiment of the Occupation; an alien, militarised, and undeniably American presence in postwar Japan. The jeep, being the omnipresent transportation of General Headquarters of the Supreme Commander of Allied Powers (GHQ) personnel, also traverses the entire landscape of Occupation. As well as being the 'steed' which bore everything the Occupation brought, the jeep itself also exerted other direct influences on Japan during the years 1945-1952. Some of these were cultural, influencing many Japanese people's ideas about personal transportation and automobiles in general. Others were clearly economic, with the maintenance, refurbishment, and, later, manufacture of jeeps, forming a major but rarely examined, element within the development of the postwar Japanese automotive industry. This highly symbolic (and literal) reconstruction an iconic piece of Americana in Japan was also one which laid some of the foundations of the subsequent success of several of Japan's postwar automotive giants. This chapter attempts to examine the impact of the jeep from both of these perspectives, reassessing the already well-established cultural interpretations of the jeep's impact, and detailing the hitherto neglected economic influences of the vehicle during the era.

Off the beaten track – the absence of jeeps in the historiography of the Japanese automotive industry

The postwar era growth of the Japanese automotive industry could be said, due to its high public profile, and by extension prestigious nature, to have central and almost totemic value in indicating the postwar 'success' of Japan, or even the presence of an 'economic miracle'. This prominent public perception and the postwar growth of the industry, often to the detriment of its Western rivals, has led to the mass production of studies of the origins, nature and characteristics of the industry, and particularly the larger corporations within it. The volume of such scholarship has ebbed and flowed over time and its focus has shifted occasionally, but major areas of scholarly attention to date have included: car manufacturing techniques, government and business relations, the histories and development of the major corporations, and the influence of the acquisition of foreign technology and its role in the development of the industry.[2] Each of these areas of scholarship provide significant insights into various aspects of the history of the development of the industry; however, when examining the literature produced to date, a number of gaps emerge in relation to the Occupation period in general, and regarding the influence of jeeps in particular.

In general, it could be said that the Occupation itself is not deeply explored or given much positive credit for its reforms or actions in many accounts of the growth of the automotive industry. In one sense, this is logical in that mass car ownership did not really begin in earnest until the latter 1950s, and hence in many accounts, the period immediately preceding the era of 'high speed growth' is somewhat understandably reduced to mere contextual background. A further influence on the relative lack of prominence of the Occupation could be due to its shifting policies towards the industry: ranging from initial restrictions on production and zaibatsu dissolution efforts (albeit of an eventually limited nature); to encouragement and assistance in terms of improving technological and quality standards; and finally to the mass 'special procurements' (*tokujū*) of 1950 which 'saved the industry' according to some. Some accounts thus treat the Occupation era as a restrictive and troubled period only after which the industry could take flight in the way it always allegedly aimed and planned to do.[3] This is particularly evident in some studies of Toyota which stress the 'dream' of Toyoda Kiichiro, founder of Toyota Motors, to produce high-quality, affordable Japanese cars, which was achieved *despite* the problems of the Occupation era.[4]

Within the economic history of the period the impact of the jeep itself is also underplayed. The Willys jeep was the most common form of small automotive transport present in Japan during the Occupation, and its psychological, economic, and design legacies were all highly significant. However, the latter two of these are almost unexamined within both histories of the industry and the broader Occupation, despite being of crucial importance in terms of the volume of sales, technology transfers, tie-ups, and in tracing the links of the automotive industry to U.S. procurement and the postwar Japanese security forces. For example, the central role of *tokujū* in enabling/accelerating the economic recovery of Japan, and even setting the stage for Japan's era of 'high speed growth' is virtually uncontested in the literature, but within this, the massive rebuilding and procurement programs of jeeps and other vehicles are simply bundled together with the broader *tokujū* boom, receiving almost no separate analysis despite their scale and parts of them preceding the Korean War by several years. Furthermore, the technological influence that jeeps exerted on the industry, which arguably was second in its early postwar history only to that of the mid-1950s tie-ups with European manufacturers, has gone almost entirely unstudied. Jeeps themselves are also given little attention in most studies of U.S. military procurement in Japan, with, for example, the studies of Samuels and Green making virtually no mention of the importance and role of jeeps and trucks.[5]

Part of this neglect potentially stems from both the period in which the jeeps resided, and the state of the automotive industry which maintained and produced them. They were a military vehicle, produced for the U.S. military and its allies, and used to facilitate the Occupation of Japan. The jeep's presence across Japan therefore represented a direct continuity with the Second World War. The jeep also later wove Japanese industry, through its recovery, remanufacture and manufacture, alongside that of other military vehicles, into markets across East Asia, albeit through the connections and contracts of the U.S. military. This clear military legacy arguably does not fit cleanly with narratives of the 'peaceful' postwar growth of the industry and Japan itself. The Willys jeep and its Japanese successors were also intermediary vehicles, mid-points between trucks and cars, as well as military and civilian vehicles. Again, in an industry which prides itself as a maker of high-quality civilian passenger automobiles, the direct link the jeep and its Japanese successors represent to the struggling, grimy, and distinctly unglamorous, truck industry which spawned them also doesn't fit smoothly with narratives of the rise of the car industry to global pre-eminence. The story of the manufacture and remanufacture of the Willys jeep and its Japanese cousins also reveals other transitional or intermediary elements of the industry including: the movement away from mere survival based upon U.S. military procurement; the transition from a truck to a passenger car industry; the early and successful adaption and development of designs and technology from outside of Japan; and the subsequent employment of this in producing highly desirable export-focused products for which markets outside Japan became a focus. As such, these vehicles navigated through a series of crossroads on the route through the rocky road to recovery onto the highway towards future success.

Alongside providing the necessary contextual background to the state of the Japanese automotive industry between 1945 and 1950, this chapter focuses on these major influences of the Willys jeep and its Japanese successors within the economic and cultural history of the Occupation. These include: the well documented, although not entirely unified, interpretations of the cultural impacts and legacy of the vehicle, the role of the reconstruction of jeeps within the car industry, and the highly significant results of the production of home-grown Japanese versions of the jeep.

You and the horse you rode in on – the cultural impact
of Willys jeeps during the Occupation

As the Occupation began, alongside its many trucks and a small number of civilian staff cars, the U.S. military brought with it hundreds of Willys jeeps. Their
light, fast, and functionally stylish design marked a huge contrast to the hand
carts; ox carts; and crude, spluttering, and ponderous, domestically produced
trucks, plying the streets of Japan in 1945. The jeep was a ubiquitous tool of
the Occupation, used by all its arms and for all its work, including: transporting the Atomic Bomb Casualty Commission; carrying humanitarian assistance
to bombed out cities in the immediate postwar days; carrying in tactical troops to
supress riots; helping to protect the Emperor during his newly established tours of
the country and MacArthur on his daily commute to work; through to transporting officials of the zaibatsu dissolution program on their site visits.[6] In terms of
the impact upon the population, the sight of jeeps effortlessly and freely zipping
through the streets, with Japanese policemen snapping to attention as they passed
(as they were required to do by Occupation directive when carrying officers) must
have made a significant impression on many Japanese, especially the young.[7] The
dominant interpretation of the influence of the jeep on the Japanese population in
the scholarship to date has been one of heavy stress on this psychological impact
of the vehicle. However, exactly what that impression was can also be contested.
Different scholars have emphasised the form of this impact and its lasting legacy
in different ways, framed to a degree by the field in which their research is situated
and by the narratives of the Occupation which they seek to espouse.

Scholars whose work is principally centred on the economic history of Japan or
the automotive industry in general tend to stress the interest in vehicles that jeeps
triggered amongst the population. For example, David Plath argues that the arrival
of the vehicles of the Occupation represented the first mass 'practical demonstration' of the impact and potential of motorisation in Japan:

> Before the war Japanese studied the United States example of motorization
> from a distance, through print media, newsreels, and especially Hollywood
> movies. After 1945 they were subjected to a free home demonstration of it,
> one that continued for a decade through the Occupation period and the Korean
> War. The Allied forces brought in hundreds of staff cars, thousands of trucks
> and jeeps. The image of the GIs in their versatile jeeps driving everywhere –
> on and off the roads – and obviously enjoying it – is burned into the memory
> of every Japanese I have ever talked to about those early postwar years.[8]

Penelope Francks supports and extends this argument, stating that the jeep exerted
a significant influence on Japanese automotive culture and even worldview: 'the
American love affair with the car – as symbol of freedom, individuality and mas-
culinity – began to permeate in Japan'.[9] Toyota itself also notes in one of its publications on this era that 'in a sense it was the Occupation army [and its jeeps]
that aroused the Japanese interest in cars'.[10] It is also certainly the case that many

of Japan's first postwar generation of car owners encountered the Occupation's jeeps, and the vehicle seems to have spurred a lifelong interest in automobiles in many, but arguably devoid of much explicit connection to the Occupation itself for some, as is discussed below.[11]

Other scholars stress the psychological impact of jeeps in relation to the power of Occupation itself, and especially the power differential between occupier and occupied. For example, Tessa Morris-Suzuki in her edited collection of personal accounts from the Shōwa era quotes Saitō Mutsuo – a recently demobilised pilot who recalled: 'a few days after I got home, I first saw the Occupation forces . . . an American jeep, full of soldiers, driving down a dusty road. I thought about how we'd trained in the army to go everywhere on foot, and carry all our equipment with us. And I looked at those soldiers sitting in the big powerful jeep. And I thought: "No wonder we lost the war!" [sic]'.[12] Other scholars examine the impact of jeeps upon children in Japan, also through focusing on perceptions of inequality. Dower notes children's admiration of the vehicle itself and their attraction to it by association with the chocolate bars and sweets its occupants carried, and often freely distributed. He also describes how jeep toys quickly became the most popular toy for boys in the immediate postwar period.[13] As Dower also notes, 'jeep' was also one of the first English words young children learned in this era. Dower also alleges their play, some of which was made up of mimicking jeeps, GHQ personnel, and their interactions with Japanese civilians, represented 'finding pleasure in being colonised'.[14] Takemae and Sodei also assert that, in certain circumstances, the jeep came to represent 'more coercion than good intentions' on the behalf of the Occupation.[15] They argue that in many rural areas, the vehicle became associated with the collection of back taxes (in cash or valuables) and rice crops by GHQ personnel, which were undertaken by force, if necessary.[16] Finally, one of the most negative impressions of the Occupation, and one also linked directly to the jeep, was the common image of Americans moving around in the vehicle with local young women, arousing resentment among some Japanese as noted by Dower,[17] and mixed emotions among others, as argued by Takemae:

> 'Recreation jeeps' with Japanese drivers were available to U.S. personnel for off-duty excursions. Officers sped through downtown thoroughfares in commandeered jeeps accompanied by fashionably dressed Japanese girlfriends trailing bright scarves, their insouciance a striking contrast to the gloomy faces of the hungry, ill-clad Japanese, many of them homeless, who looked on these centurions with a mixture of awe and envy.[18]

Han Sang Kim bridges the divide between the two interpretations described above by focusing on the image of the jeep (in this case, within the occupation of Southern Korea) as a symbol of U.S. power, freedom, and technological prowess, being: 'the embodiment of American state-of-the-art technologies . . . a vehicle of high manoeuvrability, as well as a self-contained unit that was not interrupted by any preassigned timetables . . . It was clear that the jeep was a symbol of both advanced technology and self-reliance'.[19] The two positions are also connected in some accounts to the hitherto underplayed economic impacts and legacies of the jeep, such as in the work of Kawahara Akira (a Ministry of International Trade and Industry (MITI) Automobile Section bureaucrat and later Toyota Motor Sales executive), who recalled: 'watching these soldiers made me wonder why anyone born American could own a car, the symbol of 20th-century civilization, but if you happened to be born Japanese, a car was beyond your reach. We needed to do something to rectify the situation'.[20]

The cultural influence of the jeep during the Occupation has therefore been afforded two distinct but somewhat related impacts. A number of interconnected reactions to the vehicle and its occupants are also noted, arguably representing a microcosm of the milieu of Japanese attitudes towards the wider Occupation, and even the U.S. itself at that time, ranging from disgust through envy to enthusiasm, awe, and desire. The dominant narrative within this analysis to date, at least among studies focusing on the Occupation, has been the latter, more negative impression that the jeep graphically demonstrated the technological, military, social, and economic power disparity which existed between the occupiers and the occupied.[21]

Despite the evidence of the vehicle having this impact on many, whether this sense of inequality was really associated directly with the jeep itself, or merely its occupants is hard to gauge, especially as the responses to the vehicle were so subjective and individual. For some, the vehicle was directly linked to the Occupation and served as a persistent reminder of defeat, inequality, and/or occupation, but for others, especially many of the young, it perhaps represented no more than a new, fast, and powerful car they hadn't seen the likes of before. As such, it could be argued that Dower overreaches (or perhaps over-revs) his position in stating that children's play, some of which involved mimicking jeeps, represented finding pleasure in 'being colonised', in that it is unlikely many children had much understanding of such alleged 'colonisation' in the first place and were merely interested in the vehicle for its own sake (or the sweets its occupants might give them).[22] Takemae and Sodei's position that the jeep came to represent Occupation coercion, at least in a rural setting, is challenged by other accounts such as that of Harada and could also be said to be perhaps a little too general in that it does not account for the appeal of, and interest in, the jeep itself, divorced from the actions of those using it and their coercive power.[23] It seems likely that many Japanese were more able to distinguish between the jeep and its occupants than some scholars give them credit for, permitting the rise of the long standing positive interest in the vehicle (and vehicles in general) noted by Plath and others above, separated, in many cases, from the jeep's association with perceived or alleged (mis)deeds of GHQ.

Struggling for traction: the Japanese motor industry to 1950

To fully appreciate the economic, as opposed to cultural, impacts of the jeep upon occupied Japan, an examination of the history of the influence of GHQ policies and procurement on the automotive industry, and the struggles it faced up to 1950, is necessary. From humble beginnings in the first years of the twentieth century, the fledging Japanese automotive industry was relatively advanced by the early 1930s and was producing, alongside trucks and buses, a number of civilian cars, which were largely models built under licence from, or with the assistance of, American or European carmakers.[24] With Japanese moves towards autarky from the later 1930s and a desire to promote the domestic production of vehicles to support its war in China, the Japanese state began to restrict the import of foreign vehicles and heavily assist domestic manufacturers.[25] These changes drastically altered the make-up of the industry in Japan. Ford and General Motors, the major foreign manufacturers, were quickly forced out of business, with both firms pulling out of the market by 1940.[26] Japanese firms stepped in to fill the vacuum, including the newly created Toyota Automotive, a spin-off of the Toyoda family's power-loom business.[27]

The industry went on to produce tens of thousands of trucks for Japanese military and civilian use until 1945. Buses and cars were still produced until 1941 and 1944, respectively, but even before this point the Japanese automotive industry increasingly focused on the production of two and four-ton military specification trucks, largely made of standardised parts.[28] Despite peaking in 1941 with the production of 42,125 trucks, the industry went into rapid decline thereafter, with only 1,758 trucks completed between April and July 1945.[29] Several factors contributed to this collapse in production, including: poor planning, the inept attempted dispersement of industry in 1944-1945, the low prioritisation placed on the industry, the shortage of raw materials, and the loss of Japan's merchant marine, and the access to overseas sources of such materials it provided.[30]

The meagre level of production which was maintained also consisted of vehicles of usually dismally poor quality, with trucks often supplied without a full set of headlights, gauges, instruments, proper suspension, or even rear brakes, and increasingly reconfigured into three-wheel layouts.[31] Of these trucks, those which survived the war were reduced to an even sorrier state as a result of the huge wear and tear they suffered on Japan's unmaintained and still largely unpaved road network.[32] This was exacerbated through a shortage of spares and parts, bald tyres, and engines modified to run on a range of fuels of last resort, including coal, gas, wood, and pine oil, producing the so-called *mokutan jidōsha* (charcoal cars) of the era.[33] Due to these factors, only around 41,000 trucks remained in serviceable condition across the whole of Japan at the end of the war, a chronic level of undersupply which in itself also 'contributed both to the decline and the chaos in the last years of the war', as Cohen notes.[34]

Thus, the Japanese motor industry in 1945 was barely able to continue its day to day operations, let alone contemplate new models. Toyota and Nissan teetered on the verge of bankruptcy with only reconstruction financing fund loans in the immediate postwar period and a further tranche of loans in 1947 saving them from collapse.[35] The overall economic situation of Japan at this time was also perilous with a dearth of available raw materials, fuel, credit and capital, and with inflation soaring between 50 and 365 percent a year.[36] These were far from ideal conditions in which to try to revive the industry, and Occupation policy soon presented what could be perceived as further challenges. First of all, Japan's import controls were abolished, allowing foreign vehicles to be freely brought into the country without duties or restrictions.[37] Moreover, despite appeals from the Automobile Control Association, the first weeks of the Occupation also saw the industry regulated, with the 25 September *Memorandum Concerning Operation of Manufacturing Industries* (SCAPIN 58) prohibiting the production of cars and limiting the total manufacture of trucks to 1,500 a month, a level judged to be sufficient 'to maintain minimum industrial and economic activity'.[38] This measure could be seen as somewhat punitive, but the industry was struggling to produce even a third of this amount of trucks, and the ban on the production of cars made sense from other perspectives too. No cars were actually being produced (or had been since 1944), and there was little in the way of raw materials, and less in the way of petrol, available for what was considered by GHQ a non-essential product. As the Japanese Motor Trade Association itself noted in 1949: 'the ban on standard passenger cars is accepted by Japanese makers as something unavoidable in the light of the prevailing condition of the country's economy'.[39]

The industry therefore continued to produce the same truck models it had since the 1930s, often with minor styling adjustments, and with a gradual return to late-1930s quality standards as raw materials slowly became more accessible after 1946.[40] However, despite these small improvements, and in a testament to how poorly the industry was performing, it failed even to meet the allegedly 'restrictive' GHQ production quota until 1948.[41] The industry was thus still struggling to stay afloat, and firms like Toyota and Nissan began to take on GHQ vehicle repair contracts for trucks and jeeps (see below) to supplement their own truck production.[42]

GHQ ended its moratorium on car production in June 1947, allowing a total of 300 small passenger cars with engine sizes of up to 1500cc to be produced by Japan per year, although these were still prohibited from public sale, being reserved for use by the government, hospitals, businesses, or as taxis.[43] Their use was also authorised as police patrol cars, an innovation linked to the use of jeeps by the Occupation's Military Policemen.[44] Following this relaxation of the ban on car production, Toyota attempted to break back into the market with its first postwar car, the 1947 Toyopet SA sedan, a streamlined design closely resembling the VW Beetle. However, sales were very poor, with only 215 being sold between 1947 and 1952.[45] As such, Toyota Automotive, despite the ambitions of its founder Toyoda Kiichiro, who even in 1945 talked of producing quality, domestically manufactured cars, remained essentially a struggling truck manufacturer with a minor, unprofitable, side-line in lacklustre small cars.[46] GHQ finally lifted all restrictions on vehicle manufacturing in 1949, and although improvements were being made the problems faced by the industry were still considerable.[47]

For example, Toyota and other manufacturers knew in 1949 that their products still weren't up international standards but they had made advances in producing smaller commercial vehicles, such as one-ton trucks, and had undertaken some modest updates to their wartime models.[48] A key form of assistance in this regard came from the U.S. military's recovery and repair programs, specifically Operations 'Rebuild' and 'Rollup'. Manufacturers involved in these Operations were able to study, and then manufacture parts and mechanisms which gradually met U.S. military quality standards as well as learn about new forms of manufacturing technology.[49] Operations 'Rebuild' and 'Rollup' together formed a hitherto little studied, but vast, program of collecting, refitting and rebuilding U.S. jeeps and other vehicles in Japan.[50] 'Operation Rollup', the first phase of this program, sought to recover the vast amounts of surplus, abandoned, and damaged U.S. Second World War vehicles and equipment left scattered around the Western Pacific. This was followed by 'Operation Rebuild', which sought to rebuild and recondition these stocks, where necessary.[51] The principal manufacturing hub for the program was Japan and despite starting from humble beginnings in 1945, by 1951, 'Rollup' and 'Rebuild' were providing contracts to 14 companies to conduct their work and were employing more than 30,000 Japanese workers.[52] The operations owed their existence to a number of factors, one of which was the fact that they offered a considerable saving for the U.S. government, with the average cost of recovery and remanufacture of each vehicle coming to around 75 percent of the cost of a new one, on top of the avoidance of the cost and time lag of shipping the vehicles back and forth to, from, and across, America.[53]

Under the auspices of these operations, Toyota and Nissan also began refitting jeeps in 1947, continuing until 1951, by which time they had refurbished 1,700 vehicles. Those working on jeeps as part of the program also included former aircraft manufacturers such as Kawanishi, under its new name of Shin Meiwa.[54] The most notable contributor was, however, Fuji Motors. Its huge plant at Oppama (termed 'little Detroit' by its U.S. staff), which initially employed a principally repatriate workforce, reached the level of refitting around 4,000 motor vehicles per month during the Korean War, and had completed a total of 187,000 rebuilds by the time the program came to an end in 1959.[55] The program also had an international legacy with thousands of vehicles being sent (back in many cases) to Southeast Asia, and to South Korea, where Kim argues they, after once more being recycled as civilian vehicles after the Korean War, hugely influenced the development of the South Korean car industry.[56]

Existing or refitted jeeps were also modified in Japan by companies like Nissan for use by the Occupation or overseas. As the Occupation became more settled, GHQ sought to improve the creature comforts of its main form of transport, providing further work for Japanese firms. Extended windscreens, road tyres, 12 (and later 24) volt electrics, doors, tops, and side flaps became standard additions to jeeps, and all were manufactured in Japan.[57] Some of these 'domestications' of the jeep, added for the comfort of an army of occupation, did paradoxically prove essential once that army returned to combat in Korea, especially the heaters and covers, which proved respectively invaluable in Korea's extremely cold winters and hot summers.[58]

However, despite the benefits of these programs the Japanese industry at this stage still lagged far behind its U.S. counterpart in terms of quality, especially outside of production for U.S. procurement orders. Nevertheless, the modest improvements of the late 1940s and the techniques learned through U.S. procurement work were significant and would play a role in the later development of the Toyota Land Cruiser and its rivals, so it could be said that the years up until 1950 were beneficial for Japanese car and truck design.

Although these were positive developments, the zaibatsu dissolution and reparations programs presented further challenges and disruption for the existing vehicle producers, and also opened a window of opportunity for new manufacturers to enter the market.[59] Many did so, including Isuzu, Hino, Fuji Seimitsu (later Prince Motors), New Mitsubishi Heavy Industries, Mazda, Suzuki, Honda, and Daihatsu.[60] Some of these new entrants were former aircraft manufacturers, and many specialised in motorcycles and three wheelers, sometimes also using the large amount of unused aircraft parts, manufacturing plants, and skilled labour left over from the war. The highly popular Mitsubishi 'Silver Pigeon' scooter and Mazda 'GB' three-wheeled motorcycle-based truck are good examples of the type of vehicle produced by these new entrants.[61]

A further problem faced by both the established companies and new entrants was that of competition from imported and surplus foreign vehicles. Some of these were permitted as direct imports by GHQ, principally for use in the taxi industry, with 126 European cars being imported in 1948, rising to 4,719 by 1951.[62] Others included vehicles brought into Japan by the Occupation forces or those bought by U.S. servicemen from the PX (Post Exchange).[63] These were sold as surplus when no longer needed, or when the servicemen left the country, again often in the case of passenger cars, to the taxi industry. The estimates of the numbers of vehicles sold in this way vary, with the British government having judged that by 1952 'several thousand' such passenger cars had already been sold, and Nissan claiming around 22,000 foreign vehicles were sold between 1946 and 1949 (although this figure also included truck sales).[64] These vehicles were certainly a problem for the domestic automotive industry in that they offered a superior quality vehicle at a price below that of domestically produced models. Those sold off by the Occupation forces, both officially and unofficially, had the further advantage of not needing to be shipped, as they were already in Japan, and were also exempt from tariffs and import duties (once these were re-imposed).[65] It could be said that permitting the import of these vehicles showed that the Occupation didn't always have the best interests of Japan at heart, especially when it came to matters relating to GHQ and its personnel's financial affairs, but this might be slightly overstating the case. The vehicles were originally brought in for use by the Occupation or its members with no consideration of the impact on the domestic automotive industry of their potential later resale. Furthermore, as detailed above, the industry struggled even to meet its production 'restrictions' until 1948 and was forbidden from producing any passenger cars at all for the open market until 1949. Therefore, these foreign imports arguably helped plug several holes in the market that Japanese manufacturers were unable to fill, especially in the case of truck production and taxi provision. GHQ's surplus sales here were actually beneficial as the shortage of trucks was acting as a brake on the rest of the economy. Moreover, the introduction of these cheaper, higher-quality foreign imports (which were actually in many cases less suitable than a jeep for Japan's rugged rural roads and narrow city streets) arguably also provided an additional spur to raise standards of production.[66]

Despite these issues, perhaps the greatest problem facing the car industry was the moribund state of the Japanese economy.[67] Much of the country was devastated; workers were exhausted and demoralised (at least in the initial postwar years); materials and petroleum were in short supply; the workforce in most factories heavily 'featherbedded' with excess unproductive labour; and hyperinflation interfered with demand, purchasing, and credit. Finally, most of the Japanese population was struggling to survive in conditions arguably approaching famine in the initial postwar years and then merely subsisting in a still unrecovered economy, so there was no genuine mass market for any cars which could have been built.[68] Furthermore, there were waves of strikes, stoppages, and demonstrations from the rapidly expanding, and increasingly militant, trade union movement.[69] The Occupation recognised the depth of the problems and sought to address some of them with the Dodge reforms of 1949.[70] Although Dodge's reforms brought inflation under control, they also triggered a deep recession and further aggravated labour problems, especially in the short term. As well as reducing demand by itself, this recession also impacted automotive firms' previous sales as most customers bought their vehicles on credit and many became unable to keep up their repayments. This cash flow problem created knock-on effects within the industry. For example, Toyota found itself unable to pay its workers' wages and suffered from months of industrial unrest, strikes, and stoppages, eventually resulting in the sacking of around 2,000 employees and the resignation of the president and founder of the company, Toyoda Kiichiro.[71]

Thus, the industry re-entered a period of acute crisis, and many firms, including Toyota, were again pushed close to bankruptcy. There were serious questions raised at the time as to whether firms should abandon their car businesses and just concentrate on trucks, or even whether automotive production in its entirety should be written off, with Toyota diversifying at this point into dry cleaning and chinaware production to maintain its income.[72] This pessimism about the industry wasn't just confined to company boardrooms, with many in GHQ being sceptical about the industry's future, Bank of Japan Governor Ichimada Hisato saying Japan should just 'depend on America for cars', and Socialist Diet member Nishio Suehiro also claiming that: 'the right policy is to go ahead and give up on making passenger cars and just depend on imports'.[73]

U.S. procurement, the Korean war, and the Japanese motor industry

Thus, until mid-1950, the Japanese automotive industry was still in a weak position, and despite the Dodge reforms aiming to put most companies and the larger economy onto a more sustainable footing, concerns remained over both the industry, and Japan's, economic viability.[74] As has been well documented, the outbreak of the Korean War in June 1950 rapidly and dramatically improved Japan, and the industry's, fortunes. The Korean War, allegedly hailed (separately and according to different sources) as a 'gift from the gods' by Japanese Prime Minister Yoshida Shigeru, the U.S. Ambassador, the Governor of the Bank of Japan, and senior figures at Toyota, proved a huge boon for the Japanese economy and, rather paradoxically for a war in a neighbouring state, arguably greatly enhanced Japan's military security.[75] Both of these developments led directly to a far greater role for the jeep within the development of the automotive industry.

The most immediate and direct benefit to the Japanese economy of the war stemmed from the massive procurement program undertaken by the U.S. inside Japan to support the UN and South Korean forces fighting in Korea. These special procurements, or *tokujū*, placed hundreds of millions of dollars of orders with Japanese companies for uniforms, ammunition, equipment, and a plethora of other goods and services. Huge contracts for the repair and refitting of damaged or worn-out vehicles were also handed to the Japanese automotive industry. This massive injection of new business pulled Japan out of recession and according to Miwa, added two percent to Japan's GNP in the second half of 1950.[76] Overall, *tokujū* amounting to $2.3 billion were awarded to Japanese companies between 1950 and 1953, and this, alongside already existing GHQ procurement and the manufacture of equipment for the newly created National Police Reserve, triggered a boom for Japanese industry.[77] The Japanese motor industry was no exception – with many firms going from the verge of collapse in early 1950 to rude health in less than six months.[78] Toyota, for example, won the first contract offered for 1,000 trucks for use in Korea, followed swiftly by another for 2,379 more, rapidly helping it return to profitability in late 1950, and pay its first dividend for seven years in 1951.[79] Some companies had so much work, often made up of many small batch jobs, that they needed to find ways to increase productivity and Cusumano and others attribute the innovations and automation instituted at this time at Toyota as being one of the key influences on its later, much-lauded, 'just-in-time' production methods.[80] A further major benefit *tokujū* gave Japanese industry in the period was a huge injection of foreign currency.[81] *Tokujū* contracts were paid in U.S. dollars rather than yen and were seen as so reliable in terms of settling payment that they were able to be used to secure credit on favourable terms. This injection of cash and credit broke the bottleneck the lack of such reserves had generated in Japan until 1950, greatly assisting, alongside further loans from GHQ, in the import of new machine tools and raw materials.[82]

Alongside the thousands of jobs generated by the *tokujū*, these orders carried on the trends of 'Operation Rebuild' and the industry and its workforce reaped further benefits in terms of acquiring both training and new forms of technical knowledge. The workforce, many of whom had not worked in the industry before, received training, which, Hanson argues, diffused skills amongst the population necessary for Japan's later economic recovery.[83] In terms of technical gains, 'Operation Rebuild' and later GHQ procurement of vehicles also introduced equipment and techniques thus far unknown or unused in Japan, such as electroplating, modern enamel painting, and the use of safety glass.[84] The quality control standards and training introduced covering all vehicles procured by the U.S. military also had the beneficial impact of helping Japanese industry to improve the quality of its manufacturing and inspection standards.[85] Thus, such procurement, as well as providing work and badly needed income for struggling companies and individuals, had the additional benefit of being what Samuels terms *kyōiku chūmon* (educational orders).[86] Chang also reinforces this point, specifically in regard to 'Operation Rebuild', by claiming: 'it is not too strong to claim that these on-base, American-military supervised production operations provided the Japanese with fundamental know-how of American mass-production procedures. This was clearly one of the foundations for future development of the Japanese motor vehicle industry'.[87]

Aside from the economic boost increased procurement brought to Japan, the Korean conflict also saw the U.S. make a concerted effort to enhance Japan's economic and military security. With the intensification of the Cold War, and especially after the 'loss' of China in 1949, Japan had become pivotal to U.S. strategy in the region due to various reasons including it being the only heavily industrialised country in Asia, its skilled, educated workforce, and its millions of trained former soldiers.[88] In the eyes of many in GHQ and Washington, Japan, Asia's 'superdomino', needed to be economically secure in order to minimise any chance of it leaning towards the communist bloc.[89] Influenced by this, the Occupation swiftly curtailed its reparations and zaibatsu dissolution programs and some efforts were made to expand Japanese trade with non-communist Asia, and Southeast Asia in particular.[90] This matched the ambitions of the automotive industry, as the Japanese Motor Trade Association and MITI were also pushing potential sales to Southeast Asia, as was cheerily suggested in a policy paper sent to GHQ in 1949: 'the industry looks forward to establishing a good reputation of its products abroad – at least, in the Asiatic market, by improving quality and reducing price, provided that a fair degree of production expansion is feasible. Some people laugh at this dream. But our motor vehicle manufacturers are both earnest and ambitious. They say: "wait and see!" [sic]'.[91] U.S. policymakers also thought that these economic ties between non-communist Asia and Japan would strengthen the economies and political stability of both parties and would put the Japanese economy on a more sustainable path. These new markets could offset those now less accessible due to the loss of Japan's Empire and Mao's victory in China, and at the same time the import of raw materials from the region could also potentially reduce some of Japan's dependence on the U.S.[92] Although not making much impact initially, in time these markets began to be further exploited by Japanese firms, and carmakers in particular, with large numbers of Japanese jeeps and trucks exported to the region from the mid-1950s onwards.[93] The heightened desire to secure Japan against the perceived threat of communist subversion during the Korean War also led to the creation of the force which would directly spur the creation of Japan's own jeeps: the Japanese National Police Reserve (NPR).

Japanese jeeps: the Toyota Land Cruiser and its rivals

The NPR was created in the days immediately following the start of the Korean War to provide internal security for Japan in the wake of the departure of virtually all U.S. tactical troops present in the country for the rapidly collapsing frontline in Korea.[94] The force was a paramilitary constabulary, being lightly armed, with arrest powers, and a training regime initially focused on riot control and internal security.[95] Japanese industry was used to outfit the new force, including the automotive industry. Toyota, for example, produced tankers, dump trucks, and other specialised vehicles for the force.[96] Demand for vehicles for the force also greatly increased when the tide temporarily turned against the UN forces fighting in Korea after the Chinese intervention. At this stage calls from the U.S. military in Washington and more hawkish elements of GHQ to swiftly expand the NPR and convert it into a force capable contributing to Japan's external security grew louder. This proposed expansion and increase in the capabilities of the NPR required the provision of huge amounts of material, equipment, and vehicles, especially if the full extent of the U.S. Army's plan of enlarging the force from its original 75,000 men to the proposed 360,000, were to go ahead.[97] Much of the NPR's original requirements had been supplied from U.S. surplus (including stocks from Operations 'Rollup' and 'Rebuild'), but such an expansion at a time when all spare equipment was either being sent to Korea or Europe (in the belief that the Korean War could be the start of a broader conflict) clearly required the procurement of a vast amount of new equipment and vehicles.[98] Linking in with U.S. desires noted above to use Japanese industry as far as possible to supply U.S. and other friendly regimes in the region, the interconnected benefit of strengthening the Japanese economy, and the relatively cheaper cost of manufacturing the items in Japan (as opposed to in the U.S., as was also the case with 'Operation Rebuild'), the decision was taken to source as much as possible of the NPR's equipment in Japan. This included a large number of new trucks and jeeps.[99]

As part of this process, a locally produced equivalent of the Willys jeep was sought for the NPR and a design contest was held to source such a vehicle from Japan's motor manufacturers. Mitsubishi, Nissan, and Toyota all put forward designs and prototypes for consideration for the new small four-wheel-drive vehicle for the NPR.[100] Nissan had produced the 'Nissan Patrol', a compact vehicle very similar in design and appearance to the Willys jeep.[101] Mitsubishi entered their version of the original jeep which they were already assembling through knock-down production using imported parts supplied through a tie-up with Willys, and Toyota entered the 'BJ', standing for 'B engine jeep'. The vehicle used Toyota's 1937 water-cooled B-type six-cylinder in-line 3,386cc four-ton gasoline truck engine, installed on an SB-type one-ton truck chassis.[102] The resulting vehicle had a slightly larger and chunkier body than the Willys jeep but was superior in a number of ways. The BJ, also known as the 'Toyota jeep', combined Toyota's large and small truck technology and the four-ton truck engine provided ample power, especially when climbing steep slopes.[103] The aforementioned GHQ led increase in levels of manufacturing quality also influenced the vehicle, with it having a relatively high standard of production as well as a much more stable and comfortable ride than the Willys jeep due to its use of a commercial small truck chassis. Despite the BJ performing well in trials and being more powerful than its competitors, GHQ and the NPR leadership decided to adopt the

Mitsubishi-Willys jeep.[104] The decision was seemingly influenced by the desire to have a single small four-wheel-drive vehicle in use by the force (which already used the jeep), the advantages of using a familiar vehicle in training and for maintenance (very important if the planned rapid expansion were to come about), and, finally, the importance of interoperability with U.S. forces which, of course, used the Willys jeep.[105]

Whether elements of preference for a manufacturer involved in a tie-up with an American firm also influenced the choice are unclear, but even if this did factor into the decision, it does seem that both in terms of compatibility and ease of introduction, the Mitsubishi jeep was the logical choice. Mitsubishi thus won the contract and supplied the first batch of 500 jeeps, and although the more hawkish elements in GHQ and the U.S. military leadership never achieved the level expansion they sought for the NPR, Mitsubishi continued to supply jeeps to the NPR and its successors, the National Safety Force, and Self Defense Force (SDF), ultimately producing over 200,000 jeeps in Japan for the SDF, and then the civilian market, until production ceased in 1995.[106]

Not winning the contract was a blow to Toyota, but the company was proud of the machine they had produced and confident its quality could translate into sales. Within six months, Toyota conducted another rigorous test run of the BJ under the supervision of members of the Japanese National Rural Police, a civil police force then responsible for policing Japan's small towns and countryside.[107] This test demonstrated the superior handling and performance of the vehicle, with test driver Taira Ichiro managing to drive the car up to the sixth station of Mount Fuji (more than 2,000 metres above sea level).[108] The BJ thus became the first ever vehicle to do so, surpassing even the Willys jeep. The National Rural Police, considering their rural jurisdiction and influenced by the abovementioned shift towards patrol-based policing connected to GHQ's use of jeeps, were impressed and adopted the BJ as their new patrol car, placing an order for just under 300 vehicles.[109] Although this was of some comfort to the senior management at Toyota, the failure to win the much larger ongoing NPR contract for the thousands of units, large amounts of spare parts, and technical support it would have entailed, necessitated a change of strategy away from reliance on GHQ/Japanese government procurement contracts.

Linking into the aforementioned U.S. and Japanese drive to economically link Japan to the non-communist regimes of Asia, Toyota decided to try to export the Toyota jeep. First targeting Southeast Asia and South America and later the U.S., Australasia, Europe and Africa, the relatively cheap, rugged, practical, reliable, and easily repairable BJ and its successors sold well, with over 12,000 units sold by the end of the decade.[110] The vehicle also did a lot to keep the Toyota brand alive in the U.S. in the late 1950s due to it not suffering from the major production quality issues which afflicted the company's other export models.[111] Although the Toyota jeep's modest sales 'kept Toyota American going' according to the model's chief engineer Iritani Saihei, the vehicle's original name itself did not survive, following claims of trademark violation by Willys over the name 'jeep'.[112] Toyota Director of Technology Umehara Hanji thus renamed the vehicle the 'Land Cruiser' in 1954, with the new name striking an intentionally superior sounding note over another of the vehicle's rivals, the British 'Land Rover'.[113]

With the successes of the Land Cruiser and its Japanese-made rivals, the Willys jeep indirectly, through GHQ/NPR procurement, spawned a direct Japanese competitor which was arguably even more successful, albeit in the commercial, rather than military sphere. The sales of the Land Cruiser proved to be the bedrock of Toyota's initial overseas success, with versions still in production into the 2010s, the longest of any model in the company's stable. The BJ and its direct successor models eventually sold more than 1.5 million units until their replacement with an entirely new Land Cruiser in 1986 (interestingly also the same year that Willys stopped producing direct successors to the original jeep in the U.S.).[114] Total sales of the Land Cruiser had exceeded five million by 2006, with almost all sold outside of Japan, where the vehicle remains relatively uncommon.[115] Toyota's post-Occupation export-orientated strategy – building on the *tokujū* boom and supported by the U.S. and the Japanese government – helped it move beyond subsistence and survival through government procurement and truck manufacture, into expanding into new markets around the world, including the United States itself.

The export of well-made, reasonably priced vehicles like the Land Cruiser helped Toyota to rise to be the largest car manufacturer in the world in the 2010s, successively surpassing its British, German, and, ultimately, American rivals.[116] As well as making a significant contribution to the origins of Toyota's rise to the top of the global car industry, the Land Cruiser also represented a major step in Japan's achievement of technological parity with the West in the field of automotive manufacture. Being able to ultimately produce a technologically equal, and, in some ways, superior machine which eventually outsold the jeep by several million units was a significant milestone for the Japanese automotive industry. Indeed, Toyoda Kiichiro saw his longstanding ambition of the production of a Japanese high-quality, low-cost, and high-performance vehicle as being achieved for the first time with the Land Cruiser.[117]

Conclusion

This chapter has argued that although the cultural impact of the jeep has long been noted, albeit in perhaps a slightly over-generalised fashion, the postwar Japanese automotive industry was also heavily influenced by the vehicle and owes something, directly and indirectly, to jeeps of both U.S. and Japanese origins.

In the critical decade *before* 1955, the sale, modification, and rebuild of tens of thousands of vehicles for the U.S. military, many of which were jeeps, provided vital business for Japan's automotive makers, ensuring their survival in some cases. This military procurement also provided a secure path through the tumultuous initial postwar years for the automotive industry. It is also important to note that the repair, modification and procurement of vehicles crucially started *prior* to the Korean War era *tokujū*, despite being greatly expanded by it. These types of work continued through the *shin-tokujū* of the post Korean War era and provided further major contracts to automotive makers to supply vehicles to the U.S. military and the non-communist regimes across East Asia.[118] These contracts also served as vehicles themselves on the path towards helping link the Japanese economy to the newly independent non-communist regimes of East Asia. The use of Japan as a key hub for U.S. military vehicle manufacturing continued into the 1960s until eventually being stopped by the U.S. Congress, partly due to rising costs, and partly due to the growth of the industry at the expense of the U.S. motor manufacturers.[119] Contracts like that for the jeeps supplied to the NPR also helped influenced the direction taken by some of the major manufacturers in the industry, with Toyota focusing more on the civilian market and Mitsubishi looking more towards military procurement after 1952.

The influence of the procurement of jeeps could also be said to represent a positive contribution by the Occupation to the Japanese economy, albeit through the production of a military vehicle largely for its own use. The Occupation contracts, payments, employment, and technical assistance which stemmed from the purchase and refitting of jeeps provided work and training for tens of thousands, helped hitherto struggling businesses to survive, and introduced new technologies and higher levels of quality control into the industry. It is also accurate to say the last of these was only matched in the postwar era in terms of foreign influence on production quality by the later tie-ups with European car manufacturers in the mid-1950s. Furthermore, the production and repair of jeeps by major companies in the industry also represented a transitional stage on the road towards a genuine mass market passenger car industry from what was, in spite of some minor and mostly unsuccessful previous domestic forays into car production, more of a truck industry.

Finally, the industry's ability (after the abovementioned assistance of GHQ in terms of procurement, technical help, and advice on quality control) to produce jeeps and later high-quality passenger cars of its own, seems to have obscured much of the occasionally negative immediate postwar cultural image of the Willys jeep. Domestically produced vehicles increasingly came to dominate most Japanese people's conception of the automobile from the mid-1950s onwards, especially among those who had no memory of the Occupation. This achievement of parity in terms of technology, and the rapid growth of the car industry and car ownership, also came to symbolise more than almost any other trend, the 'high growth era' from around 1955 onwards.[120] Although this development, alongside other factors, including the jeep's abovementioned clear foreign and military origins, have obscured or eclipsed some of the cultural and economic influences of the vehicle, this is, in a sense, perhaps fitting for the workmanlike, rugged, and above all utilitarian character of the vehicles themselves.

Notes

This chapter is partially based upon conference papers given at the *Asia-Pacific Economic and Business History Conference 2013*, Seoul, and the *Economic and Business History of Occupied Japan Conference*, Ritsumeikan University, Kyoto, 2015.

1 E. Takemae, *Inside GHQ: The Allied Occupation of Japan and its Legacy*, London: Continuum, 2002, p. 388; J. W. Dower, *Embracing Defeat, Japan in The Wake of World War II*, London: Norton, 2000, p. 419.

2 A full historiographical analysis of the vast scholarship on the postwar car industry is beyond the scope of this chapter. For an excellent summary of key trends and themes in such scholarship, see: S.C. Townsend, "The "Miracle" of Car Ownership in Japan's Era of "High Growth", 1955–73", *Business History*, Vol. 55, No. 3, August 2015, pp. 498–502.

3 For example, see: Togo and Wartman: Y. Togo and W. Wartman, *Against All Odds, The Story of the Toyota Motor Corporation and the Family that Created It*, New York: St. Martin's Press, 1993.

4 H. Kohama, *Industrial Development in Postwar Japan*, London: Routledge, 2007, p 155.

5 See: R. J. Samuels, *"Rich Nation, Strong Army", National Security and the Technological Transformation of Japan*, Ithaca: Cornell University Press, 1994; M. J. Green, *Arming Japan, Defense Production, Alliance Politics, and the Postwar Search for Autonomy*, New York: Columbia University Press, 1995.

6 Takemae, *Inside GHQ*, pp. 429, 284; Y. Ohtsuka, *Jeeps Over the Pacific, Jiipu Taiheiyō no Tabi* (The Jeep's Pacific Journey), Tokyo: Hobby Japan, 1994, p. 143; H. Harada, *MP Jiipu kara Mita Senryo-ka no Tokyo: Dojo Keisatsu-kan no Kansatsu-ki* (Seeing Tokyo Under Occupation from an MP Jeep: Observations of a Police Passenger), Tokyo: Soshisha, 1994, pp. 17–18. For an example of the daily usage of jeeps, see: Jeep Dispatch (9/1947–11/1948). National Diet Library, Tokyo (hereafter NDL), CHS(D) 201–202.

7 Supreme Commander for the Allied Powers Directives to the Japanese Government (SCAPINs) (Record Group 331), (hereafter SCAPIN) 223, 1/11/1945; Harada, *MP Jiipu*, pp. 40–41. Harada notes from his experience as a policeman that the salutes were always smartly returned, including by MacArthur himself, who apparently also returned salutes to U.S. and Japanese personnel alike through the streets during his daily movements within Tokyo. Ibid., pp. 17–18.

8 D. W. Plath, "My Car-ism: Motorizing the Showa Self", in C. Gluck and S. R. Graubard, eds., *Showa: The Japan of Hirohito*, New York: W.W. Norton & Company, 1992, p. 234. See Zsombor Rajkai's chapter in this volume for more on other influences of the 'demonstration' of American life on the Japanese population.

9 P. Francks, *The Japanese Consumer: An Alternative Economic History of Modern Japan*, Cambridge: Cambridge University Press, 2009, p. 202.

10 Toyota Jidōsha Kabushikigaisha, ed., *Sengō, Saisutāto wo Kitta, Shōwa 20 Nendai no Kokusanshatachi* (The Postwar Restart, Domestic Cars of the Shōwa 20s), Nagakute: Toyota Hakubutsukan, 1995, p. 18.

11 "Retiree's Blog About Old Car Catalogs Finds Fans", *Japan Times*, 12/11/2011; Ohtsuka, *Jeeps Over the Pacific*, p. 138.

12 T. Morris-Suzuki, *Shōwa, an Inside History of Hirohito's Japan*, London: The Athlone Press, 1984, p. 197.

13 Many of these were made from surplus GI canteens. Dower, *Embracing Defeat*, p. 110; Ohtsuka, *Jeeps Over the Pacific*, p. 138. An example of such a toy can be seen at the Shimadzu International Foundation Memorial Hall in Kyoto, see: www.shimadzu.com/visionary/memorial-hall/list/, accessed 29/3/2017.

14 Dower, *Embracing Defeat*, 2000, p. 110.

15 Takemae, *Inside GHQ*, p. 74; R. Sodei, "The Occupier and the Occupied", in W. F. Nimo, ed., *The Occupation of Japan: The Grass Roots, The Proceedings of the Eight Symposium by the MacArthur Memorial*, Norfolk, Virginia: MacArthur Memorial, 1992, p. 5.

16 These two programs and the resentment they provoked even spawned new phrases like *jeep kyōmai* (jeep rice requisitions) and *jeep chōzei* (jeep tax). Takemae, *Inside GHQ*,

p. 75; Dower, *Embracing Defeat*, p. 95. Appropriation involving jeeps also seemed to be something of a two-way street, with the future Doshisha University professor Otis Cary falling victim to a so-called '*jeep-ya*' (a thief specialising in stealing from jeeps) during his 1949 jeep tour of Japan. O. Cary, *Jeep Oku no Hosomichi* (The Jeep's Narrow Road to the Interior), Tokyo: Hosei University Press, 1953, pp. 17–19.

17 Dower, *Embracing Defeat*, p. 135.

18 Takemae, *Inside GHQ*, p. 74. Alongside (or aside from) the 'passive' influence the jeep had upon the Japanese population, numerous 'active' demonstrations of it also added to its public profile. Some of these were simply intended for entertainment purposes, such as car display events, half-time shows, and daredevil 'jeep rodeos' at baseball games. Others, such as the numerous military parades of the Occupation forces, the largest of which were the annual 4 July parades in front of the Imperial palace, were clearly intended as demonstrations of the power and prestige of its owner, the occupier. See: Ohtsuka, *Jeeps Over the Pacific*, pp. 149–153.

19 H. S. Kim, "My Car Modernity, What the U.S Army Brought to South Korean Cinematic Imagination about Modern Mobility", *The Journal of Asian Studies*, Vol. 75, No. 1, 2/2016, p. 69.

20 A. Kawahara, *The Origin of Competitive Strength: Fifty Years of the Auto Industry in Japan and the U.S.*, Tokyo: Springer, 1998, p. 13. See also, ibid., p. xiii.

21 T. Morris-Suzuki, *Shōwa*, p. 197.

22 Dower, *Embracing Defeat*, p. 110.

23 Takemae, *Inside GHQ*, p. 74; Sodei, "The Occupier and the Occupied", p. 5. Harada describes a friendly and curious attitude towards the jeep from the residents of then rural Setagaya in his memoir, see: Harada, *MP Jiipu*, p. 74.

24 Around 60 percent of all cars in Japan in 1937 were produced by either Ford or General Motors, see: ESS Industrial Files, Motor Vehicle "Brief History", Report No. TB-1238–50, n.d. NDL, ESS(D) 1246–48.

25 Automobile Control Association to MacArthur, The Automobile Industry, 17/09/1945. NDL, FOA 3256; Motor Car Manufacturing Enterprise Act, Law No. 33, 29/5/1936. NDL, FOA 3256. Article one of the law states that 'the object of this act shall be to firmly establish the nation's motor car industry enterprise in order to adjust national defense and develop the nation's industry'.

26 J. Halliday, *A Political History of Japanese Capitalism*, New York: Pantheon, 1975, p. 147.

27 ESS Industrial Files, Motor Vehicle "Brief History", n.d. NDL, ESS(D) 1246–48.

28 K. Okada, K. Ono and F. Adachi, *The Automobile Industry in Japan, A Study of Ancillary Firm Development*, Tokyo: Kinokuniya / Oxford University Press, 1988, p. 38; N. S. Roberts, *Japan: Economic and Commercial Conditions in Japan*, London: Her Majesty's Stationery Office, 1952, p. 50.

29 J. B. Cohen, *Japan's Economy in War and Reconstruction*, Westport: Greenwood Press, 1973, p. 247.

30 Interestingly, Allied air raids were arguably not directly responsible, at least in terms of direct bomb damage, with the automotive industry being a low-priority target. Toyota's main factory, for example, was attacked and superficially damaged only once, on the penultimate day of the war. Historical Section, GHQ, *History of the Non-Military Activities of the Occupation of Japan, Vol. 16, Industry Part A: Heavy Industries*, Tokyo: SCAP, 1951 (hereafter *History of the Non-Military Activities*), pp. 113, 115; J. Bowen, *The Gift of the Gods: The Impact of the Korean War on Japan*, n.p.: Old Dominion Graphics Consultants, Inc., 1984, p. 5; Cohen, *Japan's Economy*, p. 246.

31 M. Ruiz, *The Complete History of the Japanese Car: 1907 to the Present*, New York: Portland House, 1986, p. 171; GHQ/SCAP, Selected Data on the Occupation of Japan, 1950. NDL, ESS(B) 2672–2677, p. 64; GHQ/SCAP, Selected Data on the Occupation of Japan, 1950. NDL, ESS(B) 2672–2677, p. 64; M. Weston, *Giants of Japan: The*

Lives of Japan's Most Influential Men and Women, New York: Kodansha America, 1999, p. 61.

32 Kawahara estimates only eight percent of Japan's road system was paved in the early 1950s, see: Kawahara, *The Origin of Competitive Strength*, p. 8. For more on the poor quality of Japan's roads until the 1970s, see: Townsend, "The "Miracle" of Car Ownership", pp. 498, 506. Townsend also notes the highly suitable nature of jeeps for Japan's roads, Ibid., p. 505. Otis Cary, his wife Alice, and their six-month-old daughter Beth travelled to his birthplace in Hokkaidō from Kyoto in a surplus military jeep in 1949, suffering numerous punctures on the way due to the poor road conditions and eventually also concluding that even in 1953 the jeep, as a former military vehicle, was the best form of transport for Japan's basic road system, see: O. Cary, *Jeep Oku no Hosomichi*, pp. 9, 13, 20, 21, 74, 75, 215, 256.

33 GHQ/SCAP, Selected Data on the Occupation of Japan, 1950. NDL, ESS(B) 2672–2677, p. 64.

34 *History of the Non-Military Activities*, p. 113; Cohen, *Japan's Economy*, p. 250.

35 Kohama, *Industrial Development*, p. 191; K. Kumaki, *Nihon Shuyō Sangyō, Toyota Jidōsha* (Japan's Principal Industries, Toyota Motors), Tokyo: Tenbosha, 1959, p. 89; M. A. Cusumano, *The Japanese Automobile Industry, Technology and Management at Nissan and Toyota*, Cambridge, MA: Harvard University Press, 1989, p. 19.

36 Kohama, *Industrial Development*, p. 173; Cohen, *Japan's Economy*, pp. 447, 459–460; B. Gao, "Arisawa Hiromi and His Theory for Managed Economy", *Journal of Japanese Studies*, Vol. 20, No. 1, Winter 1994, p. 136.

37 Cusumano, *The Japanese Automobile Industry*, p. 7.

38 Automobile Control Association to MacArthur, The Automobile Industry, 17/09/45. NDL, FOA 3256; SCAPIN 58, Operation of Manufacturing Industries, 25/9/1945; Kohama, *Industrial Development*, p. 142; Toyota Jidōsha, *Sengō, Saisutāto wo Kitta*, p. 20.

39 Motors Trade Association, The Problem of Small-Sized Passenger Cars, 23/8/1949. NDL, ESS(D) 5297.

40 E. Toyoda, *Toyota, Fifty Years in Motion*, Tokyo: Kodansha International, 1987, p. 100.

41 Kohama, *Industrial Development*, p. 143.

42 Toyoda, *Fifty Years in Motion*, p. 100; Toyota Motor Corporation, ed., *Sōzō Kagirinaku: Toyota Jidōsha 50 Nen-shi* (Limitless Creation: A 50 year History of Toyota Motors), Tokyo: Dai Nippon Printing, 1987, p. 246.

43 SCAPIN 1715, Application for Permission to Manufacture Small-Sized Passenger Cars, 3/6/1947; Toyota Jidōsha, *Sengō, Saisutāto wo Kitta*, p. 22; Kohama, *Industrial Development*, p. 142.

44 See: Harada, *MP Jiipu*, pp. 105–106.

45 Toyota Jidōsha, *Sengō, Saisutāto wo Kitta*, p. 7. Total nationwide car production only amounted to 60 vehicles in 1947, see: Ministry of Commerce and Industry, Monthly Production Output of Motor Vehicles during 1947, n.d. NDL, ESS(D) 12426.

46 Kohama, *Industrial Development*, p. 155.

47 SCAPIN 2053, Application for Permission to Manufacture Small-Sized Passenger Cars, 25/10/49; Cusumano, *The Japanese Automobile Industry*, p. 19.

48 Kase to Hynick, Exhibit of Light Motor Vehicles at the Export Bazaar, 2/8/1949. NDL, ESS(D) 5297.

49 Okada, Ono and Adachi, *The Automobile Industry in Japan*, p. 42.

50 For example, Green makes a brief and inaccurate reference to the programs (confusing 'Roll-up' with 'Rebuild' and misstating the start date of the former). Green, *Arming Japan*, p. 31.

51 Far East Command, Headquarters, Japan Logistical Command, "Operation Rollup-Operation Rebuild, 14 Aug 1945–30 Jun 1952", in *U.S. Army Center of Military History Historical Manuscripts Collection: The Korean War*, Wilmington: Scholarly Resources, n.d. NDL, YF-A4, Reel 11.

52 T. E. Hanson, *Combat Ready? The Eighth U.S. Army on the Eve of the Korean War*, College Station: Texas A&M University Press, 2010, p. 38; Chang, *The Japanese Auto Industry*, p. 44.

53 Hanson, *Combat Ready*, p. 39.

54 Samuels, *"Rich Nation, Strong Army"*, p. 199. Samuels mistakenly uses the company name 'Nakanishi' here.

55 Chang, *The Japanese Auto Industry*, pp. 44–45. See Steven Ivings's chapter in the current volume for more on the postwar employment of repatriates.

56 Ohtsuka, *Jeeps over the Pacific*, pp. 138, 155–157, 163; Offshore Procurement and Effects of Chamberlain Amendment on Nagoya Automakers, Telegrams from Nagoya Consulate to State Department, Central Files of the Department of State, 8/23/1963, in H. Masuda, ed., *Rearmament of Japan, Part 2: 1953–1963*, Tokyo: Congressional Information Service and Maruzen, 1998 (hereafter cited by NDL call number, YF-A17), 2-G-52; Kim, "My Car Modernity", p. 69.

57 Ohtsuka, *Jeeps Over the Pacific*, pp. 158, 167, 160; Kobe Base Ordinance Deport APO 317, 18/1/1947. NDL, ESS(D) 5036.

58 Ohtsuka, *Jeeps Over the Pacific*, pp. 160, 173.

59 See Steven Ericson's chapter in this volume for more on zaibatsu dissolution.

60 *History of the Non-Military Activities*, p. 114; Y. Maeda, "High-Level Growth and the Development of the Open Economy", M. Sumiya, ed., *A History of Japanese Trade and Industry Policy*, Oxford: Oxford University Press, 2000, pp. 410, 411.

61 Daihatsu, Meiwa Automobile, Mitsubishi Heavy Industries Nagoya (Silver Pigeon), 3 Wheelers, n.d. NDL, ESS(D) 5035; Toyota Jidōsha, *Sengō, Saisutāto wo Kitta*, pp. 4, 8. Mase Hajime, Chief of the Auto Industry Division, Machinery Bureau in the Ministry of Commerce and Industry, claimed the principal reason scooters like the Pigeon did well was their excellent fuel efficiency. Mase to Melyan, Production of Motor Scooters, 11/11/1948. NDL, ESS(D) 12426.

62 Townsend, "The "Miracle" of Car Ownership", p. 506.

63 Kawahara, *The Origin of Competitive Strength*, p. 13.

64 Nissan Jidōsha Kōgyō K. K., *Nissan Jidōsha Sanjūnenshi* (Thirty-Year History of Nissan Motor Vehicles), Tokyo: Nissan Jidōsha Kōgyō KK., 1965, p. 138; Roberts, *Japan: Economic and Commercial Conditions*, p. 51. Cusumano claims 27,000 trucks were sold by GHQ in Japan between 1946 and 1949. Cusumano, *The Japanese Automobile Industry*, p. 19.

65 C. S. Chang, *The Japanese Auto Industry and the U.S. Market*, New York: Praeger, 1981, p. 40.

66 Townsend, "The "Miracle" of Car Ownership", p. 507.

67 *History of the Non-Military Activities*, p. 119.

68 C. Aldous, "Contesting Famine: Hunger and Nutrition in Occupied Japan, 1945–1952", *Journal of American-East Asian Relations*, Vol. 17, No. 3, 2010, pp. 230–255; Toyota Jidōsha, *Sengō, Saisutāto wo Kitta*, p. 22.

69 Cohen, *Japan's Economy*, pp. 450–451; Cusumano, *The Japanese Automobile Industry*, p. 73.

70 H. B. Schonberger, *Aftermath of War, Americans and the Remaking of Japan 1945–1952*, London: Kent State University Press, 1989, pp. 201–205.

71 Toyoda, *Fifty Years in Motion*, pp. 100–102; Toyota Motor Co., Ltd, 3/51. Ishida to Ikeda, Application for the Loan from the United States Counterpart Fund, 3/1951. NDL, ESS(D) 7356.

72 Toyoda, *Fifty Years in Motion*, pp. 100–102; Weston, *Giants of Japan*, p. 61.

73 Quoted in: Kohama, *Industrial Development*, p. 143; Competition with Foreign Cars, Japanese Automobile Industry Faces a Very Serious Period, n.d. NDL, ESS(D) 1246.

74 Records of the Office of Northeast Asian Affairs, Relating to the Treaty of Peace with Japan, Subject File, 1945–1951, Miscellaneous State Department Material, "Japanese

Economic Prospects", 4/8/1949. NDL, YF-A10, Reel 11, pp. 10–11. See also Steven Ivings's chapter in this volume.

75 Toyoda, *Fifty Years in Motion*, p. 114; A. Forsberg, *America and the Japanese Miracle: The Cold War Context of Japan's Postwar Economic Revival, 1950–1960*, Chapel Hill: University of North Carolina Press, 2000, p. 48; M. Schaller, *Altered States: The United States and Japan Since the Occupation*, Oxford: Oxford University Press, 1997, p. 49; W. S. Borden, *The Pacific Alliance: United States Foreign Economic Policy and Japanese Trade Recovery, 1947–1955*, Madison: University of Wisconsin Press, 1984, p. 146.

76 R. Miwa, "The Reorganisation of the Japanese Economy", in M. Sumiya, ed., *A History of Japanese Trade and Industry Policy*, Oxford: Oxford University Press, 2000, p. 229.

77 R. B. Finn, *Winners in Peace, MacArthur, Yoshida, and Postwar Japan*, London: University of California Press, 1992, p. 267; T. French, *National Police Reserve: The Origin of Japan's Self Defense Forces*, Leiden: Global Oriental, 2014, pp. 109–119.

78 Toyota Motor Corporation, *Sōzō Kagirinaku*, p. 248.

79 Ibid, p. 246; Toyoda, *Fifty Years in Motion*, p. 113.

80 Cusumano, *The Japanese Automobile Industry*, pp. 274–276. See also: E. Daito, "Automation and the Organization of Production in the Japanese Automobile Industry: Nissan and Toyota in the 1950s", *Enterprise and Society*, Vol. 1, No. 1, 3/2000, p. 141.

81 MacEachron to Macy, Question of Economic Aid for Japan in FY 1954, Records of the Bureau of Budget, 13/6/1952, in H. Masuda, ed., *Rearmament of Japan, Part 1: 1947–1952*, Tokyo: Congressional Information Service and Maruzen, 1998 (hereafter cited by NDL call number, YF-A16), 4-A-7.

82 Marquat to Ministry of Finance, Counterpart Fund Loans to the Automotive Industry, 31/3/1951. NDL, ESS(D) 7323; L. E. Hein, "Growth Versus Success, Japan's Economic Policy in Historical Perspective", in A. Gordon, ed., *Postwar Japan as History*, Berkley: University of California Press, 1993, p. 110; Toyota Motor Corporation, *Sōzō Kagirinaku*, p. 247; Marquat to Ministry of Finance, Counterpart Fund Loans to the Automotive Industry, 31/3/1951. NDL, ESS(D) 7323; Reed to Marquat, 31/3/1951. NDL, ESS(D) 7323; Watanbe to ESS, Application for the Release of a US Fund for a Loan to the Toyota Jidōsha K.K. (Loan of Yen Fund for Machinery Export), 30/3/1951. NDL, ESS(D) 7323; Watanbe to ESS, Application for the Release of a US Fund for a Loan to the Nissan Motors Ltd (Loan of Yen Fund for Machinery Export), 30/3/1951. NDL, ESS(D) 7323; Toyota Motor Co., Ltd, 3/51. Ishida to Ikeda, Application for the Loan from the United States Counterpart Fund, 3/1951. NDL, ESS(D) 7356.

83 Hanson, *Combat Ready*, p. 38.

84 Chang, *The Japanese Auto Industry*, p. 46.

85 Dr. W. Edward Deming's work is well known in this field; see: Townsend, "The "Miracle" of Car Ownership", p. 508; Hein, "Growth Versus Success", p. 110; Toyota Motor Corporation, *Sōzō Kagirinaku*, pp. 248–249.

86 Samuels, *"Rich Nation, Strong Army"*, pp. 137, 138.

87 Chang like Green, confuses 'Rollup' and 'Rebuild'. Chang, *The Japanese Auto Industry*, pp. 46.

88 A. Iriye, "The United States as a Pacific Power", in G. T. Hsiao, ed., *Sino-American Détente and its Policy Implications*, New York: Praeger, 1974, pp. 11–13.

89 J. Dower, "The Superdomino in Postwar Asia: Japan in and Out of the Pentagon Papers", in N. Chomsky and H. Zinn, eds., *The Pentagon Papers, Vol. 5, The Senator Gravel Edition*, Boston: Beacon Press, 1972, pp. 101–103.

90 The Cold War, was not however the only consideration here, see the chapters by Steven Ericson and Takahiro Ohata in this volume.

91 Motors Trade Association, The Problem of Small-Sized Passenger Cars, 23/8/1949. NDL, ESS(D) 5297; Kase to Hynick, Exhibit of Light Motor Vehicles at the Export Bazaar, 2/8/1949. NDL, ESS(D) 5297; Mori to Malyan, Passenger Car Production Program, 16/8/1949. NDL, ESS(D) 5297.

92 Schaller, *Altered States*, pp. 3–4; B. Gao, "The Postwar Japanese Economy", in W. Tsutsui, ed., *A Companion to Japanese History*, Malden: Blackwell, 2007, p. 506.
93 Japan Economic Report No. 6, June 1952, 09/07/1952. Foreign Office, FO 371/99417; Department of the Army / ESS, *Program for a Self-Supporting Japanese Economy*, Washington, DC: Department of the Army, 1/1949, pp. 14–15; Schaller, *Altered States*, p. 49; Togo and Wartman, *Against All Odds*, pp. 148–149.
94 French, *National Police Reserve*, pp. 156–157.
95 T. French, "Contested 'Rearmament': The National Police Reserve and Japan's Cold War(s)", *Japanese Studies*, Vol. 34, No.1, May 2014, pp. 30–33.
96 Toyota Motor Corporation, *Sōzō Kagirinaku*, p. 249.
97 French, *National Police Reserve*, pp. 229–237.
98 Conference on Japanese National Police Reserve, Minutes of Conference, Records of Army Staff, Operations, 1/3/1952. YF-A16, 1-B-16.
99 Ridgeway to Department of the Army, Records of the Joint Chiefs of Staff, 27/1/1952. YF-A16, 1-A-134; Memorandum: NPRJ Support from US and Japan, 25/1/1952. NDL, TS 150.
100 Maebara to Carter, 14/4/1951. NDL, ESS(F) 1345; Production Estimate, Toyota Motor co., 1/1951. NDL, ESS(F) 1346–1347; Production Schedule of 4 Wheeled Motor Vehicles, Nissan, 14/4/1951. NDL, ESS(F) 1345.
101 Nissan Jeep Specifications, 1951. NDL, ESS(F) 1345. By 1952, Nissan was also making around 50 jeeps a month from scratch for the Occupation, see Samuels, *"Rich Nation, Strong Army"*, p. 137.
102 Togo and Wartman, *Against All Odds*, p. 148; Data of Vehicles for National Police Reserve Force, Toyota Jidōsha, Toyota BJ, 1951. NDL, ESS(F) 1347.
103 The BJ was not the first 'jeep' that Toyota had produced. Besides the GHQ repairs and procurement mentioned above, the company had also made the AK-10, a reverse engineered vehicle based upon a precursor to the Willys jeep, the Bantam BRC-40, one of which was captured intact during the war and given to the company to examine. The AK-10 was produced in very small numbers and curiously doesn't seem to have influenced subsequent Toyota truck or jeep development. Toyota Motor Corporation, *Sōzō Kagirinaku*, p. 249; Ohtsuka, *Jeeps over the Pacific*, p. 2. The same vehicle, acquired this time through lend-lease also heavily influenced the Soviet designed GAZ 67-B, see: C. Bishop, ed., *The Encyclopaedia of Weapons of World War II*, London: Amber Books, 2007, p. 109.
104 Toyota Motor Corporation, *Sōzō Kagirinaku*, p. 249.
105 Memorandum: NPRJ Support from US and Japan, 25/1/1952. NDL, TS 150; Toyota Motor Corporation, "Prologue, Birth of The Toyota Jeep BJ", *Toyota Land Cruiser Data Library, History, Figures and Photo Material Collection*, 2007, (hereafter TLCDL). Toyota's application was also rather lacklustre when compared to the competing bids, with no cover letter and containing few documents, most of which were in Japanese; see: Production Estimate, Toyota Motor Co., 1/1951. NDL, ESS(F) 1346–1347.
106 Offshore Procurement and Effects of Chamberlain Amendment on Nagoya Automakers, Telegrams from Nagoya Consulate to State Department, Central Files of the Department of State, 8/23/1963. YF-A17, 2-G-52; O. Kigure, "Rikujojietai no Jiipu" (The Ground Self Defense Force's Jeep), in M. Fry and T. Kosai, eds., *Indestructible Jeep, Jiipu: Fumetsu no Sentōsharyo* (Jeep: Indestructible Combat Vehicle), Tokyo: Sankei Publications, 1981.
107 For more on the National Rural Police, see: C. Aldous, *The Police in Occupation Japan, Control, Corruption and Resistance to Reform*, London: Routledge Studies in the Modern History of Asia, 1997.
108 Toyota Motor Corporation, "Prologue, Birth of The Toyota Jeep BJ", TLCDL.
109 Harada, *MP Jiipu*, pp. 105–106; Toyota Motor Corporation, "Prologue, Birth of The Toyota Jeep BJ", TLCDL. The purchase of these vehicles would have helped to offset the problems that a shortage of vehicles had caused the Japanese police during the

Occupation and their effective off-road performance was ideal for the rural jurisdiction of the National Rural Police, see: Aldous, *The Police in Occupation Japan*, p. 63; Memorandum, Graves to Chief, PSD, "Statistics on Vehicles to be used by Japanese Police", Records of the Supreme Commander for Allied Powers, 18/7/1949. YF-A16, 1-D-137.

110 Togo and Wartman, *Against All Odds*, pp. 148–149; Toyota Motor Corporation, "History of Production/Sales", TLCDL. Townsend also notes the ruggedness of vehicles such as the Land Cruiser helping sales in markets whose road systems were as undeveloped as Japan's. See: Townsend, "The "Miracle" of Car Ownership", p. 506.

111 Kawahara, *The Origin of Competitive Strength*, pp. 25–31; Togo and Wartman, *Against All Odds*, p. 148.

112 Toyota Motor Corporation, "Comments from Mr Saihei Iritani", TLCDL. In contrast Togo and Wartman claim the modest sales of the vehicle did little to offset the mounting losses of Toyota's American arm, see: Togo and Wartman, *Against All Odds*, p. 148.

113 Toyota Motor Corporation, "Episode, The Man Who Named It", TLCDL.

114 Toyota Motor Corporation, "Model 40, Full-Scale Expansion in Variation", TLCDL; S. Bull, *Encyclopedia of Militiary Technology and Innovation*, Westport: Greenwood, 2004, p. 137.

115 Toyota Motor Corporation, "Worldwide Annual Sales", TLCDL.

116 "Toyota Seen Recapturing No. 1 Spot", *Japan Times*, 16/1/2013.

117 Toyota Motor Corporation, "Prologue, Birth of The Toyota Jeep BJ", TLCDL. See Kohama for more on Toyoda Kiichiro's ambitions: Kohama, *Industrial Development*, p. 155.

118 Samuels, *"Rich Nation, Strong Army"*, p. 137.

119 Offshore Procurement and Effects of Chamberlain Amendment on Nagoya Automakers, Telegrams from Nagoya Consulate to State Department, Central Files of the Department of State, 8/23/1963. YF-A17, 2-G-52.

120 Maeda, "High-Level Growth", p. 400; Townsend, "The "Miracle" of Car Ownership", pp. 498–501.

6 The Japanese cotton spinning industry and economic recovery under SCAP

Takahiro Ohata

Introduction

The United States government, at least until 1948, did not regard Japan's economic recovery as an official or central goal and instructed the General Headquarters of the Supreme Commander for the Allied Powers (SCAP) to 'not assume any responsibility for the economic rehabilitation of Japan or the strengthening of the Japanese economy'.[1] It was important for Washington to carefully formulate policies to reform the undemocratic and militaristic influences in Japan's politics, economy, and society. However, the majority of the Japanese, suffering under an intense food shortage, had to pay stronger attention to their survival rather than social remodelling. The Japanese basically requested from SCAP, not aid in the form of finished products, but rather the supply of raw materials to produce them, the import of food, and permission to rehabilitate repairable productive facilities. Moreover, air raids by the United States forces were not as destructive to the Japanese industries as was expected, enabling such potential economic activity.[2]

Despite Washington's instructions, SCAP came to consider the rehabilitation of Japanese industry to be one of its primary policy goals. Fortunately, Washington permitted SCAP, upon the instruction of the Joint Chiefs of Staff (JCS), to import commodities in order to 'prevent such widespread disease or civil unrest as would endanger the occupying forces or interfere with military operations'.[3] In addition, Washington was generally not informed of the actual conditions of Japanese industry in detail and had not specifically instructed SCAP how to handle each industry, except in the case of the arms industries. SCAP utilised such provisions and the asymmetry of flows of information to achieve its goals.

SCAP seldom executed conspicuous policies to rebuild Japan's industries, such as intervening to direct the fiscal expenditure of the Japanese government. The measures to support the reconstruction of industries were complex and varied. Seemingly, SCAP's policies towards industries were also sometimes unclear as to what specific goals SCAP sought. Indeed, SCAP supported various industries' reconstruction, in many cases, by systematic and organisational measures and through long term perspectives, not necessarily always in ways the Japanese desired, but in the way SCAP wished to act.

It is very difficult to understand the functions of SCAP's policy towards economic recovery from either the English and Japanese literature on the Occupation.[4] The majority of previous works on the economic aspects of the Occupation are based upon the supposition that from 1945 to 1947, the United States government and SCAP focused their main policy goals upon reform. In this period, the Japanese government controlled the economy but was not able to inhibit mass inflation. In October 1948, the National Security Council approved NSC13/2, which recommended a change of the direction of Occupation policy from reform to economic recovery. In December 1948, the Nine Point Stabilisation Program based upon NSC13/2 was sent to SCAP. Additionally, to implement such new policies effectively, Joseph M. Dodge came to Japan. His policies curbed inflation, but brought about a recession from 1949 to 1950. This recession ended with the 'special procurements' of the Korean War. Based on such an overview, SCAP's economic policy is relegated to the background of narratives of the Occupation.[5]

This paper confines its attention to policies supporting specific industries (i.e. industry-supporting policy) within SCAP's economic policies. A policy which promotes the growth of an industry is generally called an 'industrial policy'. However, at present, the concept of 'industrial policy' includes both measures to arrange inter-industry structures (public redistribution of resources from a certain industry to another) and sometimes competition policies, such as the antitrust policy. Such competition policies tend to improve the economy slowly over time.[6] By contrast, this paper emphasises that SCAP's industry-supporting policy yielded a beneficial economic effect in a relatively short time of about five years.

The cotton spinning industry is an excellent case study here in that it had the following three characteristics which were important for the Japanese economy under the Occupation. First, it was one of the typical industries towards which SCAP implemented an industry-supporting policy, as examined below. The Japanese were aware that the industry received special treatment from SCAP, which was more supportive of its reconstruction than it was towards many other sectors. Second, the cotton spinning industry was able to exert great influence upon the Japanese economy. In pre-war Japan, it was one of the largest industries, and many spinners diversified into weaving on an enormous scale.[7] The cotton textile industry not only employed many workers because of its labour-intensive characteristics, but also stimulated production within the related industries such as dyeing, trading, and transport. It also directly fulfilled the population's need for cotton textiles within Japan.

Finally, the cotton spinning industry had long been one of the main sources of foreign currency earnings for Japan. It supplied cotton yarn to the cotton weaving industry, which was competitive internationally. Indeed, from 1933 to 1941, Japan had been the largest exporter of cotton fabrics in the world, overtaking the UK.[8] Foreign currency gained by the export of cotton textiles was absolutely necessary for the import of Japan's requisites. Certainly, Japan had to import a large amount of other raw materials and essential goods. However, provided the Japanese subdued domestic consumption of cotton textiles and increased exports of them, the cotton spinning industry could earn large sums of foreign currency, exceeding payments for the import of raw cotton. Moreover, in the late 1940s, textile goods were scarce around the world, so there was a great demand for cotton goods.[9] Therefore, the cotton spinning industry deserved reconstruction in the eyes of SCAP.

Meanwhile, from the outset of the Occupation, the future of the cotton spinning industry was full of uncertainty which arose partly from the industry's adaptation to the controlled economy of wartime, and partly from SCAP's reforms. Below, the transfiguration of the cotton spinning industry and hindrances to its recovery from 1937 to about 1950 are examined, followed by SCAP's policies towards the industry.

Adaption to the wartime-directed economy and the restart of the industry under the Occupation

Active military operations, especially from the outbreak of the Sino-Japanese War in 1937 onwards, required the Japanese government to transform the usual peacetime economy into a wartime-controlled economy.[10] After the disruption of foreign trade increased in 1941, the Japanese government implemented two principal policies towards cotton spinners in the spheres of production and distribution. First, in order to exert extensive control over the textile industry, new intermediate entities called 'Control Associations' were founded in 1942 for each of the four textile categories (wool, hemp, cotton and staple fibre, and chemical fibres).[11] In 1943, these four Control Associations were consolidated into the Textile Control Association, and all operating spinners were requested to participate in the association and were officially organised under a 'chain of command'.

Second, the government led spinners to merge with each other and to convert their textile factories to munitions plants, as it aimed to prevent their collapse and to focus scant resources upon effective companies and factories.[12] The state also ordered spinners to deliver a large number of their spindles and looms for scrap. Although there were 78 spinners in 1937, the state forced them to unite with each other into ten companies (the 'Big Ten' spinning companies: Dainippon, Toyo, Shikishima, Daiwa, Kurashiki, Daiken, Kanegafuchi, Fuji, Nisshin, and Nitto) by 1943. The Big Ten were still, however, forced to convert some textile factories to munitions work and diversify into manufacturing military aircraft parts and so on. In addition, they sold and rented some factories to other munitions companies. In 1937, the spinners owned a total of 285 cotton factories and 12,367,695 spindles.[13] However, in August 1945, the Big Ten owned only 38 cotton factories and 3,665,366 spindles, of which 2,005,366 remained operable. The rest of those spindles were heaped up in corners of factories, requiring the Big Ten to reinstall and repair them. In 1940, the number of looms owned by the spinners numbered 114,005 (the highest before 1945), whereas in August 1945, the Big Ten owned 42,749, of which 23,178 were operable. Approximately 600,000 spindles and 8,000 looms were lost due to war damage such as from air raids, although most spindles and looms were forcibly sold to the state for scrap.

At the end of war, the Big Ten decided to close their munitions factories and reopen their main cotton textile businesses. However, there were many obstacles. They had little raw cotton, labour, and few materials to repair their damaged machinery and factories.

The cotton spinning industry, additionally, received five major shocks due to SCAP's democratisation and demilitarisation program. First, the public payment of huge wartime indemnity to companies had been virtually cancelled, pursuant to SCAP's order in July 1946.[14] The Japanese government had withdrawn the payment of both public insurance for war damage and unpaid supply of goods to the state. Therefore, thousands of companies were short of funds and thus not able to repay their debts to the banks and others and hence likely to become bankrupt. In order to prevent a large number of bankruptcies, some special laws were enforced. Such laws stipulated the following: the designated companies, including the Big Ten, had two balance sheets (old accounts and new accounts). They moved the debts derived from wartime indemnity into their old accounts and operated normally under their new accounts. The right of creditors to charge for the debts of the designated companies had been stopped. When the designated companies had the prospect of both the acquisition of sufficient money and the repayment of such debts (other debts were permitted to be incurred by shareholders and creditors), they applied to both the Japanese government and SCAP for permission to unite their two sets of accounts and resume the financial right to act freely. However, their financial rehabilitation basically had to be accomplished by themselves.

Second, the Big Ten spinners were designated as restricted concerns, following SCAP's orders. Restricted concerns needed government and SCAP permission for the following: transfer and dissolution of companies under their banner, change of capital, sale of securities and property, borrowing, and so on. Therefore, the Big Ten spinners' applications to rehabilitate their productive facilities were reviewed by SCAP. Indeed, some of those applications were rejected.[15] Third, some directors from the Big Ten were also purged from their official positions for several years. Such directors included, for example, presidents and chairpersons of the Big Three spinning companies (Dainippon, Toyo, and Kanegafuchi), which were among the larger spinners of the Big Ten. Fourth, the Big Ten were subject to SCAP's reorganisation program (to dissolve larger companies into smaller units), as described below. Fifth, there was a possibility that spindles and looms in Japan would be removed by the Allied reparations program. Particularly, the final report of the United States reparation mission (published in November 1946), led by Edwin W. Pauley, stipulated that Japan was permitted to own only 3,000,000 spindles and 150,000 looms. The Japanese spinners clearly saw the reparation program as a threat,[16] although ultimately, their machinery was not removed.

If SCAP's industry-supporting policy towards spinners had not succeeded in the end, their resentment towards SCAP could have remained. The Japanese hostility towards Allied nations, which had been greatly elevated in wartime, may have also persisted in the bottom of the hearts of the Japanese people if an unsuccessful or more punitive approach had been taken by SCAP towards such a crucial industry.

Imports of raw cotton from 1946 to 1948

From 1945 to 1947, the United States government was largely uninterested in Japan's economic recovery. However, MacArthur's staff assumed the responsibility for such a recovery. One of the industries in which SCAP placed much value was the cotton spinning industry. Within SCAP, the section which held jurisdiction over much of the Japanese economy was Economic and Scientific Section (ESS), which was established on 2 October 1945.[17]

From the outset, ESS regarded economic recovery and reform as its main policy target. As early as 17 August 1945, the first Chief of ESS (October to December 1945), Colonel Raymond C. Kramer, implied to his superior, the Deputy Chief of Staff of SCAP, that it was necessary to found a new section to handle the Japanese economy.[18] Kramer stated that SCAP had to deal with various major problems, such as who had the primary responsibility for Japan's recovery. In September 1945, he argued, in papers submitted to the Chief of Staff of SCAP, that such a section should 'make recommendations to insure maximum production of, and equitable distribution of, essential goods among the civil population' and 'make recommendations for the ultimate form of and restoration of the Japanese economy'.[19] He envisaged the maximisation of civilian industry as a clear goal alongside other related duties within the economic reconstruction of postwar Japan. Such ideas were expressed in formal documents to stipulate the work and policies of ESS.[20] Obviously, the cotton spinning industry was one such potential civilian industry in Japan.

ESS also gradually came to comprehend the dire condition of the cotton spinning industry. From September 1945 onwards, Kramer conferred with Japanese officials and business managers to obtain information and data. On 27 September 1945, he and his staff met seven representatives of the textile industry including four directors of cotton spinning companies.[21] They explained to Kramer that they had shrunk their productive facilities during wartime and detailed how much machinery and raw materials they held at that time. They also informed Kramer that the stock they held was sufficient to keep the mills running for approximately two months at the present rate of production. On 13 October, the Japanese representatives also 'explained the present situation of the cotton industry' to the ESS official Harold S. Tate, who became first Chief of the Textile Division in 1946, as described below.[22] Officially, the Japanese government requested that ESS import raw cotton on three separate occasions around this time: 21 September, and 9 and 15 November 1945.[23]

ESS, at last, decided to request the import of raw cotton from Washington. On 23 November 1945, ESS asked the Department of the Army (DA) to ship raw cotton to Japan 'because of extreme importance of textile industry in Japan [sic]', and stated that such an import had to be hastened as raw cotton stocks in Japan would be exhausted by approximately January.[24] In early December, the DA agreed to supply raw cotton to Japan, because of both large surpluses of American raw cotton and a worldwide shortage of textiles.[25] However, the first shipment of raw cotton was not so easy to carry out. ESS and the DA discussed by radiogram the terms, quality, and quantity of raw cotton to be shipped for some time, and even by January 1946, the situation remained unchanged.[26] While the DA said clearly on 12 January 'the requirements stated as necessary to prevent disease and unrest will be procured and financed by [the DA]', it did not state definitively how and when raw cotton was to be shipped.[27] Recognising that raw cotton stocks in Japan were 'practically exhausted', ESS urged the DA to speed up on 14 and 17 January.[28]

Finally, in February 1946, the government agencies within Washington finished arranging the supply of raw cotton to Japan. While discussing the provision of cotton, the Department of State (DOS) dispatched a 'textile mission' to Japan, something which Britain, China and India had demanded.[29] The purpose of this mission was to research the condition of the Japanese textile industry and to determine how much raw cotton the United States needed to supply. Eventually, Washington decided to supply surplus raw cotton owned by the Commodity Credit Corporation (CCC).[30] In February 1946, the inter-agency contract stipulating the terms of raw cotton supply was signed by the Department of Agriculture, the DA, the DOS, and the United States Commercial Company (USCC, which was founded in 1942 for procuring strategic goods and food, and for executing policies according to the National Defense Plan).[31]

Next, ESS aimed at determining the total amount of raw cotton to be shipped in 1946 under this agreement. ESS called on the DA to send 890,000 bales of raw cotton, which was based upon an estimate by the Japanese, and gained agreement from the textile mission, who were then present in the country.[32] These 890,000 bales of raw cotton were imported from June 1946 to October 1947,[33] at a time when this CCC raw cotton was the only raw cotton imported into Japan (see Tables 6.1 and 6.2).

The next plan for the import of raw cotton for 1947 was also not easily determined. From October 1946, ESS often asked the DA to plan for shipment of another 890,000 bales of raw cotton the following year.[34] However, Washington hesitated to approve such a plan, because of financial problems procuring raw cotton, bad prospects for future cotton textile sales, and a shortage of dollars in foreign cotton textile markets.[35] Additionally, the CCC had no surplus raw cotton.[36] From March to April, Washington informed SCAP of the difficulty of supplying more to Japan. On 15 April, SCAP replied in strong terms, 'request immediate action to be taken to procure American cotton. Any further delay will have a damaging effect upon the textile industry of Japan'.[37] After this intervention, Washington more seriously considered planning for the further supply of cotton to Japan. The formulation of such a program was promoted by conferences between the DA, the DOS, and a 'large group of senators from cotton growing states'.[38] In such conferences, they 'manifested decided concern over maintaining at least historic pos [position] of U.S. raw cotton in occupied areas'.[39] After the adjustment of the terms of shipment between the DA and SCAP, by August, it was determined that the CCC was able to procure 350,000 bales of raw cotton for Japan from the market, and that according to these new conditions the CCC raw cotton agreement of 1946 would be revised. From October 1947 to February 1948, pursuant to the

Table 6.1 Raw Cotton Imports to Japan

	United States	India	Pakistan	Egypt	Mexico	Others	Total (1,000lbs)
1946 Jun	100%	–	–	–	–	–	32,759
Jul to Sep	100%	–	–	–	–	–	214,241
Oct to Dec	100%	–	–	–	–	–	111,638
1947 Jan to Feb	100%	–	–	–	–	–	72,035
Apr to Jun	100%	–	–	–	–	–	21,257
Jul to Sep	100%	–	–	–	–	–	6,973
Oct to Dec	64.3%	35.8%	–	–	–	–	189,924
1948 Jan to Feb	96.5%	–	–	1.7%	–	–	92,828
Apr to Jun	18.6%	38.0%	–	43.4%	–	–	6,997
Jul to Sep	36.8%	63.2%	–	–	–	–	68,171
Oct to Dec	86.6%	0.6%	–	12.8%	–	–	48,177
1949 Jan to Feb	93.7%	0.7%	–	4.4%	–	1.2%	96,195
Apr to Jun	71.1%	8.2%	15.1%	4.2%	–	1.4%	195,576
Jul to Sep	72.2%	9.8%	–	11.4%	–	6.5%	103,311
Oct to Dec	60.5%	0.8%	18.5%	9.8%	–	10.4%	39,137
1950 Jan to Feb	88.4%	7.3%	3.7%	2.2%	1.7%	0.2%	190,987
Apr to Jun	82.3%	5.9%	9.5%	0.0%	–	2.2%	178,883
Jul to Sep	76.9%	0.0%	16.6%	0.7%	1.9%	3.8%	206,148
Oct to Dec	72.6%	0.1%	13.3%	1.6%	8.6%	3.8%	223,371
1951 Jan to Feb	35.8%	–	24.2%	4.7%	20.0%	15.2%	337,545
Apr to Jun	41.9%	6.0%	20.7%	3.1%	12.0%	16.2%	209,031
Jul to Sep	21.5%	6.6%	4.2%	5.2%	26.6%	35.8%	98,642
Oct to Dec	82.2%	–	3.2%	1.7%	10.4%	2.4%	205,891
1952 Jan to Feb	63.4%	–	29.7%	2.5%	1.1%	3.4%	259,549
Apr to Jun	66.4%	4.6%	12.7%	3.2%	7.1%	6.0%	208,831

Sources: *Menka Geppō* (The Cotton Journal), Vol.1, No. 1 to Vol. 2, No. 6, Osaka: Nihon Menka Yunyū Kyōkai (The Japan Cotton Importers Association), 1946 to 1947; *Menka Tōkei Geppō* (The Cotton Statistical Journal), Vol.1 to Vol. 58, Osaka: Menka Keizai Kenkyūjyo (The Cotton Economics Research Institute), 1948 to 1952.

CCC raw cotton agreement of 1947, 350,000 bales of American raw cotton were shipped to Japan. This raw cotton from the CCC was equal to almost all of the raw cotton imported to Japan through 1947 (Table 6.1). Indian raw cotton was the exception. Although not much of it was imported during the Occupation, Indian raw cotton was necessary to blend with various types of cotton for the purpose of making cheaper but high-quality yarn, as had been done in pre-war Japan.

In 1947, ESS sought to procure such Indian raw cotton. After ESS received a request in February for raw cotton exports from the representatives of the Indian liaison mission in Tokyo,[40] ESS arranged the imports with the DA and negotiated with the Indian representatives.[41] In October, a barter agreement to import 170,000 bales of Indian raw cotton was signed between the Indian government, the Japanese government, and SCAP.[42] This cotton was imported in 1947. In November, a similar barter agreement to import 5,000 bales of Egyptian raw cotton (which was generally necessary to produce fine yarn) was signed with the

Table 6.2 Funds, Contracts, and Agreements Related to American Raw Cotton Imported to Japan

Fund	1946		1947		1948		1949		1950		1951		Total	
a. CCC	704,710	100	426,149	100	123,402	41.2							1,254,261	30.4
b. QM					49,117	16.4							49,117	1.2
c. OJEIRF					78,893	26.4	336,237	46.0	188,244	16.2			603,374	14.6
d. PL820							55,401	7.6	171,400	14.8			226,801	5.5
e. ECA							47,938	6.6	2,588	0.2			50,526	1.2
f. EROA							92,993	12.7					92,993	2.3
g. UNICEF							808	0.1	1,470	0.1			2,278	0.1
Total	704,710	100	426,149	100	251,412	84.0	533,377	73.0	363,702	31.4			2,279,350	55.3
Private Trade					47,813	16.0	197,001	27.0	796,160	68.6	800,189	100	1,841,163	44.7
Total	704,710		426,149		299,225		730,378		1,159,862		800,189		4,120,513	

Unit: Bales. Notes: a. to d.: See text of this paper. e.: ECA (Economic Cooperation Administration) of the United States government provided this raw cotton. f.: This raw cotton was purchased with the EROA (Economic Rehabilitation in Occupied Area) Fund of the United States government. g.: UNICEF (United Nations International Children's Emergency Fund) provided this raw cotton for Japanese children.

Sources: *Menka Geppō* (The Cotton Journal), (see sources of Table 6.1); *Menka Tōkei Geppō* (The Cotton Statistical Journal), (see sources of Table 6.1); The Section of Trade, Economic Stabilization Board "Paper No. 8", Reel No. 9 (Trade, Exchange, Foreign Capital), Records of the Postwar Economic Policy of the Economic Stabilization Board, housed by Tokyo University; E. Arita, *Ekonomisuto no Tame no Bōseki Nyūmon* (Introduction of the Cotton Spinning Industry for Economists), Osaka: Seisensha, 1954, pp. 119–120.

Egyptian government.[43] After these agreements, Indian, Pakistani, and Egyptian raw cotton was frequently shipped to Japan (Table 6.1). Consequently, Indian and Egyptian raw cotton supplemented the somewhat unstable supply of American raw cotton from 1947 to 1948 (see Table 6.1).

Import of raw cotton to Japan throughout 1948 remained at low levels (Table 6.1). The main reason was because the CCC raw cotton agreement did not continue, owing to the withdrawal of the USCC. As a temporary measure, imports from the Quarter Master (QM) of raw cotton from U.S. military stocks were arranged by the DA (Table 6.2). In March and early April 1948, the Textile Division of ESS proposed that the Foreign Trade Division of ESS send a mission to India in order to procure Indian raw cotton, because of both a shortage of raw cotton and the advantage of not needing to settle imports from India in dollars.[44] Additionally, the Indian mission in Tokyo was inadequate to make a further contract for raw cotton. In April, ESS decided to dispatch the mission.[45] Its dispatch was decided upon by SCAP without Washington's prior consent.[46] Staff from ESS along with some Japanese representatives made the trip to India and Pakistan in May and June and purchased about 100,000 bales of raw cotton.[47]

Later in 1948, the shift of Occupation policy from reform to economic recovery within Washington decisively swung things in favour of the Japanese cotton spinning industry. Undersecretary of the Army, William H. Draper, Jr., especially, took the initiative in giving Japan loans for raw cotton which were based upon the Occupied Japan Export-Import Revolving Fund (OJEIRF) and the Public Law 820 of the 80th Congress (PL820).[48] The OJEIRF was originally established by SCAP in August 1947 to facilitate the import of materials such as raw cotton, rubber, and wool.[49] In June 1948, an agreement based upon the OJEIRF was signed between the DA and American Banks, which provided that the DA accept a loan of 60 million dollars for raw cotton shipments to Japan. The PL820 passed the Congress in June 1948 and stipulated that the United States government loan funds for shipment to Japan of raw cotton, wool, and so on. From 1949, raw cotton was imported almost continuously by virtue of these loans, other aid (see Table 6.2), and the development of foreign trade treaties.

About 60 percent of American raw cotton shipped to Japan by 1950 was based upon the CCC raw cotton agreement, the OJEIRF, and the PL820 (Table 6.2). These three loans required a system of total control over the Japanese cotton textile industry, as described below.

Formation of the postwar control system

The three main raw cotton agreements (the CCC raw cotton agreement, the OJEIRF, and the PL820) resembled each other in giving SCAP a heavy responsibility to reimburse the loans to buy American raw cotton in dollars. Initially, the responsibility was indirect. The CCC raw cotton agreement stipulated the following: the CCC would deliver raw cotton to the USCC, which the USCC would then export to Japan. The Japanese government would accept and take ownership of it. The Japanese would then, under the supervision of SCAP, produce cotton textiles such as yarn and fabrics from the CCC raw cotton and deliver more than 60 percent of these textiles to the USCC. The USCC would then export the textiles to foreign countries and use earnings from this to reimburse the debt to the CCC in dollars.[50]

In Japan, ESS was responsible for the processing and transporting of the raw cotton. Moreover, most export activities of cotton textiles were actually conducted by ESS and the Japanese, not the USCC.[51] After January 1948, the USCC transferred to SCAP the direct responsibility to repay the debt. Therefore, SCAP took the heaviest responsibility of the American parties to the CCC raw cotton agreements. These conditions were also basically passed on to subsequent agreements.

In mid-1946, ESS established a control system to force the Japanese to both produce cotton textiles from CCC raw cotton and export them. In April 1946, ESS authorised only the Board of Trade to handle all of Japan's foreign trade, and ordered that most of the activities of the Board of Trade should be placed under SCAP's control.[52] Next, in June, ESS directed the Board of Trade to take ownership of the CCC raw cotton and formulate plans (such as import, production, domestic distribution, and export) regarding the CCC raw cotton, coordinating with both the Textile Bureau of the Ministry of Commerce and Industry and the Japanese Textile Association (which had represented textile industrial groups and followed the Textile Control Association during the war).[53] According to these orders, the Japanese created the control system for the CCC raw cotton, which included various industrial groups related to cotton, centring on those three entities.[54] From May 1947, functions of some trade industrial groups were transferred to the Textile Trade Kodan, because the Antitrust Law promulgated in April 1947 (enacted in July) forbade various functions to be exercised by the industrial groups. At the outset, this system did not permit the Japanese to directly participate in export and import.[55] However, after the second half of 1947, most trade activities were transferred to the Japanese, and then ESS chiefly conducted trade negotiations with other countries and supervised the Japanese trade activities. After about 1949, as foreign trade on a private basis increased and trade on a government-to-government basis like the CCC raw cotton agreement decreased, such a control system gradually diminished. For example, the Textile Foreign Kodan was dissolved in December 1950.

In June 1946, ESS established a new division to supervise the textile industry, the Textile Division (TD), mainly due to the increasing amount of administrative work related to both the textile industry and the import of raw cotton.[56] ESS/TD basically supervised the sphere of production within the textile industry. Particularly, the Cotton Branch (or the Cotton and Wool Branch) within ESS/TD had jurisdiction over the cotton spinning industry. However, the Foreign Trade Division (or the Foreign Trade and Commerce Division, FT), which had been founded within ESS in late 1945, supervised the sphere of foreign trade of textiles and raw materials like cotton. ESS/TD operated until November 1949, and after that its functions were transferred to ESS/FT and the Industry Division of ESS.

Thus, by about early 1947, ESS/TD had built a control system which was hierarchically organised, made up of the Japanese government (chiefly, the Textile

Bureau of the Ministry of Commerce and Industry, and the Board of Trade), industrial groups, cotton spinning companies, and cotton textile factories (Figure 6.1). This system enabled ESS/TD to do the following. First, ESS/TD was efficiently able to issue instructions and gather necessary information. ESS/TD was also able to acquire comprehensive statistics and information concerning the cotton spinning industry submitted by the Japanese (Table 6.3). ESS/TD was informed about such statistics regularly and relatively quickly (approximately two weeks later with regard to weekly reports, and approximately one month later with regard to monthly reports). In addition, these statistics were almost the same as those which the Japanese published later.[57] ESS/TD was able to gather exact statistics regularly.

ESS/TD was also able to foster cooperation with the Japanese. The spinners' requirements for raw cotton were fulfilled through ESS; however, this fact did not necessarily mean that the Japanese always cooperated with ESS. This was due to the fact that Japan was forced to export more than 60 percent of its products (actually, the average of every quarter from July 1946 to 1949 was more than 75 percent), although Japan was short of clothing at that same time. ESS/TD had some staff who were eager to cooperate with the Japanese, and these staff frequently held meetings with them (Table 6.4).[58] These meetings were also beneficial for instructing the Japanese and gathering information efficiently. Such a system was not however a fully top-down organisation, but a system within which ESS/TD and the Japanese were able to communicate and cooperate with each other.

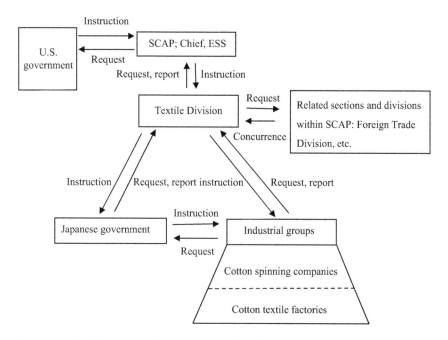

Figure 6.1 The Hierarchical Control System of the Cotton Spinning Industry

Table 6.3 Japanese Statistics Concerning the Cotton Spinning Industry Submitted Regularly to the Textile Division from 1946 to November 1949 (Dissolution of the Textile Division)

	Representative Title	*Report Frequency*	*Time Lag**	*Period*
1	Weekly Report of Yarn and Fabric Produced by CCC Cotton	Weekly	12 days (7–20 days)	From August 1947 to July 1948
2	Production of Cotton Yarn by Count	Monthly	29 days (23–62 days)	From December 1946
3	Production of Cotton Yarn	Monthly	26 days (24–45 days)	From September 1946
4	Production of Cotton Fabrics for Export using CCC Cotton	Monthly	28 days (24–54 days)	From November 1946
5	Cotton Yarn Production per Day per Spindle	Monthly	29 days (23–40 days)	From October 1946
6	Production and Delivery Status of Cotton Yarn	Monthly	37 days (18–74 days)	From January 1947
7	Explanation on Monthly Report	Monthly	23 days (20–27 days)	From November 1946
8	Cotton Spinners' Weekly Report	Weekly	9 days (7–30 days)	From January 1947
9	Cotton Spinners' Report	Monthly	23 days (17–34 days)	From November 1947

Notes: 1. These statistics were written in English. 2. * The 'time lag' is the difference between the final day covered by the data and the day of submission. '(○ – ○ days)' shows the maximum and minimum time lag. In the cases that there were some statistical modes, these are averaged.

Sources: ESS(B) 09035–09038, National Diet Library, Tokyo (hereafter NDL); ESS(C) 07138–07165, 07178, 07179, 07186–07199, NDL.

Other policies of ESS towards the cotton spinning industry

Aside from the measures examined above, ESS's industry-supporting policies took various other forms as well. First, ESS permitted the cotton spinning industry to retain their productive facilities on the basis of a plan formulated by ESS. After the war, the Big Ten spinners sought to rehabilitate their machinery. However, as they were designated as restricted concerns, they had to gain permission from SCAP regarding loans from banks for rehabilitation. Moreover, they longed for assurances that their plant would not be removed as reparations. In October 1946, the spinners officially applied for permission to acquire rehabilitation loans for their productive facilities.[59] In order to reply to their requests, ESS/TD started to examine the future status of the productive facilities of the cotton industry. In January 1947, ESS/TD finished a plan which stipulated that the Japanese would need four million spindles for the time being.[60] In this plan, ESS/TD estimated the cotton yarn per year, which was necessary for domestic consumers, industrial

Table 6.4 Meetings between the Textile Division and Japanese Officials/Industry Personnel

Period	Number of Meetings	Organisation				Subject of Meeting									Inspections by the Cotton Branch
		Officials	Industrial Groups	Companies	Labour Union	Raw Materials	Production, Distribution	Export Facilities	Financing	Coal/Electricity	Labour	Dyeing/Finishing	Examination	Others	
1946 Aug. to Sept.	5	3	4	2			3						1	1	1
Oct. to Dec.	47	20	28	14	1	2	20	9	3	2	1	6	3	1	
1947 Jan. to Mar.	20	5	8	8		4	4	5	2			3	3	1	3
Apr. to Jun.	14	5	11	3		5	2		2					1	4
Jul. to Aug.	3	1	2				1	1				1			2
Sep. to Nov.	17	6	7	5	1		6	4		1	1		1	1	4
1948 Dec. to Feb.	66	19	25	26	3	12	26	3	4	2	7	2	2	1	1
Mar. to May.	33	5	23	7	1	6	11	3			4	5		2	1
June, July, Sept., Dec.	4	3			1		2			1	1				6
1949 Jan. to Mar.	51	27	14	16		13	33	1					1	1	2
Apr.	4	1	3	1		1	3								1

Notes: 1. The period is generally divided by quarters, but other periods are used depending on the statistical distribution of the remaining documents. 2. The number of each category does not mean the total number of participants, but the number of meetings in which persons belonging to each category's organisation participated.

Sources: ESS(C) 07073, 07138–07140, 07142, NDL; ESS(E) 03541–03560, 03589, 03600–03603, 03647–03650, 03652, 03669, 03670, NDL.

requirements, and export. Next, these amounts were divided by an estimated production per spindle. As a result, domestic necessities were calculated to require about 3.5 million spindles. ESS/TD also added 500,000 spindles for 'the possibility of a moderate expansion in exports in the next few years' to the 3.5 million required.[61]

During this process, ESS/TD had to give considerable attention as to whether Washington was going to remove the spinning machinery as reparations. However, things took a more favourable turn following Paulay's mission in 1945. Washington actually became less likely to order SCAP to confiscate the machinery because that would have hampered reimbursement of the cost of the CCC raw cotton. When the mission led by Clifford S. Strike was dispatched to Japan by the DA for investigation of the reparations program in January and February 1947, SCAP must have been informed that the mission did not suggest the removal of spindles and looms. Indeed, the report of Strike mission, which was sent to SCAP on 18 February and to the DA on 24 February, did not consider the productive facilities of the cotton spinning industry to be targets for reparation.[62]

SCAP eventually determined the following orders for spinners' capacities independently, without Washington's prior permission. From February to mid-1947, ESS/TD issued some directives regarding spinners' capacities to the Japanese government. In February, ESS/TD permitted Japan to possess up to four million spindles and an unlimited number of looms.[63] Each of the Big Ten spinners was permitted to possess only their present number of spindles (3,665,366 in total).[64] This meant that formally, the Big Ten were confined to their present number of spindles and to owning the same number of spindles going forward.

Additionally, in 1947, ESS/TD directed the Japanese government to distribute the difference between the four million total permitted spindles and those presently owned by the Big Ten (a total difference of 334,634 spindles) to new companies.[65] The government then allowed the admission of 25 new spinners (*Shinbō*) into the cotton spinning industry after reviewing the applicants.[66] This measure was deemed necessary for ESS/TD because of the dissolution of the oligopoly of the Big Ten. ESS/TD's industry-supporting policy here was also influenced by the economic idealism predominant in the early Occupation. Subsequently, under the circumstances of a shortage of materials to repair their assets, the Big Ten and *Shinbō* spinners struggled to rehabilitate and install their spindles.

The Japanese and other divisions of ESS sometimes insisted that the limit of four million spindles should be raised.[67] ESS/TD certainly viewed the furtherance of rehabilitating spinners' capacities as facilitating the economic recovery of Japan, which was short of clothing. Indeed, in November 1946, the Chief of the Cotton Branch told the Chief of ESS/TD that, 'it is most important that the 2,359,000 spindles get in operation just as soon as possible', and 'we not only need this production for the credit side of our foreign trade account but we need the production of this Japanese economy as well'.[68] Nevertheless, ESS/TD opposed the expansion of the industry beyond a certain level after taking into consideration the amount of imported raw cotton, the existence or non-existence of dollars in export markets and the opposition of the cotton textile manufacturers in the United States and Britain.[69] In addition, the spinners' pace of rehabilitating themselves was slow; therefore, ESS/TD considered promoting rehabilitation of the present spindles to be more essential than adding new ones.[70]

By 1949, the problems of both the import of raw cotton and the terms of export were gradually being resolved. Additionally, in early 1950, the opposition of cotton textile manufacturers in the United States and Britain cooled down, and a letter from the Senate urging the expansion of the number of Japanese spindles was sent to SCAP.[71] In June, that letter directly resulted in the repeal of directives restricting the spinners' capacities.[72]

Within its other activities connected to the cotton industry, ESS also involved itself in the coordination of production. From 1946 to 1949, imports of raw cotton were not stable (see Table 6.1). In some months, the volume was high, whereas in other months, it was low. ESS/TD generally controlled raw cotton consumption through supervising the production and distribution plans submitted by the Japanese. However, when such standard control methods were impossible, ESS/TD ordered increases or decreases in the consumption of raw cotton (that is to say, production of cotton yarn) in accordance with the amount of imported raw cotton available.

In late 1946, ESS/TD instructed the Japanese to increase production, however the spinners were not able to do so, despite the mass imports of raw cotton at that time. In October, ESS/TD held a conference with the Japanese and determined what ESS/TD, the Japanese officials, and the spinners could do to increase production.[73] Owing to this, the Japanese government conducted measures to promote production, such as additional rations of food to employees in the cotton textile factories.[74] The spinners also established a special commission to inspect each other's factories. ESS/TD requested that other divisions in ESS import necessary parts for spindles, raise wages for the employees, and provide additional rations of food.[75] As a result, the production of cotton yarn in December doubled compared to that in August.[76]

The pre-war Japanese cotton spinning industry carried out a cartel based curtailment of yarn production 11 times because of overproduction. However, in the late 1940s, the cotton spinning industry executed the same curtailment twice because of shortages of raw cotton, pursuant to SCAP's orders. The authorities' intervention was indispensable for such a curtailment because the Antitrust Law forbade industrial groups to execute cartel based behaviour akin to that used in the pre-1945 era. In summer 1947, as the import of CCC raw cotton decreased, stocks became scarce. Therefore, ESS/TD ordered the Japanese to slow down the production of cotton yarn.[77] In early 1948, as raw cotton imports decreased, ESS/TD again instructed the Japanese to diminish their production.[78] According to these orders, the Japanese decreased the cotton yarn production,[79] but in doing so maintained a degree of stability in terms of production and the use of labour.

ESS/TD also played a role in influencing the judgement of the Deconcentration Review Board (DRB), which mitigated its plans to dismantle most large Japanese companies, such as the Big Ten spinners. This plan had been formulated by the Antitrust and Cartels Division (AC) of ESS. The decision process of the reorganisation plan was full of twists and turns. From April 1947, ESS/AC initiated the reorganisation plan, and in December compelled the Japanese government to enact the Deconcentration of Excessive Economic Power Law in order to dissolve companies efficiently.[80] According to the law, the Holding Company Liquidation Commission (HCLC), which was composed of Japanese individuals, was supposed to conduct the reorganisation plan, however, ESS/AC had virtually decided the plan by itself by April 1948. From mid-1947, some key personalities in Washington strongly opposed the reorganisation plan, and Undersecretary of the Army, William H. Draper Jr. dispatched the DRB to Japan in May 1948.[81] In Japan, the DRB took on the final authority to decide the organisation plan. However, the DRB consisted of only five committee members and had no supporting researchers. Therefore, they basically depended upon information submitted to them by SCAP and the Japanese.[82]

ESS/TD initially resisted the reorganisation plan because, in their opinion, there was 'no textile group in any of the Big Ten companies that is so large as to be called a monopoly'.[83] In 1947, ESS/TD reluctantly gave assent to ESS/AC's reorganisation plan of the Big Ten. However, in mid-1948, ESS/TD reversed its position and completely opposed ESS/AC's plan, withdrawing its support for ESS/AC.[84] Eventually, in November 1948, ESS/AC sent the reorganisation plans for seven of the Big Ten spinners to the DRB and awaited its ruling. On 9 February 1949, the Chief of ESS/TD expressed a dissenting view on dismantling these seven spinners to the DRB, and said that the Big Ten 'were highly competitive'.[85] It is not known exactly how he explained this to the DRB at that meeting due to the absence of a precise record. However, because ESS/TD was able to obtain information and views from the Japanese under the control system, he must have explained to the DRB about the similar opinions on the side of the companies themselves.

In February 1949, the DRB concluded that one of the seven spinners, Daiken, should be dissolved, but that the others should not be dismantled.[86] Most of the reasons described in the DRB's recommendation were identical to those described in the documents which the HCLC submitted in order to oppose the ESS/AC's plan.[87] Additionally, in that recommendation, the DRB referred to the fact that there was no monopoly in the cotton spinning industry. This was also identical to the view of the Chief of ESS/TD. Therefore, ESS/TD can be seen to have influenced the DRB's recommendations.

The accomplishment of reconstruction

By 1950, the cotton spinning industry had been fully revived. How was this expedited through SCAP's industry-supporting policy? The following three points deserve examination: the repayment of loans for American raw cotton, the rehabilitation of cotton productive facilities, and the construction of a stable structure to make profits.

First, the three main loans of American raw cotton were reimbursed by 1950. This fact can be confirmed by elucidating foreign currency accounts under SCAP's control. The first foreign currency account which was used for Japan's settlement of foreign trade was the SCAP Trust Fund set up by the DA in October 1946.[88] This was a part of the DA's financial system utilised by SCAP.[89] The DA established such an account in order to deposit the proceeds in dollars of Japan's exports to the United States and to disburse it to pay for imports into Japan. However, the SCAP Trust Fund did not offer the functions of commercial banking services such as the payment of bills, which were necessary for general trade operations.[90] SCAP, after obtaining permission from the DA, created the SCAP Commercial Account in the Tokyo Branch of the National City Bank of New York in September 1947 because private trade reopened partly in August 1947 and SCAP considered control of its own accounts as desirable in order to promote foreign trade.[91] The SCAP Commercial Account became a major exchange settlement account for Japan's trade. In the end, SCAP Commercial Accounts were opened in approximately ten foreign banks.[92] SCAP also controlled various other accounts, for example, government-to-government open accounts and the SCAP Cotton Textile Account.[93]

Through these accounts, all the loans for American raw cotton were paid off by 1950. The repayment of the main three loans was as follows: the loan of CCC Cotton amounted to 185,547,800.81 dollars, including interest, and over 99 percent of that debt was repaid by December 1948, with the total fully paid off by mid-1949.[94] Raw cotton was procured by the OJIERF especially in early 1949 and at the outset of 1950. The loan based upon the OJIERF amounted to approximately 93 million dollars and was also repaid by April 1950.[95] Finally, a loan based upon PL 820, aggregating to approximately 53.8 million dollars, was appropriated for Japan in 1949.[96] This loan was repaid in 1950. From around 1950, Japan basically did not depend upon the American credit for imported raw cotton and allotted foreign currency obtained from exports for the import of raw cotton.

The SCAP accounts system was, however, a separate institution. SCAP directly controlled it, entirely separately from Japanese government or industry control. The Japanese thus did not comprehend the actual conditions as to how their business activities for foreign trade produced foreign currency. Furthermore, as the Japanese government under this system was allowed to take no account of the real exchange rate, it fixed the prices of imports lower and the prices of exports higher than real (black market) prices.[97] Hence, public expenditure grew, and inflation accelerated. Nevertheless, the SCAP accounts system supported the smooth handling of the cotton textiles trade and certainly contributed to the expansion of such trade in the late 1940s.

The permitted level of cotton productive facilities was almost reached by 1950 (with regard to the Big Ten spinners, see Table 6.5). However, after the limit on the number they could add was abolished in June 1950, the Big Ten did not play a leading role in the acquisition of new spindles. In the business upswing after the Korean War broke out, in addition to the 25 *Shinbō* spinners, about 100 new spinners gained entry to the market by 1953.[98] Such emerging start-up spinners

Table 6.5 The Rehabilitation Plans of the Big Ten Spinners in 1947 and Their Achievements

	Cotton Spindles		Cotton Looms	
	Estimated Completion of Rehabilitation	Date Accomplished	Estimated Completion of Rehabilitation	Date Accomplished
Dainippon	Jun 1948	Jun 1949	Mar 1948	Aug 1950
Toyo	Jun 1949	Dec 1950	Dec 1948	Oct 1951
Shikishima	Jun 1949	Jan 1951	Jun 1949	*
Daiwa	Aug 1949	Feb 1951	Mar 1948	Dec 1949
Kurashiki	Sept 1949	Oct 1950	Jun 1948	Feb 1948
Daiken	Sept 1948	Nov 1949	Jun 1948	Sept1950
Kanegafuchi	Jun 1949	Mar 1951	Dec 1949	Apr 1952
Fuji	Jun 1948	Jan 1950	Dec 1948	July 1949
Nisshin	Jul 1948	Jun 1949	Jun 1949	Nov 1949
Nitto	Aug 1948	Feb 1950	Mar 1948	May 1951

Notes: * Shikishima did not accomplish its plan to rehabilitate its looms.

Sources: Y. Tawa, ed., *Nihon Bōsekigyō no Fukkō* (The Reconstruction of the Japanese Cotton Spinning Industry), Osaka; Nihon Bōseki Kyōkai (Japan Spinners' Association), 1948, pp. 43–44; Nihon Bōseki Kyōkai (Japan Spinners' Association), ed., *Menshi Bōseki Jijyō Sankōsho* (Report of Statics of the Cotton Spinning Industry), Osaka: Nihon Bōseki Kyōkai, 1948 to 1952.

simultaneously started to increase their number of spindles. As a result, in the early 1950s, the Big Ten were anxious about the overproduction of yarn and thus restrained increases in cotton production capacity, while the larger companies such as the Big Three gradually placed an emphasis on diversification into other businesses such as synthetic fibre production.

The Big Ten spinners also constructed a stable structure to make profits from cotton textiles by 1950. This can be clarified by examining the financial condition of their profit and loss statements. Table 6.6 demonstrates that almost all of the Big Ten earned profits during the early Occupation. However, such profits might have been gained from their spinoff business such as chemical textiles and non-fibre production. Regarding this point, the case of Shikishima spinning company, which produced only cotton textiles, should be analysed. Shikishima showed a deficit until 1947, however after 1948, it ran a surplus. Consequently, sales from cotton textiles exceeded costs from about 1948. This means that the price controls of the Japanese government under SCAP's supervision basically helped spinners make a profit. This price control of cotton textiles lasted until 1951. The government raised cotton textile prices several times because of intense inflation. As a result, rising prices offset inflation and generated income. By virtue of such profits, by the late 1940s the Big Ten spinners had good prospects for reimbursing the debts incurred in 1946 (see above). After the deterrence of expansion of the reorganisation program, this return to profitability and solvency allowed the Big Ten to gain permission to unite their two balance sheets (pre-1946 and post-1946, see above) in late 1949.[99]

Table 6.6 Financial Condition (Profit and Loss Statement) of the Big Ten Spinning Companies (1946–1949)

Dainippon	1946–47	1947	1948	1949
Gross Profit	156	227	1,107	1,343
Net Operating Profit	91	95	802	890
Net Profit	34	14	511	418

Toyo	1946–47	1947	1948	1949
Gross Profit	239	279	777	2,723
Net Operating Profit	163	167	408	1,603
Net Profit	36	70	66	1,026

Shikishima	1946–47	1947	1948	1949
Gross Profit	−2	55	209	717
Net Operating Profit	−23	18	142	576
Net Profit	−41	−26	30	467

Daiwa	1946–47	1947	1948	1949
Gross Profit	26	66	228	741
Net Operating Profit	36	30	95	534
Net Profit	−0.4	−1	69	287

Kurashiki	1946–47	1947	1948	1949
Gross Profit	168	137	257	1,224
Net Operating Profit	104	65	143	835
Net Profit	46	51	96	247

Daiken Sangyō	1946–47	1947	1948	1949
Gross Profit	160	356	1,534	2,384
Net Operating Profit	15	119	866	1,468
Net Profit	0.02	18	262	781

Kanegafuchi	1946–47	1947	1948	1949
Gross Profit	477	471	631	1,670
Net Operating Profit	369	352	322	918
Net Profit	119	138	292	577

Fuji	1946–47	1947	1948	1949
Gross Profit	85	51	293	1,286
Net Operating Profit	58	28	212	735
Net Profit	16	22	22	543

Nisshin	1946–47	1947	1948	1949
Gross Profit	33	43	255	782
Net Operating Profit	3	9	41	317
Net Profit	0.9	7	41	156

Nitto	1946–47	1947	1948	1949
Gross Profit	145	107	250	630
Net Operating Profit	112	18	42	321
Net Profit	38	14	77	249

Unit: Millions of Yen. Notes: The period of '1946–47' is from August 1946 to a set month in the second half of 1947. The period of '1947', '1948', and '1949' varied for each spinner.

Sources: Dainippon: ESS(A) 10605, 10606, 10608, ESS(D) 12576, NDL; Toyo: ESS(D) 09316, ESS(I) 01075, NDL; Shikishima: ESS(D) 12757, ESS(F) 04601, 04637, NDL. Daiwa: ESS(C) 11528, ESS(D) 12609, NDL; Kurashiki: ESS(F) 04712, 04713, NDL; Daiken Sangyō: ESS(E) 09162, 09175, NDL; Kanegafuchi: ESS(D) 09423, 09424 ESS(H) 01801, NDL; Fuji: ESS(D) 12632, ESS(F) 04602, NDL; Nisshin: ESS(A) 12645, ESS(F) 04687, NDL; Nitto: ESS(A) 10700, 10704, 12672, NDL.

Conclusion

SCAP's industry-supporting policy did not directly conduct the reconstruction of the Japanese cotton spinning industry. Of course, the most hard-working and active entities within the recovery were Japanese. SCAP, however, was an efficient facilitator in the rebuilding of the industry. Realising Japan's adversities, SCAP requested Washington send raw cotton to Japan, imported their raw cotton from the United States, and enacted policies to speed up the rehabilitation of the industry.

SCAP's industry-supporting policy can be divided into two aspects, production and foreign trade. As for the production, ESS indirectly supported the cotton spinning industry. On the other hand, SCAP's industry-supporting policy with regard to foreign trade was a form of direct support. In the late 1940s, SCAP rebuilt the Japanese trade institutions and led moves towards the construction of the control system closely related to the trade of cotton. Without sufficient support from SCAP, the industry would have expended more resources on reconstruction and arguably might have expanded too rapidly.

The top management of the cotton spinning industry expressed gratitude towards SCAP's support and considered it to be diligent and dedicated. In 1950, when spinners were recovering and receiving the benefits from SCAP's support, their managers referred to the positive impact of SCAP (or U.S.) support and expressed a feeling of thankfulness in articles written for economic magazines. The examples of such articles from presidents of the Big Three spinners included: Hara Kippei, president of Dai Nippon Bōseki, saying in 1950: 'I cannot ignore the immeasurable kindness of SCAP which supplied raw cotton and reopened trade'.[100] Abe Kojiro, president of Toyo Bōseki, also said in 1951: 'after the end of the Pacific War, the Japanese cotton industry achieved reconstruction thanks to the provision of American raw cotton by the United States'.[101] Also, Muto Itoji, president of Kanegafuchi Bōseki, claimed in 1951: 'though we received American aid of 1.8 billion dollars by June last year, it was appropriated mainly for food and clothing' and 'the 400 million dollars a year accepted from the United States was invested in industries directly or indirectly, so that we attained the present economic recovery'.[102]

Even after over 20 years had passed since the end of the Occupation, some did not forget SCAP's achievements. Tawa Yasuo, who worked in the Japan Spinners' Association during the Occupation and later became a managing director, remembered in his reminiscences in 1976 that Harold S. Tate, the first Chief of the Textile Division of ESS, 'was entirely an amateur in textiles, but he was not a bad person and considered the reconstruction of the cotton industry really deeply'.[103] In addition, Tawa said that William R. Eaton, Chief of the Cotton Branch of the Textile Division, 'handled most favourably' each raw cotton loan and the imports of raw cotton, and even that he 'was very pro-Japanese and a never-to-be-forgotten person in thinking of the reconstruction of the Japanese cotton spinning industry'.[104] The effective acceleration of economic recovery by SCAP's policies in the context of the cotton industry certainly mitigated some hostility among the

Japanese towards the United States and therefore partly helped improve the attitude of the postwar Japanese towards the United States.[105]

Previous studies which attached importance to the change of the United States Occupation policy from reform to economic recovery around 1948 undervalue the contribution of SCAP towards Japan's economic reconstruction. The recovery of the cotton spinning industry, which was one of the most important industries for the Japanese economy, was based upon SCAP's support prior to this date.

SCAP's support, however, did not assure the long term prosperity of the cotton spinning industry. In the early 1950s, the entry of about 100 new spinners into the industry caused excessive competition, so that after 1955, the Japanese government regulated the increase of spindles owned by spinning companies and decreased the total number of spindles.[106] Also, after the late 1960s, international low-cost competition promoted its decline.[107] The reason for the success of the Occupation's support for the reconstruction of the industry was that SCAP concentrated its policy upon helping not to create new competition, but to realise the industry's remaining potential, thus accomplishing a simple but difficult task. The Japanese cotton spinning industry after the 1950s was not able to build further upon the initial success of its reconstruction, and did not succeed in effectively innovating, or in other strategies such as in massive foreign direct investments in which some Japanese spinners had previously been successful in China in the pre-war years.[108]

Notes

This paper is based upon the author's book published in Japanese. T. Ohata, *GHQ no Senryō Seisaku to Keizai Fukkō: Saikō Suru Nihon Menbōsekigyō (GHQ's Occupation Policy and Economic Recovery: The Rehabilitation of the Japanese Cotton Spinning Industry)*, Kyoto: Kyotodaigaku Shuppankai, 2012.

1 JCS1380/15, "Basic Initial Post-Surrender Directive to Supreme Commander for the Allied Powers for the Occupation and Control of Japan", 1/11/1945, Division of Special Records, Foreign Office, Japanese Government, ed., *Nihon Senryō Oyobi Kanri Jyuyō Bunshōshū (Documents Concerning the Allied Occupation and Control of Japan)*, Vol. 1, 1949, (Hereafter JCS1380/15), p. 136.
2 U.S. Strategic Bombing Survey, *The Effects of Strategic Bombing on Japan's War Economy*, Washington DC: U. S. Government Printing Office, 1946, Chapter 5.
3 JCS1380/15, p. 151.
4 K. Yamamura, *Economic Policy in Postwar Japan: Growth Versus Economic Democracy*, Berkeley: University of California Press, 1967, Chapter 1 to 3; M. Schaller, *The American Occupation of Japan: The Origins of the Cold War in Asia*, New York and Oxford: Oxford University Press, 1985; T. Igarashi, *Tainichi Kōwa to Reisen: Sengo Nichibei Kankei no Keisei (The Treaty of Peace With Japan and the Cold War: The Foundation of Postwar Relationship between Japan and the United States)*, Tokyo: University of Tokyo Press, 1986; H. B. Schonberger, *Aftermath of War: Americans and the Remaking of Japan, 1945–1952*, Kent and London: The Kent State University Press, 1989; R. Miwa, "The Reorganization of the Japanese Economy", M. Sumiya, ed., *A History of Japanese Trade and Industry Policies*, Oxford and New York: Oxford University Press, 2000 (first published in Japanese in 1994).

5 Some historians placed a high value upon SCAP's economic policy. Steven J. Fuchs pointed out that the economic policy not of the United States government but of SCAP had fulfilled the crucial functions within Japan's economic recovery; see "Feeding the Japanese: Food Policy, Land Reform, and Japan's Economic Recovery", M. E. Caprio and Y. Sugita, ed., *Democracy in Occupied Japan: The U.S. Occupation and Japanese Politics and Society*, Oxford: Routledge, 2009. He deemed the central SCAP economic policy to be its food policy from 1945 to 1947. However, this paper focuses upon SCAP's furtherance of Japan's economic recovery by supporting industries such as the cotton spinning industry from 1945 to 1950. Yamazaki Hiroaki pointed out that SCAP also promoted the reconstruction of the Japanese chemical textile industry; see "Sengo Kaikaku to Kasen Sangyō" (The Postwar Recovery and the Chemical Textile Industry), *Sengo Kaikaku, (Postwar Reform)*, Vol. 8, Tokyo: Tokyodaigaku Shuppankai, 1975, pp. 279–320. However, he did not explore the system and organisational characteristics of SCAP's policies.

6 Eleanor M. Hadley pointed out that the antitrust policy during the Occupation was one of the main factors which generated rapid economic growth in the 1960s. E. M. Hadley, *Antitrust in Japan*, Princeton: Princeton University Press, 1970.

7 Even during the Occupation, spinners produced about half of the cotton fabrics in Japan. See, Nihon Bōseki Kyōkai (Japan Spinners' Association), ed., *Menshi Bōseki Jijyō Sankōsho* (*Report of Statics of the Cotton Spinning Industry*), every half year version (1946 to 1952).

8 Nihon Bōseki Kyōkai (Japan Spinners' Association), *Bōkyō Hyakunenshi* (*The History of the Past Century of Japan Spinners Association*), Osaka: Nihon Bōseki Kyōkai, 1982, p. 122.

9 During the Occupation, the concept that there was a worldwide demand for cotton textiles made in Japan was common in Japan and the United States. Even Jerome B. Cohen in 1949, who doubted the significance of SCAP's policies towards Japan's cotton spinning industry, agreed that there was a demand for cotton textiles sufficient for it 'to remain the largest single export item . . . over the next five years'. J. B. Cohen, *Japan's Economy in War and Reconstruction*, Minneapolis: University of Minnesota Press, 1949, p. 489 (selected and with a new introduction by J. Hunter, *Japanese Economic History 1930–1960*, Vol. 2, London and New York: Routledge, 2000).

10 A. Hara "Senji Tōsei Keizai no Kaishi" (The Start of the Wartime Controlled Economy), *Iwanami Kōza Nihon Rekishi* (*The History of Japan*), Vol. 20, Tokyo: Iwanami Shoten, 1976.

11 Tsūshō Sangyōshō (Ministry of International Trade and Industry), ed., *Shōkō Seisakushi* (*The History of Commercial and Industrial Policy*), Vol. 16, Tokyo: Shōkō Seisakushi Kankōkai, 1972, pp. 182–189.

12 J. Watanabe, "Restructuring in Cotton-spinning Companies", *Japanese Research in Business History*, Business History Society of Japan, Vol. 22, 2005, pp. 55–81; J. Watanabe, *Sangyō Hatten Suitai no Keizaishi: Jyūdaibō no Keisei to Sangyō Chōsei (The History of Japanese Industrial Development and its Decline: The Formation of Big Ten Spinning Companies and Industrial Adjustments)*, Tokyo: Yuhikaku, 2010, pp. 45, 56–86.

13 Nihon Bōseki Kyōkai (Japan Spinners' Association), ed., *Menshi Bōseki Jijyō Sankōsho, the first half of 1940*; Y. Tawa, ed., *Nihon Bōsekigyō no Fukkō* (*The Reconstruction of the Japanese Cotton Spinning Industry*), Osaka: Nihon Bōseki Kyōkai, 1948, pp. 1, 15, 17–18; Japan Spinners' Association, *The Statistics of the Japanese Cotton Industry, 1903–1949*, Japan Spinners' Association, 1951, Table 1.

14 *History of the Nonmilitary Activities of the Occupation of Japan, 1945–1951*, Vol. 40, Tokyo: Nihon Tosho Senta, 1990 (reprint); Okurashō (Ministry of Finance), ed., *Shōwa Zaiseishi: Haisen kara Kōwa Made* (The History of Finance in the Shōwa period: From the End of War to the Peace Treaty), Vol. 11, Tokyo: Tōyō Keizai Shinpōsha, 1983.

15 For example, see Nitto Bōseki (Nitto spinning company), *Kaiko Sanjyūnen (Reminiscences of 30 years)*, Tokyo: Nitto Bōseki, 1952, pp. 117–118.
16 Tawa, ed., *Nihon Bōsekigyō no Fukkō*, p. 21.
17 SCAP, "General Order No. 3, Economic and Scientific Section", 2/10/1945, *History of the Nonmilitary Activities of the Occupation of Japan, 1945–1951*, Vol. 2, Tokyo: Nippon Tosho Senta, 1990 (reprint), Appendix 5, A.
18 Asst. to DC/S to DC/S, 17/8/1945. National Diet Library, Tokyo (hereafter NDL), ESS(E) 00812. Almost all of the Records of SCAP (RG 331) housed by the National Archives and Records Administration have been copied to microfiche by Japan's National Diet Library since 1985. When the documents in the RG 331 are referred to in this paper, the call number of the National Diet Library is used.
19 Asst. to DC/S to DC/S, "Draft Directive for Economic and Scientific Section", 14/9/1945. NDL, ESS(E) 00812; R. C. Kramer to Chief of Staff, "Establishment of Economic and Scientific Board", 9/9/1945. NDL, ESS(E) 00812.
20 SCAP, General Order No. 3.
21 "Memo for Record", 28/9/1945. NDL, ESS(E) 00850.
22 Nihon Seni Rengōkai (Japanese Textile Association), ed., *Seni Nenkan Shōwa 22 Nenban (The Year Book of Textile, 1947)*, Tokyo: Seni Nenkan Kankōkai, 1947, p. 15.
23 Tsūshō Sangyōshō (Ministry of International Trade and Industry), ed., *Shōkō Seisakushi*, Vol. 16, pp. 253–254.
24 Scap to Warcos [DA], CA55231, 23/11/1945. NDL, ESS(C) 00729.
25 Washington (CAD) [DA] to CINCAFPAC ADV [SCAP], WX86987, 6/12/1945. NDL, ESS(C) 00729.
26 Washington (CAD) to CINCAFPAC, W85103, 25/11/1945. NDL, ESS(C) 00729; ESS, "Memorandum for Record", 19/12/1945. NDL, ESS(C) 00729; SCAP to WARCOS, CA56255, 21/12/1945. NDL, ESS(C) 00729.
27 Washington (CAD) to CINCAFPAC, WX92507, 12/1/1946. NDL, ESS(C) 00728.
28 ESS, "Memorandum for Record", 14/1/1946. NDL, ESS(C) 00728; SCAP to WARCOS, ZA12917, 14/1/1946. NDL, ESS(C) 00728; SCAP to WARCOS, CA56998, 17/1/1946. NDL, ESS(C) 00728.
29 JCS 1588, "Visit of a Textile Mission to Japan", 26/12/1945, Record of the Joint Chiefs of Staff, Part 2: 1946–1953, Reel. 1, University Publications of America, 1980; ESS, Executive Division, "Memo for Record", 28/3/1946. NDL, ESS(C) 00728.
30 JCS 1566/3, "Guidance to SCAP Regarding Shipment of Raw Cotton to Japan", 10/4/1946, Record of the Joint Chiefs of Staff, Part 2: 1946–1953, Reel. 1.
31 Regarding the USCC, see the following: *United States Government Manual, 1945, First Edition*, Washington, DC: Division of Public Inquiries, Office of War Information, p. 67.
32 ESS to WARCOS, C59402, 30/3/1946. NDL, ESS(C) 00727; ESS, "Memorandum for Record", 23/3/1946. NDL, ESS(C) 00727; Tawa, ed., *Nihon Bōsekigyō no Fukkō*, p. 54.
33 Ibid., p. 65. Most of the 890,000 bales had been imported to Japan by the early half of 1947.
34 SCAP to Washington (WDSCA ES), C66493, 23/10/1946. NDL, ESS(C) 00733; SCAP to Washington (WDSCA), Z34758, 12/3/1947. NDL, ESS(C) 00832; Foreign Trade Division, ESS, "Memorandum for Record", 20/3/1947. NDL, ESS(C) 00834.
35 ESS, "Memo for Record", n.d. (estimated to be in April 1947). NDL, ESS(B) 00838.
36 WAR to CINCFE, WAR94319, 20/3/1947. NDL, ESS(B) 00834; Chief, Foreign Trade Division, to Chief, ESS, "Amendment to Cotton Contract", 23/6/1947. NDL, ESS(B) 00846.
37 SCAP to WASHINGTON (WDSCA ES), C51828, 15/4/1947. NDL, ESS(B) 00838.
38 WAR (WDSCA ES) to SCAP, W97334, 2/5/1947. NDL, ESS(B) 00840.
39 Ibid.
40 Political Representative of India in Japan, Indian Liaison Mission, Tokyo, to Chief, ESS, 12/2/1947. NDL, ESS(B) 00910.

41 For example, see, SCAP to WAR (WDSCA ES), C54446, 31/7/1947. NDL, ESS(B) 00850; WAR (WDSCA ES) to SCAP, W84419, 16/8/1947. NDL, ESS(B) 00857.

42 "Agreement for the Mutual Sale and Delivery of Indian Raw Cotton and Japanese Products", 28/10/1947. NDL, ESS(A) 05172.

43 "Contract for Purchase of Egyptian Cotton and Payment Therefore by Sale of Japanese Products", 1/11/1947. NDL, ESS(C) 07118.

44 TD to FT, "Japanese Cotton Buying Mission to India", 25/3/1948. NDL, ESS(B) 09027; TD to FT, "Trip to India for Procurement of Cotton", 7/4/1948. NDL, ESS(B) 09026.

45 FT to TD, "Trip to India for Procurement of Cotton", 10/4/1948. NDL, ESS(B) 09026.

46 SCAP to DA, Z46281, 22/4/1948. NDL, ESS(C) 05086. This short radio message informed the DA about the dispatch of a mission and had no radiogram number for reference from Washington. This indicates that there were no prior discussions between SCAP and Washington.

47 W. Eaton to Chief, ESS, "Preliminary Report of the SCAP Trade Mission India and Pakistan", 18/6/1948. NDL, ESS(A) 05435.

48 Schonberger, *Aftermath of War*, Chapter 6.

49 SCAP, "Circular No. 9, Establishment of Occupied Japan Export-Import Revolving Fund", 15/8/1947. NDL, ESS(B) 07208; SCAP to WASHINGTON (WDSCA ES), C69902, 7/2/1947. NDL, ESS(B) 07208.

50 JCS 1566/3, "Guidance to SCAP Regarding Shipment of Raw Cotton to Japan".

51 Y. Tawa, ed., *Sengo Bōsekishi (The Postwar History of the Cotton Spinning Industry)*, Osaka: Nihon Bōseki Kyōkai (Japan Spinners' Association), 1962, p. 34.

52 Supreme Commander for the Allied Powers Directives to the Japanese Government (SCAPINs) (Record Group 331), (hereafter SCAPIN) 854, 3/4/1946, E. Takemae, ed., *GHQ Shirei Sōshūsei (The Corpus of SCAPIN)*, Vol. 4, Tokyo: Emuthi Shuppan, 1994.

53 ESS to Board of Trade, BT-2, "Raw Cotton Regulation", 15/6/1946. NDL, ESS(C) 00726.

54 *Nihon Bōseki Geppō (The Monthly Report of Japan Spinners' Association)*, Vol. 1, Osaka: Nihon Bōseki Kyōkai, 11/1946, pp. 24–28; Tsūshō Sangyōshō (Ministry of International Trade and Industry), ed., *Shōkō Seisakushi*, Vol. 16, pp. 254–257.

55 Nihon Seni Rengōkai, ed., *Seni Nenkan Shōwa 22 Nenban*, p. 87, 90.

56 Maganga to Chief, ESS, "Justification of Textile Division", 7/6/1946. NDL, ESS(E) 00814; ESS, Administrative Order No. 10, 19/6/1946. NDL, ESS(E) 00772.

57 For example, those statistics were as almost the same as those in *the Report of Statics of the Cotton Spinning Industry* published by the Japan Spinners' Association during the Occupation, and *the Yearbook of Statistics of Textiles (Seni Tokei Nenppo) 1953* published by the Ministry of International Trade and Industry in 1954, which includes statistics during the Occupation. Moreover, the Japanese sometimes submitted the revised statistics later.

58 Ohata, *GHQ no Senryō Seisaku to Keizai Fukkō*, pp. 162–163.

59 E. Takemae, ed., *GHQ he no Nihon Seifu Taiō Bunsho Sōshūsei (The Corpus of Correspondences of the Japanese Government to SCAP)*, Vol. 7, Tokyo: Emuthi Shuppan, 1994, p. 5634.

60 Chief, ESS to Chief of Staff of SCAP, "Interim Level of Japanese Cotton Textile Production", 3/1/1947. NDL, ESS(A) 00433.

61 Ibid.

62 Okurashō (Ministry of Finance), ed., *Shōwa Zaiseishi: Haisen kara Kōwa made* (The Shōwa History of Finance: From the End of War to the Peace Treaty), Vol. 1, Tokyo: Tōyō Keizai Shinpōsha, 1984, pp. 351–370.

63 SCAPIN 1512, 7/2/1947. NDL, ESS(E) 03587.

64 SCAPIN 1562, 8/3/1947. NDL, ESS(E) 03587. In July, this order was revised partly. TD to Textile Bureau, Ministry of Commerce and Industry, TD-17, 15/7/1947. NDL, ESS(E) 03587. Other orders also were partly revised.

65 TD to Textile Bureau, Ministry of Commerce and Industry, TD-7, 13/3/1947. NDL, ESS(E) 03587.

66 Tawa, ed., *Nihon Bōsekigyō no Fukkō,* pp. 46–50.

67 C. Campbell to Chief, ESS, "Cotton Ring Spindle", 7/6/1948. NDL, ESS(C) 01022.

68 W. Eaton to H. Tate, "The Necessity of Full Operation of Present Cotton Spindles", 12/11/1946. NDL, ESS(E) 03543.

69 "Brief of Letter from Mr. W. C. Plantz, the Cotton-Textile Institute to Mr. Willard L. Troop, U. S. Dept. of State 24 March 1947", n.d. NDL, ESS(B) 00841; W. Eaton to H. Tate, "Future Level – Cotton Spinning Industry", 22/4/1947. NDL, ESS(E) 03588; H. Tate to Chief, ESS, "Comments on Discussion Presented by the Cotton-Textile Institute, Inc.", 16/5/1947. NDL, ESS(B) 00841; Industry Division to Deputy Chief, ESS, 3/5/1950. NDL, ESS(A) 01278; Y. Yasuhara, "Rengōkoku no Senryō Seisaku to Nihon no Bōeki" (The Allied Occupation Policy and Japan's Trade), Tsūshō Sangyōshō (Ministry of International Trade and Industry), ed., *Tsūshō Sangyō Seisakushi (The History of Policies of International Trade and Industry)*, Vol. 4, Tokyo: Tsūshō Sangyō Chōsakai, 1990, pp. 29–31.

70 W. Bushee to Chief, TD, "Rehabilitation Program Cotton Spinning Industry", 3/12/1948. NDL, ESS(E) 03587.

71 "Nichibeiei Mengyō Kaidan Kiroku" (Records of the Cotton Conference among Japan, the United States, and Britain), *Nihon Bōseki Geppō,* Vol. 41, 6/1950; Chief, ESS, "Memo for record", 24/6/1950, NDL, ESS(B) 03342; SCAP to DA, C56768, 24/6/1950. NDL, ESS(B) 03342.

72 SCAPIN 2109, 27/6/1950, E. Takemae, ed., *GHQ Shirei Sōshūsei (The Corpus of SCAPIN)*, Vol. 4, Tokyo: Emuthi Shuppan, 1994, p. 7078.

73 W. Eaton to Chief, TD, "Report on Conferences Held in Osaka with the Big Ten Spinning Companies at the Request of Japan Textile Bureau for Investigation of Low Production", 9/10/1946. NDL, ESS(E) 03544.

74 Tawa, ed., *Nihon Bōsekigyō no Fukkō,* pp. 97–106.

75 TD, "Meeting Held on 15 October 1946 to Discuss the Current Textile Production Problems", 15/10/1946. NDL, ESS(E) 03544.

76 Nihon Bōseki Kyōkai, ed., *Menshi Bōseki Jijyō Sankōsho,* the second half of 1946.

77 TD, "Report of Meeting held 17 April 1947", 18/4/1947. NDL, ESS(E) 03545; TD, "Production of Cotton Yarn", 30/6/1947. NDL, ESS(C) 07140.

78 TD to Chief, ESS, "Consumption of American Cotton", 26/4/1948. NDL, ESS(C) 01051; Japan Cotton Spinning Association to TD, "Restraint Plan of Yarn Production from July to September – 1948", 2/8/1948. NDL, ESS(C) 07145.

79 Tawa, ed., *Nihon Bōsekigyō no Fukkō,* pp. 109–114; Nihon Bōseki Kyōkai, ed., *Menshi Bōseki Jijyō Sankōsho,* 1947 and 1948.

80 Okurashō (Ministry of Finance), ed., *Shōwa Zaiseishi: Haisen kara Kōwa made (The Shōwa History of Finance: From the End of War to the Peace Treaty,)*, Vol. 2, Tokyo: Tōyō Keizai Shinpōsha, 1982, pp. 456–577; T. Cohen, *Remaking Japan: the American Occupation as New Deal*, New York: Free Press, 1987.

81 Schonberger, *Aftermath of War*, Chapter 6.

82 Regarding SCAP's antitrust policy, see Steve Ericson's chapter in the current volume.

83 H. Tate to Chief, AC, "Reorganisation Plan of Toyo Bōseki", 22/7/1947. NDL, ESS(C) 14715.

84 Chief, AC to Chief, TD, "Memo to Mr. Williams", 27/8/1948. NDL, ESS(C) 14714; Chief, AC to Chief, ESS, "'Big Ten' Spinning Companies and Deconcentration Policy", 27/8/1948. NDL, ESS(C) 14714.

85 Deconcentration Review Board Log Book, 9/2/1949, MacArthur Papers. NDL, MMA-3, Roll No. 17.

86 DRB, "Recommendations of ESS/AC with Reference to Seven of the 'Big Ten' Spinning Companies", 24/2/1949. NDL, ESS(C) 14698. Daiken was recommended to separate its trading business from its textile business.

87 HCLC, "The Ten Cotton Spinning Companies and the Deconcentration Law", 1/1949. NDL, ESS(D) 13022; Ohata, *GHQ no Senryō Seisaku to Keizai Fukkō*, pp. 204–205. See Steven Ericson's chapter in the current volume for more on the HCLC.

88 SCAP, *History of the Nonmilitary Activities of the Occupation of Japan, 1945–1951*, Vol. 52, Tokyo: Nihon Tosho Senta, 1990 (reprint), p. 182.

89 SCAP, "Report on Examination of Foreign Exchange Funds for the Period From September 2, 1945 to March 31, 1951", 16/7/1951, p. 35. NDL, OOC 01052–01053.

90 ESS to Chief of Staff, "SCAP Commercial Account", 28/8/1947. NDL, ESS(A) 00388.

91 FT, "Memorandum for Record", 12/3/1947. NDL, ESS(A) 00381; Headquarters of Far East Command, "Report on Examination of Foreign Exchange Funds for the Period from 1 April, 1951 thru 30 September 1951", 15/8/1952. NDL, OOC 01051–01052, p. 35.

92 SCAP, *History of the Nonmilitary Activities of the Occupation of Japan, 1945–1951*, Vol. 52, Tokyo: Nihon Tosho Senta, 1990 (reprint), p. 183.

93 Okurashō (Ministry of Finance), ed., *Shōwa Zaiseishi: Haisen kara Kōwa made* (The History of Finance in the Shōwa period: From the End of War to the Peace Treaty), Vol. 15, Tokyo: Tōyō Keizai Shinpōsha, 1976, pp. 189–193.

94 "Report on Examination of Foreign Exchange Funds for the Period from 1 April, 1951 thru 30 September 1951", p. 13. NDL, OOC 01051–01052; Ohata, *GHQ no Senryō Seisaku to Keizai Fukkō*, pp. 172–173, 175.

95 "Report on Examination of Foreign Exchange Funds for the Period from September 2, 1945 to March 31, 1951", 16/7/1951, p. 33. NDL, OOC 01052–01053; Ohata, *GHQ no Senryō Seisaku to Keizai Fukkō*, pp. 176, 178–179.

96 "Report on Examination of Foreign Exchange Funds for the Period from September 2, 1945 to March 31, 1951", 16/7/1951, p. 34. NDL, OOC 01052–01053; SCAP, *History of the Nonmilitary Activities of the Occupation of Japan, 1945–1951*, Vol. 52, p. 198.

97 Tsūshō Sangyōshō (Ministry of International Trade and Industry), ed., *Shōkō Seisakushi* (The History of Commercial and Industrial Policy), Vol. 6, Tokyo: Shōkō Seisakushi Kankōkai, 1971, p. 380.

98 Tawa, ed., *Sengo Bōsekishi*, p. 57; Watanabe, *Sangyō Hatten Suitai no Keizaishi*, pp. 186, 202–203.

99 Tawa, ed., *Sengo Bōsekishi*, pp. 50–52.

100 K. Hara, "Menseihin Bōeki no Gendankai to Nihon no Tachiba" (The Present Stage of Cotton Goods Trade and the Position of Japan), *Tōhō Keizai*, Vol. 11, No. 1, 3/1950, p. 9.

101 K. Abe, "Saikin no Beimen Jijyō" (The Current Affairs of American Raw Cotton), *Keizai Sekai*, Vol. 1, No. 3, 6/1951, p. 23. The company presidents under the Occupation seem to have tended to offer compliments to SCAP. However it would be undeniable that their words expressed genuine feelings of thankfulness.

102 I. Muto, "Shinnen no Kadai Futatsu" (There are Two Tasks in the New Year), *Seni Geppō* Vol. 8, No. 1, 1/1951, p. 24. 'Clothing' meant the supply of raw cotton, because the United States exported little clothing.

103 T. Yasuo, *Bōkyo 45 Nen* (*45 Years in Japan Spinners' Association)*, Osaka: Osaka Seni Gakuen Shuppanbu, 1976, p. 119.

104 Ibid., p. 125. On the other hand, Tawa resented an impolite attitude of one SCAP's official engaged in antitrust operations towards the Japanese spinners' presidents in a meeting. Ibid., p. 127.

105 John Dower pointed out persuasively in *Embracing Defeat* that the Japanese under the Occupation suffered from '*Kyodatsu*' (a state of mental/psychological collapse) (p. 89) and converted its recognition to an aspiration for peace and democracy, which paradoxically resulted in the positive acceptance of SCAP's early idealistic reforms. However, it is necessary to examine further how the Japanese eased hostility towards

SCAP and the United States before or after they accepted the reforms. First of all, it is easy to think that food imports by the United States eased hostility. Moreover, SCAP's industrial policy towards various industries is estimated to have exerted the same effect especially upon business managers (and employees). J. W. Dower, *Embracing Defeat: Japan in the Wake of World War II*, New York and London: W. W. Norton, 1999.

106 Tawa, ed., *Sengo Bōsekishi*, pp. 73–107; Watanabe, *Sangyō Hatten Suitai no Keizaishi*, Chapter 4, 5.
107 Nihon Bōseki Kyōkai, *Bōkyo Hyakunenshi*, pp. 132–136.
108 N. Takamura, *Kindai Nihon Mengyō to Chūgoku (The Modern Japanese Cotton Industry and China)*, Tokyo: Tokyodaigaku Shuppankai, 1982.

Part 3

Socioeconomic changes in the Occupation era

7 The economic reintegration of former colonial residents in postwar Japan

Steven Ivings

Introduction

For many strewn across the vast expanse of Japan's wartime and colonial empire, Japan's defeat was characterised by its abruptness and the confusion which ensued thereafter. The immediate repercussions of defeat would vary for the multitude of Japanese military and civilian populations who found themselves in areas where Japanese authority was rapidly collapsing. In some parts of the former empire, such as Manchuria, a military onslaught had ensued before Japan's formal surrender, and with the Japanese military in retreat, colonial settlers found themselves bearing the brunt of local acts of retribution and an advancing Red Army. Elsewhere, open and protracted violence was less pervasive, but a great level of uncertainty remained as to what fate would befall those who, as the Japanese empire disintegrated, found the borders shifting beneath their feet.[1] On paper at least, the map of Northeast Asia could effectively be redrawn overnight, yet the human aspects of decolonisation were a much more complicated and protracted affair, involving the 'repatriation' of over six million Japanese from battlefields and now former colonies across Asia and the Pacific and the deportation of over a million former colonial subjects from Japan to what was considered to be their appropriate home countries.[2]

The process of repatriation itself and the often tragic personal accounts of the struggles of 'repatriates' (*hikiagesha*) to return to Japan have gained a degree of scholarly attention. They have also come to play a prominent role in the public memorialisation of Japanese defeat and occupation, serving as a powerful strand within the narratives of Japanese victimhood.[3] Yet, little scholarly attention has so far been given to the process of reintegrating former colonial residents into the socio-economic landscape of postwar Japan even though their repatriation marked one of the largest cases of post-colonial migration in history. The reintegration of such a large and rapid population influx was an enormous challenge for the initially dislocated and unstable economy of a defeated Japan. This chapter seeks to shed light on this little appreciated feature of Japanese postwar socio-economic history by focusing on one aspect of this issue, the employment experiences of ordinary civilian repatriates in Hokkaidō who had been residents of the former colony of Karafuto. In addition, a contrast will be made between the experiences of ordinary residents of the former colony of Karafuto and the former colonial elite of the same territory. Making use of repatriate association registers, and a national survey conducted by the Ministry of Health and Welfare (hereafter MHW), this paper examines how repatriates negotiated the passage through wartime to postwar and how former colonial residents fared in the first decade of Japan's economic reconstruction.

An outline of postwar repatriation

The desirability of the repatriation of the nationals of defeated nations had been agreed upon by the Allied powers prior to Japan's surrender. Indeed, in Europe, population transfers involving tens of millions of people – particularly, but not exclusively, ethnic Germans – were already taking place. Though these population transfers came to involve levels of violence and disorder that shocked many contemporary observers, it was thought that the removal of certain ethnic minorities from fledgling postwar states would provide a more stable platform for long term peace in a continent which had been torn by war.[4] This logic was extended to Asia, as the Allied powers sought to unmake the Japanese empire, with the result that Japan would be reduced to the territorial boundaries it had held prior to the first Sino-Japanese War (1894-95).[5] The process of undoing 50 years of Japanese imperial expansion was not the same everywhere. In the areas of the Pacific and Southeast Asia that Japan had occupied following Pearl Harbor, it entailed the removal of a primarily military presence which was, in theory at least, to be swiftly replaced by the reinstated colonial rule of one of the Allied powers. Elsewhere in East Asia, the dismantling of the Japanese empire was more complex, involving the removal of sizeable Japanese civilian communities from more longstanding formal and informal colonies, including Taiwan, Korea, Manchuria, and Karafuto. These territories were either supposed to become independent, as in the case of Korea, or to be 'returned' to either China (Taiwan and Manchuria) or the Soviet Union (Karafuto). This erasure of Japanese colonial rule was complicated by emerging Cold War politics, but whichever hands these territories found themselves in after Japanese defeat, their new status rendered unwelcome the sizeable Japanese civilian presence, at least in the long term. As a result, the preferences of Japanese civilians regarding repatriation or staying on were given little, if any, thought, if indeed there was much doubt regarding such preferences.

The basis for Japanese repatriation was to be found in the Potsdam declaration which the Allied powers had signed on 26 July 1945, and Japan had accepted as the terms of its surrender on 14–15 August. Article 9 of the declaration in particular referred to the issue and though it primarily addressed military personnel, as part of broader processes of demobilisation and disarmament, in practice it was also extended to overseas civilian Japanese, who, it stated, 'shall be permitted to return to their homes with the opportunity to lead peaceful and productive lives'.[6] Indeed, within a few months of the Japanese surrender, a program to repatriate Japanese civilian and military personnel was swiftly implemented by the Japanese government and the Occupation authorities (SCAP), even though no concrete plan appears to have existed prior to surrender. In late August 1945, the grim state of affairs in post-surrender Japan meant that the interim government – operating before the Allied Occupation was formally set up – initially discouraged the repatriation of overseas Japanese. In September, it began to make plans for evacuation and repatriation, whilst stressing the need for overseas Japanese to remain where they were, for the time being at least. By late September, the interim government began to communicate to SCAP its plans for repatriation. However, this Japanese government initiative was soon superseded by SCAP authority, as in mid-October 1945, SCAP issued its first orders regarding the repatriation of Japanese nationals. Thereafter, SCAP took charge of the negotiation with local authorities across Asia over the return of overseas Japanese, providing physical materials – most importantly ships – and formulating a set of instructions to oversee the process.[7]

This did not mean that the Japanese government was no longer involved, as the day-to-day administration of the repatriation (and deportation) program fell to the MHW, which established and managed quarantine facilities, refugee camps, and regional repatriation centres at a number of ports across Japan. The first of these repatriation centres was in operation by late November 1945, and by the end of the year, ten such centres had been established. Stretching from Kagoshima in the south to Hakodate in the north, a total of 15 ports eventually served as centres of repatriation between late 1945 and 1958, when the final repatriation centre in Maizuru (Kyoto Prefecture) was closed along with the official repatriation process.[8] The exact numbers of people who passed through these repatriation centres is unknown, but it is estimated that 6.28 million Japanese had been repatriated by the end of 1958. Once the repatriation program was up and running, it proceeded relatively rapidly. Between late 1945 and the end of 1946, as many as 5.09 million people were able to return to Japan, climbing to 6.24 million by the end of 1949.[9]

This meant that over 99 percent of those who returned via official channels had done so by 1950. Yet, whilst the vast majority were able to return to Japan within five years of defeat, these numbers conceal the complicated nature of the repatriation process for many who returned and say nothing of the considerable numbers who perished along the way. The continued, if much reduced, influx of repatriates in the 1950s kept the repatriation issue in the public eye to some extent, and served as a constant reminder of the complicated nature of the human aspects of decolonisation. Among the repatriates from these later years were the remnants of the Japanese prisoners of war from Soviet zones who had been detained in order to utilise their labour in the reconstruction of the war-torn Soviet economy.[10] At one time thought to number over 600,000, their delayed repatriation provided a source of tension between the U.S. and Soviet occupying forces and further damaged the Soviet Union's reputation in Japan, ultimately affecting Japan's stance in the emerging Cold War.[11] Repatriation from Soviet zones, which began in December 1946 and continued long into the 1950s, was not just limited to internees. It also incorporated numerous civilian population transfers from (and to a lesser extent, bound for) Manchuria, North Korea, and Sakhalin.

Among this flow, civilian repatriation from Sakhalin in particular highlighted the complicated nature of repatriation on officially imposed lines of nationality/ethnicity and the complications involved due to the influence of the looming Cold War. In this case, most Japanese returned before 1950, but some families of Japanese-Korean mixed marriages were repatriated in smaller numbers thereafter. In a small number of cases, Japanese stayed behind in Sakhalin, often alongside Korean spouses, and they were joined by thousands of Korean families (approximately 23,000 individuals) – many of whom had been mobilised or forced to migrate to, and then work in, Karafuto during the war. For these Koreans, repatriation was delayed and then ultimately prevented by the escalating Cold War and the intensification of conflict on the Korean peninsula.[12] Repatriation from China also proved to be a protracted affair in some cases. Late arrivals from China included military and technical experts who had remained behind for a number of years following Japanese surrender and could be found on both sides of the Chinese Civil War.[13] It also involved Japanese women in Manchuria who had married Chinese, often as a means to survive in the postwar chaos, and Japanese children who had either been orphaned by the conflict in Manchuria or handed over to Chinese families as their fleeing biological parents thought this the best way to ensure their children's survival. Some of these later cases would resurface long after official repatriation had ended, as children and parents alike sought the family from which they had long been separated by war.[14]

Existing literature and popular images of repatriation

Research into the repatriation phenomenon has been limited until recent years and has tended to focus on the process of returning to Japan. Characteristic of the bulk of this literature are the official histories produced by the MHW and local repatriation centres – which tend to celebrate the achievements of these administrative bodies – and a growing body of tragic personal accounts, either published individually as personal histories (*jibunshi*) or in annotated collections of personal testimonies.[15] These emotive narratives of the struggle to get home – and for the authorities, the struggle to cope with the huge influx – are given the majority of coverage in these works, and these narratives have gone on to become prominent features of war memory in contemporary Japan.[16] This is reflected in the displays of prominent Tokyo museums such as the Peace Memorial Museum (*Heiwa Kinen Tenji Shiryōkan*) in the bustling Shinjuku district and at the National Shōwa Museum (*Shōwakan*), located a stone's throw away from the Imperial Palace. In both these museums, the struggle of repatriates to return to Japan is given considerable coverage alongside other war victims. Additionally, at Maizuru, on the site where a repatriation centre once stood, there is a museum specifically dedicated to commemorating repatriation. Here, too, the focus of the museum's displays rests on the epic struggle to get home and is joined by a narrative of the warm welcome repatriates received upon arrival. Little attention is given to the more problematic aspects surrounding the issue of postwar repatriation such as the (sometimes involuntary) deportation of former colonial subjects from Japan, the discrimination faced by repatriates after their return, or the history of colonial expansion, which was intertwined with the emergence of these large Japanese communities overseas in the first place.

Thankfully, these relatively unproblematised depictions of repatriation have been countered in recent years by scholarly enquiry. At the forefront here was the 1991 account (republished in 1995) by Wakatsuki Yasuo which critically examined repatriation from a very broad perspective for the benefit of a general readership. This work has been built on by more recent works in English by Lori Watt (2009) and in Japanese by a group of scholars, centred on Araragi Shinzō, who examine various aspects of postcolonial migration – including the repatriation and deportation processes – across multiple localities and time frames, and from numerous perspectives.[17] These recent works have been accompanied by a great effort led by Katō Kiyofumi to make materials related to repatriation available.[18] Among this recent work, Watt's account in particular has problematized the fate of repatriates and their reintegration into postwar society by highlighting the construction of a media stereotype surrounding repatriates. She elucidates the cold reception many repatriates felt after their return, and the multitude of ways that Japanese society 'othered' them as a distinct social category. This included discrimination faced by female repatriates who, it was thought, may have been 'polluted' by their time overseas, either due to the sense that the moral standards of life in overseas territories (*gaichi*) were not up to those of mainland Japan (*naichi*) or to the possibility that they had suffered rape during their displacement. For male repatriates who had been detained by the Soviet Union, there was also discrimination, especially based on the fear that they may have become indoctrinated with communist ideology during their internment and would become agitators upon their return.[19] Indeed, this concern with 'red repatriates' was also held by the SCAP authorities, whose G-2 section closely monitored returning repatriates from Soviet zones, singling out individuals for the dual purposes of obtaining intelligence information and to head-off communist agitators.[20] This recent research activity has done much to problematise the issue of repatriation; however, the primary focus continues to be on the process of returning home. Even though Watt's work more explicitly tackles the reintegration problem, hinting that this process was less than smooth, she stops short at media representations, offering little in terms of a detailed examination of repatriates' actual prospects and outcomes in Japan's postwar socio-economic landscape. This chapter works towards addressing this void by focusing specifically on former colonial residents who were civilian repatriates.

The socio-economic reintegration of former colonial residents

It is estimated that 3.21 million Japanese civilians and 3.67 million Japanese military personnel were spread across Japan's colonial and wartime empires at the war's end. This represented about nine percent of Japan's 1945 population, and as such, the scale of postwar repatriation rendered the reintegration process one of the most salient challenges in the early postwar years.[21] This challenge was all the greater considering the war-torn state of Japan at the time. Several years of warfare against the world's most populous country, its largest empire, and its largest economy had taken its toll on Japan with its economic structure fully geared towards total war. Moreover, having been the target of urban fire bombing and the world's first cases of atomic bombing, Japan's urban, industrial, and transportation infrastructures had taken a battering. Housing and basic consumer goods were in short supply, and having lost most of its merchant marine during the conflict, Japan found itself cut off from international trade. Defeat also severed Japan from its former colonies, such as Taiwan and Korea, which had provided an important source of food imports, deepening a food crisis that was already being felt towards the end of the war. Defeated, demoralised, hungry, dispossessed, and dislocated were shared feelings among a great deal of the general population in Japan, and not uniquely held by those being repatriated from Asia and the Pacific. In this context, public sympathy and recognition of any special suffering on the part of repatriates were not especially high, and the ability of the Japanese economy to absorb them was far from given.

Repatriates were rarely able to bring anything but a few basic personal items with them back to Japan. They had to abandon most of their overseas assets, boarding repatriation vessels with baggage limited to what they could carry and a maximum of 1,000 yen per person, which itself was a paltry sum in a country that faced rampant inflation. After disembarkation and processing at a regional repatriation centre, repatriates were given special tickets to board trains bound for 'home' at which point they were more or less on their own.[22] Left to their own devices, many became dependent, temporarily at least, on the benevolence of relatives and friends for food and shelter and help finding work. Many repatriates were able to benefit from employment in public works schemes, and, for those without relatives, emergency shelter. However, for the most part, the Japanese government, constrained by the limited resources available to it, played little role in assisting repatriates' reintegration. The association of repatriates with Japanese imperialism also meant that, initially at least, the stance of SCAP was for the most part far from sympathetic to their plight. Indeed, even for civilian repatriates, official recognition of their loss and suffering had to wait until 1957, when the Japanese government passed a law (*hikiagesha kyūfukin tō shikyū hō*) that granted a special payment to repatriates on low incomes. This payment amounted at best to no more than an average urban family's monthly income, and a more comprehensive compensation program – this time without income restrictions – was not implemented until 1967.[23]

Evidence of how repatriates fared economically in the initial postwar years is scant, but there is a sense that as the Japanese economy recovered the problem was resolved. Whether this came as quickly as the early to mid-1950s – when Japan surpassed its pre-war peaks in industrial production (1951), real gross GNP (1951), and real per capita GNP (1953) – or later, has yet to be firmly established.[24] Nonetheless, the conventional wisdom suggests that by the era of high economic growth in the 1960s, the resulting labour shortage more or less dissolved any lingering economic disadvantage felt by repatriates. Utilising information in the

1950 national census – the only census which included repatriates as a separate category – Odaka Konosuke has demonstrated that the overall unemployment rate among repatriates stood at 2.4 percent, a rate not dramatically higher than the equivalent for the general population (1.9 percent).[25] This data suggests that there was a rather smooth transition into employment for the vast majority of repatriates in Japan. This especially appears to be the case when compared to ethnic German refugees in West Germany who had fled or been expelled from Eastern Europe following the collapse of the Nazi regime. In 1950, the general unemployment rate in West Germany stood at 4.9 percent, but for refugees the rate was more than double the average, standing at a shocking 12.5 percent, five times greater than the contemporary equivalent for Japanese repatriates.[26] At this point, refugees made up 16.1 percent of the population in West Germany, but accounted for a disproportionate share of the unemployed, with over a third of those out of work but actively seeking employment drawn from this group.[27] Even if the unemployment rate of repatriates in Japan was greater than that of the general population, in comparison at least, it appears to be a minor difference.

Whilst by 1950, the Japanese economy appears to have been comparatively successful in absorbing the surplus labour of repatriates, the rate of employment/ unemployment says nothing of the type of work which repatriates were able to obtain. In this regard, the 1950 census data presented by Odaka which display the employment of repatriates by sector are indicative, if not wholly satisfactory. Census data shows that agriculture formed the largest sector of employment for repatriates, employing 28.7 percent of the total, however this was far below the equivalent share for the general population (46.7 percent). This was most likely a reflection of the fact that, especially for former colonial residents, many had come from non-agricultural backgrounds and/or had moved abroad permanently, meaning that they had no farm to return to. In this way, civilian repatriates are likely to have ended up in more marginal positions in the agricultural sector after return, working as agricultural labourers on other people's land, renting land from friends or relatives, or participating in projects to clear and settle hitherto uncultivated land (*sengo kaitaku*), which was often of marginal quality and tended to produce far from satisfactory results.[28] Although underrepresented in the agricultural sector, elsewhere in the economy repatriates appeared slightly overrepresented in the manufacturing (which employed 17.9 percent of repatriates compared to 15.8 percent of the general population), small-scale commerce (12.8 percent to 11.0 percent), service (9.7 percent to 8.5 percent), and construction (5.9 percent to 4.2 percent) sectors. Moreover, they appear particularly overrepresented in the civil service (7.8 percent of repatriates compared to 3.5 percent of the general population), transportation and public works (8.0 percent to 4.8 percent), and mining (3.5 percent to 1.5 percent) sectors.[29]

Whilst this is important macro-data which gives a sense of the general trends, it also carries with it several important limitations. Firstly, it gives a snap-shot of the situation five years after the war had ended, and as such tells us little about how repatriates negotiated the initial postwar years and thereafter. Secondly, the focus on the sector of employment tells us little of the types of work and position of repatriates within each sector respectively. If repatriates were at a disadvantage in the labour market, as they were in sectors such as agriculture, then they may have ended up in more marginal types of employment, on temporary contracts or employed by smaller firms whose employment conditions carried less security or fringe benefits, and, in most cases, a significantly lower salary. Finally, the data presents a national trend which may mask significant variations of experience both locally in Japan and among repatriates from specific areas of the former empire. In order to address these concerns, an approach which provides local detail and an expanded temporal frame is required. Yanagisawa Asobu has shown the benefits of such an approach in the closing section of his work that examined the Japanese commercial community in Dairen (Dalian), Manchuria, in which he traced the fortunes of a number of Japanese merchants after their repatriation. Yanagisawa was able to demonstrate that whilst many initially returned to their ancestral villages upon return to Japan, they remained mobile and soon made their way to the major cities, for the most part successfully re-establishing themselves in commerce and coming to manage small and medium-sized enterprises.[30] In the sections that follow a similar approach will be offered by looking at civilian repatriates from one specific colony, Karafuto, but unlike Yanagisawa, attention will be directed onto a single destination prefecture, Hokkaidō, where the focus will be broadened to include all types of former colonial residents, rather than solely the commercial class.

Leaving Karafuto: evacuation, flight, and repatriation

Karafuto, located in southern Sakhalin, was a Japanese colony that had been acquired following the Russo-Japanese War of 1904-1905. Under Japanese colonial rule, it developed rapidly based on the exploitation of rich forestry, marine, and coal resources, and, to a lesser extent, on agriculture. In this period, the population of Karafuto expanded rapidly from a few thousand in 1905 to over 400,000 by the early 1940s. Unlike the other colonies in Japan's formal empire, Karafuto had a small existing population, and so Japanese settlers were quickly in the majority, accounting for as much as 97 percent of the colony's population by the end of the 1920s.[31] This was significant for the make-up of Japanese society in Karafuto, where Japanese settlers from various social backgrounds could be found in large numbers, quite in contrast to Japanese settler communities elsewhere in the empire, where a sizeable colonial bureaucracy and business elite oversaw or employed much larger populations of colonial subjects.[32] The idea that, among Japan's formal colonies, the social structure of Karafuto most closely resembled that in the metropole is significant here because it means that an examination of the former colonial residents of Karafuto provides an opportunity to observe the postwar experiences of repatriates from all walks of life, including those from modest backgrounds.

The course of repatriation from Karafuto attests to the fact that the human aspects of decolonisation are often a complex and protracted affair. The Soviet Union entered the war against Japan on 9 August 1945, and within days, a battle front had opened in Karafuto. Fighting between Soviet troops and the hastily organized Japanese resistance continued until late August, long after the Emperor's radio broadcast that announced Japan's defeat to a stunned public. During the conflict, the local administration (*Karafuto-chō*) began to implement an evacuation program which prioritised women, children, and the elderly. These efforts at evacuation took place between 12 and 23 August – by which point the Soviet Union, now in effective control, halted the evacuation – and it is thought that approximately 88,000 people left Karafuto in this way.[33] Evacuation, however, was not without incident. In three cases, an unidentified submarine torpedoed vessels carrying evacuees from Karafuto. Two of these ships sank, with the other sustaining heavy damage, but still being left able to reach port at Rumoi, Hokkaidō. If the unaccounted for are included, then the death toll of these incidents stands at 1,708 individuals, with 3,274 survivors.[34] To organised evacuation we must also add flight, as a number of Karafuto residents – particularly those with access to fishing boats – decided to risk the journey across the Sōya straits to Hokkaidō, rather than live under Soviet occupation or get caught up in the fighting. Official statistics on flight are unlikely to be exact but do suggest that over 24,000 people returned this way between August 1945 and September 1946, sometimes paying substantial fees to brokers for their passage.[35]

This combination of emergency evacuation and individual flight meant that Karafuto had lost between a quarter and a third of its population before 'official repatriation' commenced in December 1946 – a fact that is confirmed in the impressions of those who escaped Karafuto and were interrogated by SCAP authorities.[36] As Jonathan Bull has argued, this would have important consequences for the integration of former Karafuto residents in places like Hokkaidō, because it meant that when the official repatriates arrived, an extensive structure to handle them was already in place involving local officials and organised repatriate groups.[37] Meanwhile in Karafuto itself, the conflict had initially displaced many of the colony's residents, with a number of isolated, but bloody, attacks on civilian targets – notably during the aerial bombing of Toyohara station and the amphibious landings at Maoka. Nevertheless, such conflict and displacement appears to have been relatively short-lived, and, as the Soviet Union established effective control, life on the island swiftly regained a semblance of normality with those fleeing conflict areas returning to their homes. The harassment of civilians by Red Army troops, initially a serious problem, appears to have been brought under control and economic production restarted with the Soviet authorities also making efforts to import rice from North Korea, with the result that Japanese residents on Soviet-occupied Karafuto probably enjoyed a favourable ration compared to that on offer in Japan.[38] As the economy in Karafuto was returning to normal, Soviet settlers started to flood in. This created a housing shortage that meant many Japanese had to share their accommodation with these Soviet newcomers, while they awaited the scheduling of their repatriation to Japan.[39] Relations between these new neighbours were not always bad – indeed, sometimes, genuine friendships seemed to have emerged – but there could be little hiding that these newcomers were replacements for the Japanese residents, a crucial part of Sovietisation.[40] In January 1946, Karafuto as an administrative district, was dissolved by the Soviet Union, and along with the Kurile Islands, it was merged with North Sakhalin in January 1947, creating Sakhalin Oblast in its current form. However, more than these administrative adjustments, it was the influx of Soviet settlers and the official repatriation of the Japanese population which ensured that Karafuto rapidly became Soviet Sakhalin. The official repatriation process took place between December 1946 and July 1949, involving 266,872 civilians and 12,484 military personnel who were transported from Maoka (Kholmsk) to the regional repatriation centre in Hakodate.[41]

After escape, evacuation, or the repatriation centre: housing, mobility and settlement

Whether evacuee, escapee, or official repatriate, for the vast majority of those returning from Karafuto, the first action after arrival was to return to their family home, or when not possible, to call on friends or extended family. Yet, when compared to repatriates from some other parts of the empire, those from Karafuto were characterised by the comparatively long time spent outside of Japan, and as a result, there were a comparatively high number who returned without any local connections at all, and thus without a place to return to. These people, known as *muenkōsha*, are thought to have made up about a third of all repatriates passing through the Hakodate repatriation centre. Over half of these muenkōsha were to be relocated in a program implemented by the MHW and prefectural authorities which saw 60,115 individuals relocated, with Hokkaidō absorbing 70 percent of the total, and the remaining 30 percent shared almost entirely among the six prefectures of Japan's northeast.[42] This program was only one part of the broader story of resettlement in which Hokkaidō played a key role. Indeed, Japan's northernmost prefecture accounted for almost 60 percent of the initial destinations of those returning from Karafuto (see Table 7.1), reflecting the fact that many Karafuto residents originally hailed from and/or had long-standing connections with Hokkaidō.[43] The remainder of those repatriated from Karafuto initially were bound for the six prefectures which make up Japan's northeast (Aomori, Akita, Yamagata, Iwate, Miyagi, and Fukushima), which, in combination, accounted for 25.9 percent of the total. Very few former residents of Karafuto went to any of Japan's 40 other prefectures, including the capital Tokyo, the tenth most common initial destination, which drew in only 0.8 percent of the total. To some extent, the continued mobility of repatriates would see more than the initial numbers drift to urban centres like Tokyo, but with almost 85 percent of Karafuto repatriates initially absorbed in Hokkaidō and the northeast, resettlement would prove to be a geographically concentrated affair.

Hokkaidō's role as a place for resettling repatriates was not limited to those from Karafuto. According to the 1950 national census, Hokkaidō had the highest number of repatriates in the country, absorbing 11 percent of the national total. The extensive connections that Karafuto repatriates had with the prefecture helps to explain why so many settled there, but there were other reasons why Hokkaidō

Table 7.1 Initial Planned Destination of Evacuees from Karafuto and Official Repatriates Leaving the Hakodate Regional Repatriation Centre

Destination Prefecture	Official Repatriates	Evacuees (Incl. Escapees)	Total	Share of Total (%)
Hokkaidō	171,121	65,791	236,912	58.7
Aomori	24,903	5,098	30,001	7.4
Akita	15,904	3,799	19,703	4.9
Yamagata	15,025	2,204	17,229	4.3
Iwate	13,378	1,737	15,115	3.7
Miyagi	9,557	1,885	11,442	2.8
Fukushima	9,542	1,573	11,115	2.8
Niigata	5,718	1,369	7,087	1.8
Toyama	3,174	976	4,150	1.0
Tokyo	2,723	643	3,366	0.8
Other	39,759	7,564	47,323	11.7
Total	310,804	92,639	403,443	100.0

Note: The official repatriate data likely include approximately 37,200 military personnel, 4,000 repatriates from the Kurile Islands, as well as small numbers of non-Japanese.

Source: Zenkoku Karafuto Renmei, *Karafuto Shūsenshi*, 1973, pp. 596–597.

was an appealing destination for repatriates and the bureaucrats looking to resettle them, regardless of where they came from. The main reasons were that Hokkaidō had suffered comparatively little damage during the war. In the case of housing, for example, nationally speaking, 15 percent of homes had suffered war damage, which compared to a mere one percent in Hokkaidō.[44] Moreover, Hokkaidō had additional capacity to absorb excess population, having itself only really been settled extensively from the Meiji period onwards. As a result, there was a strong perception that there was plenty of land available in Hokkaidō, which, with proper management, could be successfully brought under cultivation, providing a solid foundation for resettlement, and also contributing towards alleviating Japan's food security problems. The wider attraction of Hokkaidō to repatriates in general aside, former residents of Karafuto made up the majority of the prefecture's repatriate population, accounting for almost 60 percent of all repatriates in the prefecture in 1950.[45] Despite the limited war damage and the perception of having extra space, the reality of housing such a large incoming population – one source estimated that repatriates made up 12 percent of Hokkaidō's overall population – in such a short period of time meant that a housing shortage was felt in some parts of Hokkaidō in the initial postwar years.[46] Repatriates with family and friends in Hokkaidō were often able to find temporary shelter with or through their local connections; however, the situation was different for muenkōsha, who often ended up in temporary shelters.

Those who had fled or were evacuated from Karafuto in 1945 were faced with a particularly trying situation as they arrived before a coordinated response could be organised. Hundreds at a time, these arrivals flooded into ports like Wakkanai in late August 1945, with the authorities ill-prepared to handle them. Others still came ashore in fishing boats at various points across the northern stretches of Hokkaidō's coast often without much in the form or provisions or documentation. According to a report published by a repatriate group, the Karafuto Association (*Karafuto Kyōkai*), mobilised to handle the situation, by 25 October 1945 approximately 84,750 had been repatriated from Karafuto via evacuation and flight. The report suggests that almost all evacuees were able to find a place to stay through their connections, but that among the evacuees there were precisely 2,171 (approximately 2.5 percent of the total) who had no connections whatsoever, requiring special provision to be provided for them on the part of the authorities.[47] These were the first to be called muenkōsha and appear to have initially been housed in temporary lodges or temples. Indeed, at the time of the report, six temples in Sapporo were listed as housing 540 people and, in Iwamizawa, seven temples housed 604. Most evacuees were either women, children or the elderly, and thus many of those housed in temples were without regular work, subsisting on a small daily allowance provided to them by local authorities and later, wherever available, on wages from employment as cleaners and maids, etc.[48] The vast majority of those who had been evacuated had found shelter via connections, most likely with friends or relatives who took them in, but there were also cases where the evacuated dependants of employees of major firms and public bodies in Karafuto were housed by their employer. Among these cases was the Oji paper and pulp co. – a heavyweight of Karafuto's pre-war economy – which housed approximately 670 family members of their Karafuto-based staff in facilities on the site of its factory at Ebetsu. Similarly, the family of staff employed at the Karafuto Railway Office who otherwise had nowhere to go were housed at various facilities in Hokkaido, including in Shibetsu, Nayoro, Sapporo, and elsewhere.[49]

As official repatriation got under way, many families were reunited, but this meant that Hokkaidō's civilian repatriate population swelled from 100,000 in May 1946, to 371,125 by February 1950, further accentuating the housing shortage.[50] These reunited families would, from both a practical and psychological perspective, find it more difficult to continue to depend on friends or relatives for their shelter. Moreover, the return of male family members of working age boosted the ability of many a family to re-establish themselves independently, increasing the demand for private housing. Indeed, data regarding the housing situation in 1950 presented elsewhere by Jonathan Bull suggest that at that point, 78.6 percent of all repatriates residing in Hokkaidō were living in private or rented accommodation. However, the data also show that 26 percent of repatriates resided in what was deemed to be 'temporary' accommodation, and that as many as 12.3 percent (46,477 people) resided in group shelters which had been set up on various sites such as warehouses and converted military facilities.[51] These included sites around the Okadama airfield north of Sapporo, and the barracks of the former Seventh Division of the Imperial Army at Asahikawa. The latter, having been constructed in the late nineteenth century, was not in a good state and was served by poor sanitation facilities, and outbreaks of tuberculosis among inhabitants were reported. At its peak, the former barracks at Asahikawa, known locally as 'welfare village' and managed by city authorities, housed about 2,000 people, all of whom would later need to be rehoused.[52] In order to meet the growing demand for private housing on the part of repatriates and to phase out the group shelters, local authorities began to construct special housing complexes in and around Hokkaidō's urban areas. Dubbed 'repatriate housing' (*hikiagesha jūtaku*), these efforts would contribute to the closure of temporary accommodation facilities, especially for those households on welfare and without family members of working age. Albeit in reduced form, repatriate housing continued to be a problem at least into the late 1960s.[53]

On the whole, most repatriate households were able to solve their own housing situation without official assistance by utilising connections to secure temporary housing then finding employment, which allowed them to secure long term housing arrangements. In order to achieve this, many repatriates had to remain relatively mobile, willing to move wherever work and favourable housing was available. Table 7.2 shows data compiled from an extensive MHW survey into the economic situation of repatriate households (*hikiagesha zaigai jujitsu chōsa*, hereafter HZJC) conducted in 1956 as part of the preparation for the 1957 bill mentioned above, which granted a modest welfare payment to some repatriate households.[54] Amongst other information, the survey asked households to list their first place of residence after leaving the repatriation centre and their current address. This information provides an insight into the distribution of repatriates in Hokkaidō and their mobility over time. It shows that repatriates tended to establish themselves in major cities such as Hakodate, Sapporo, Otaru, and Asahikawa, where work was more readily available. These four cities all remained in the top

Table 7.2 Mobility and Residence of Former Residents of Karafuto Who Were Resident in Hokkaidō in 1956

First Private Residence After Repatriation		*Current Residence (1956)*	
Ten Most Common Places of Residence			
Hakodate	16.9%	Hakodate	18.5%
Sapporo	10.6%	Sapporo	14.6%
Wakkanai	10.4%	Wakkanai	11.0%
Otaru	10.1%	Otaru	10.4%
Asahikawa	7.7%	Asahikawa	9.7%
Aomori Prefecture	5.9%	Monbetsu	7.7%
Obihiro	4.5%	Yubari	7.2%
Kamiiso	4.5%	Sorachi (Various)	6.3%
Monbetsu	4.5%	Ashibetsu	4.7%
Akita Prefecture	4.1%	Bibai	4.5%
Subtotal for Top Ten	39.3%	Subtotal for Top Ten	47.1%
Other	60.7%	Other	52.9%

Compiled from: HZJC files for Hokkaidō residents who came from Shinkai and Chitose villages, Maoka town (surnames beginning with a, i, u, e, o) in Karafuto five places of residence in 1956, with each growing slightly in share of the total, and they were also joined by Wakkanai, the closest city to Sakhalin in Hokkaidō, where repatriates became an influential force in local politics and the economy.[55]

Hidden by the consistency of the top five concentrations of repatriates in Hokkaidō between repatriation and 1956 is a more general mobility. Indeed, among the households in the HZJC sample utilised in Table 7.2 it is found that only 54.6 percent of repatriates lived in the same city/town/village in 1956 as they had done directly after repatriation. As the survey does not include any other intermediate addresses between repatriation and 1956, it is not certain whether these households moved at some point. Nonetheless, what is certain is that 44.2 percent of households moved at least once, a rate of mobility far in excess of the norm amongst the general population. This mobility included Karafuto repatriates who first returned to Honshū only to re-migrate to Hokkaidō – ten percent of the sample, for example, first went to Aomori or Akita prefectures before coming to Hokkaidō – and significant levels of migration within Hokkaidō itself. Of the latter, the coal mining districts of Hokkaidō in particular became sites of resettlement, with Yūbari, Ashibetsu, Bibai, and other parts of the Sorachi district absorbing large numbers by 1956. This was brought about by the comparatively favourable economic situation in coal mining districts. With the priority production system in place from 1947, the government placed special emphasis on the recovery and expansion of the coal mining industry.[56] In this way, substantial funding was provided to the mining sector, allowing it to expand thereafter, and miners were given extra rations, rendering mine work more attractive.[57] As Kimura has shown, residing in mining towns appealed to repatriates as it provided good access to food, fuel, and shelter, with most mining companies offering employees company housing which was relatively comfortable by the standards of the time.[58] Nonetheless, the influx of repatriates to mining districts was a result of the employment opportunities the sector offered. With little or no assets to tie them down, repatriates were more mobile than the general population, willing to relocate wherever work was readily available.

The employment of former colonial residents of Karafuto

The reemployment of repatriates was the most important factor in their economic reintegration. If adequate work could be found, repatriate households were able to solve most of the other material problems that they faced, including their housing situation. Therefore, the question becomes, how did repatriates fare in the labour market? Here, evidence is hard to come by, but the evidence that does exist suggests that repatriates' pre-war and wartime employment experiences and personal connections (social capital) combined with the general economic situation to determine the course of their integration into the labour market. The mining sector offers a good example of this, with mining companies being an important employer in Karafuto. Mitsui and Mitsubishi mining actively recruited among repatriates, including many who had worked at the mines these companies had operated in Karafuto. Having a relationship with the firms who were recruiting surely helped repatriates secure jobs, but in the mining sector at least, this rehiring of staff previously employed in the colonies stemmed from more than a sense of paternalistic corporate responsibility. It also made economic sense, because as experienced workers, those who were rehired required little or no training. In addition, the large scale rehiring in mining reflected the basic economic conditions faced in the sector, with mining benefitting from the priority production system and facing an acute labour shortage. During the war years, mining in Hokkaidō had employed 92,000 miners, including approximately 42,000 Chinese and Koreans, many of whom were forced labourers. However, with these workers and a further 12,000 Japanese labourers abandoning Hokkaidō's mines in the wake of Japan's defeat, when the sector was finally up and running again, there was plenty of work to be had.[59]

The early recovery and labour shortage felt in mining were not conditions commonly shared throughout the economy, and as a result, some sectors were less able to absorb repatriates than others. Reflecting considerable variations in the structure of local economies, higher rates of unemployment were felt by repatriates in certain localities. Hokkaidō was such a case with local data suggesting that in 1950, 6.9 percent of working age repatriates were unemployed and actively seeking work, compared to just 2.4 percent of repatriates nationally.[60] Unlike mining, some of Hokkaidō's other main industries were less than vibrant in the postwar years, and as a result, former residents of Karafuto who had worked in these sectors in the pre-war period struggled to reintegrate, often having to switch employment sectors. This picture is clear from Table 7.3, which shows the occupational

Table 7.3 Occupational Structure by Sector of Former Residents of Karafuto when Resident in the Colony and in Postwar Hokkaidō

	Main Occupation when Resident in Karafuto	Occupation in Hokkaidō, 1956
Agriculture	14.2%	16.4%
Fishing & Marine Products	30.4%	13.5%
Forestry	2.1%	1.3%
Labour & Construction	4.6%	16.4%
Mining	2.3%	6.7%
Manufacturing	13.4%	12.0%
Transport & Communications	10.4%	5.7%
Commerce	5.9%	7.6%
Civil Service	5.7%	6.6%
Education	1.3%	2.6%
Professional	4.8%	6.2%
Military/Police	1.1%	0.2%
Services	3.9%	4.8%
Working in the Same Sector to that in Karafuto		47.2%
Working in a Different Sector to that in Karafuto		52.8%

Note: The sample used is composed of 892 households where the pre and postwar occupations could be determined.

Compiled from: HZJC files for Hokkaidō residents who came from Shinkai and Chitose villages, Maoka town (surnames beginning with a, i, u, e, o), and miscellaneous settlements (surnames beginning with 'a, i, u, e, o' or 'ka, ki, ku, ke, ko') in Karafuto.

structure of former residents of Karafuto when they lived in the colony and in Hokkaidō in 1956, utilising HZJC data compiled from the former residents of various settlements in Karafuto. Table 7.3 indicates a degree of consistency across the pre and postwar periods with employment in manufacturing, agriculture, forestry, commerce, services, education, civil service, and professional white-collar occupations all registering less than a 2.5 percent change, positive or negative, in their overall share of employment. Nonetheless, this apparent smooth transition masks a greater degree of occupational change within the sample. When each individual household's transwar occupational transition is analysed, it turns out that the sample is split almost exactly down the middle, with half able to find employment in the same sector in which they were employed in the pre-war period and the other half switching. As Table 7.3 indicates, a significant decline in the share of same sector employment was registered in transport and communications (from 10.4 percent to 5.7 percent), and fishing and marine products (30.4 percent to 13.5 percent).

The decline in fishing reflected the saturation of Hokkaidō's fishing industry, which had suffered from falling catches in the pre-war period due to overfishing. Moreover, in the pre-war period, Hokkaidō-based fishing operators had been very active in the seas north of the island, often operating around Karafuto, Soviet Sakhalin, the Kurile Islands, and as far as Kamchatka. Whilst it is clear that Japan's pre-war pelagic empire made a comeback elsewhere, with the de facto loss of Karafuto and the Kurile Islands to the Soviet Union, and the postwar geo-political situation, Hokkaidō-based fishing interests were no longer able to tap these rich fishing grounds as they had done previously.[61] Faced with these difficult conditions, the fishing sector in postwar Hokkaidō was unable to absorb much additional labour, and thus, Karafuto's fishermen often struggled to find reemployment in fishing. Though it is difficult to assess with a high degree of accuracy, a number of the individual household returns from the HZJC sample also point to a trend among those who were reemployed in which reemployment entailed a drop in status. Many of Karafuto's independent fishermen found themselves working as ordinary fishing labourers on the boats of Hokkaidō's operators in 1956. Others still left sectors like fishing entirely, with some taking up work in mining (which almost tripled its share of employment to 6.7 percent of the total) or as general labourers, usually employed in construction. The later sector saw its share of employment in the HZJC sample grow more than any other, expanding from 4.6 percent to 16.4 percent, making it the largest employer of Karafuto repatriates in Hokkaidō alongside agriculture. This was not a positive development for the repatriate community, as most cases in the HZJC sample indicate that many repatriates took up work in this sector as day labourers, an occupation considered to be at the bottom of the labour market for unskilled labour, characterised by high seasonal variation in work availability, low job security, and poor working conditions. The prevalence of this type of work indicates that whilst most repatriates had re-entered the labour force, and half in a sector in which they had skills and experience, a significant underclass of repatriate labour emerged. Indeed, such work was particularly common among the most vulnerable segments of the repatriate community, as revealed in a 1949 survey into the conditions at Asahikawa's 'Welfare Village Number One', which found that over a third of the group shelter's working residents were employed as day labourers.[62]

The HZJC sample data suggest that this underclass of repatriate labour continued to exist in 1956 in places like Hokkaidō, but this should not be interpreted as evidence of widespread absolute poverty among repatriates. In this regard, HZJC data also indicates that among the repatriate households from Karafuto who resided in Hokkaidō in 1956, only 3.7 percent were receiving public aid (*seikatsu hogo*), many of which were headed by widowers or elderly day labourers. The national equivalent for the general population was exactly equal to this level and so repatriate families do not appear particularly hard-pressed.[63] Though a significant number of repatriates became employed in less desirable sectors of the economy and/or marginal positions within them, for the most part as growth spread throughout the economy they found work and did not become dependent on the public purse. Moreover, it would be a mistake to suggest that the transwar occupational transition made by the majority of former colonial residents was fraught with prolonged difficulty. Clearly, there was a significant minority which ended up at the bottom of the labour market. However, the transwar experience of former colonial residents was as varied as colonial society itself, and this was also reflected in the process of economic (re)integration.

Table 7.4 presents occupational data compiled from a 1949 roster of leading members of the *Zenkoku Karafuto Renmei* (known as Kabaren) which emerged

Table 7.4 Occupational Structure by Sector of Leading Members of Kabaren when Resident in Karafuto and in 1949

	Main Occupation in Karafuto	*Occupation in 1949*
Agriculture	0.8%	1.3%
Fishing & Marine Products	1.3%	1.7%
Forestry	0.8%	0.9%
Labour & Construction	1.6%	2.4%
Mining	1.3%	1.7%
Manufacturing	9.0%	7.9%
Transport & Communications	1.7%	1.3%
Commerce	2.4%	4.3%
Civil Service	23.4%	14.8%
Education	39.8%	40.8%
Professional	14.2%	21.8%
Military/Police	3.8%	1.1%
Services	0.0%	0.0%
Working in the Same Sector to that in Karafuto		72.5%
Working in a Different Sector to that in Karafuto		27.5%

Note: The sample used is composed of 633 prominent members of Kabaren. The sample does not include a handful of those who were listed in the source but were yet to be repatriated to Japan.

Compiled from: Zenkoku Karafuto Renmei, *Karafuto-jin Meikan*. Tokyo: Zenkoku Karafuto Renmei, 1949.

as the main organisation representing the interests of Karafuto repatriates in post-war Japan and was largely composed of leading members of colonial society, especially the colonial administration (Karafuto-chō).[64] These data allow us to make a comparison between the transwar occupational transition of members of the colonial elite and general repatriates, reflected in the HZJC data presented in Table 7.3. The difference of seven years between the samples does problematize the comparison somewhat, but in the absence of alternative sources of information, the data prove somewhat indicative. Overall, the difference in occupational structure between the samples is striking, with the Kabaren sample showing a high concentration of employment in white-collar occupations – particularly in the civil service, education, and professional sectors – and very few engaged by the major employers of general repatriates, namely agriculture, labour and construction, and fishing and the production of marine products. Furthermore, a closer examination of the positions held in these sectors by the individuals listed in the Kabaren roster shows another key difference with the individuals in the HZJC sample. Whereas in the latter, those employed in construction were often day labourers, in the former, they were company heads or managers. In manufacturing, a significant employer in both samples, the HZJC sample contains many working in small workshops or as ordinary factory labour, whilst the Kabaren sample lists mostly technicians, many in the employ of firms that had been active in Karafuto.

We may say that this difference is not particularly surprising given that the Kabaren sample is largely made up of colonial bureaucrats (including those employed at Karafuto-chō schools) and other members of the colonial elite. However, what is significant in the Kabaren sample is the relative stability in the occupational structure from pre-war to postwar, with over 70 percent of Kabaren's main members finding employment in the same sector in which they worked in Karafuto. Moreover, the only sector which saw a large decline in its overall share of employment was the civil service (from a 23.4 percent to a 14.8 percent share of total employment), and in this case, most of the now former civil servants were able to take up professional white-collar employment, which saw its share of total employment grow from 14.2 percent to 21.8 percent. Thus, it appears that for the most part, those who are listed in the Kabaren roster did not suffer a fall in status like that felt by many of the individuals in the HZJC sample. There were no day labourers or fishing labourers in the Kabaren sample; neither was there anyone at all employed in the service sector. This was true for both the pre and postwar occupations of those listed in the sample, and it indicates that those with high levels of human and social capital were successfully able to find suitable employment, integrating at the high end of the labour market as early as 1949.

Conclusion

The repatriation of over six million Japanese nationals from the moribund Japanese empire and their subsequent reintegration into society were among the most prominent of numerous challenges faced in early postwar Japan. The evidence presented here suggests that repatriation itself and reintegration were complex processes, and thus there was no typical repatriate experience. Nonetheless, evidence from Hokkaidō focusing on the former residents of Karafuto suggests that by the mid-1950s at least, the majority of repatriates had reintegrated, albeit with a minority stuck at the bottom end of the labour market. Despite the common claim that repatriates returned 'with only the clothes on their back', it has been argued here that the collapse of Japan's colonial empire and subsequent repatriation of its Japanese residents was not a great equalizer.[65] This is because repatriates brought back with them much more than the physical items they could carry aboard their repatriation vessel. Most importantly, they brought with them social and human capital, which enabled them to negotiate the chaotic situation in the initial postwar years and ultimately regain their pre-war social position, some better than others. In such a way, the pre-war hierarchies of colonial society survived the war years, re-establishing themselves in repatriate organisations and the labour market.

Acknowledgements

The author would like to thank the participants at the workshops organised by Martin Dusinberre in Zurich and Araragi Shinzō in Okinawa, as well as the audiences at Tokyo and Tohoku universities, who heard earlier versions of this research, for the highly valuable feedback and comments they gave. This research has also benefited from travel grants from the "Cluster of Excellence: Asia and Europe in Global Perspective" established at Heidelberg University in 2015, and the Suntory Toyota Institute of Economics and Related Disciplines at the London School of Economics in 2014. Jonathan Bull (Hokkaidō University) and Sumiyo Nishizaki (London School of Economics) also deserve special thanks for their kind help and advice in the acquisition of source materials, without which this research would have been impossible. All errors are my own.

Notes

1 L. Watt, "Embracing Defeat in Seoul: Rethinking Decolonization in Korea, 1945", *Journal of Asian Studies*, Vol. 74, No. 1, 2015, pp. 153–174.
2 L. Watt, *When Empire Comes Home: Repatriation and Reintegration in Postwar Japan*, Cambridge, MA: Harvard University Press, 2009, p. 93.
3 J. Orr, *The Victim as Hero: Ideologies of Peace and National Identity in Postwar Japan*, Honolulu: University of Hawaii Press, 2001.
4 R. M. Douglas, *Orderly and Humane: The Expulsion of the Germans After the Second World War*. New Haven: Yale University Press, 2012.
5 Two notable exceptions to this were the U.S. military occupation of Okinawa, which was returned to Japan in 1972, and the Kurile Islands, which were occupied by Soviet forces, incorporated as Soviet territory and continue *de facto* as part of the Russian Federation today, despite Japanese territorial claims on the southern part of the island chain.
6 S. Yokote, "Soviet Repatriation Policy, U.S. Occupation Authorities, and Japan's Entry into the Cold War", *Journal of Cold War Studies*, Vol. 15, No. 2, 2013, p. 32.
7 Watt, *When Empire Comes Home*, pp. 61–70.
8 Kōseishō Engokyoku, *Hikiage to Engo 30-nen no Ayumi* (30 Years of Repatriate Assistance), Tokyo: Kōseishō, 1977.

9 Ibid., p. 689.
10 A recent account of the internment of Japanese POWs in Soviet zones can be found in A. Barshay, *The Gods Left First: The Captivity and Repatriation of Japanese POWs in Northeast Asia, 1945–1956*, Berkeley: University of California Press, 2013.
11 Yokote, "Soviet Repatriation Policy", pp. 44–50.
12 On the failure to repatriate the majority of Sakhalin Koreans, see: Y. Din, "Dreams of Returning to the Homeland: Koreans in Karafuto and Sakhalin", in S. Paichadze and P. Seaton, eds., *Voices From the Shifting Russo-Japanese Border: Karafuto/Sakhalin*, Abingdon: Routledge, 2015.

   On the Japanese who remained in Sakhalin, see T. Nakayama, "Saharin Zanryū Nihonjin" (The Japanese Remaining in Sakhalin), in S. Araragi, ed., *Teikoku Igo no Hito to Idō* (Migration After Empire), Tokyo: Bensei Shuppan, 2012, pp. 733–781.
13 For a focus on military entanglements, see D. Gillin and C. Etter, "Staying On: Japanese Soldiers and Civilians in China, 1945–1949", *Journal of Asian Studies*, Vol. 42, No. 3, 1983.

   For technicians, see R. Ward, "Delaying Repatriation: Japanese Technicians in Early Postwar China", *Japan Forum*, Vol. 23, No. 4, 2011.
14 A comprehensive account of this phenomenon is provided in S. Araragi ed., *Chūgoku Zanryū Nihonjin to iu Keiken* (The Experience of Japanese Left Behind/Remaining in China), Tokyo: Bensei Shuppan, 2009.
15 The first of these official histories was produced even as repatriation was ongoing: Hikiage Engokyoku, *Hikiage Engo no Kiroku* (The Chronicle of Repatriation Assistance), Tokyo: Kōseishō, 1950. A number of personal testimonies have been published and are too numerous to list here. For an example which relates to repatriates from Karafuto, see: Sōka Gakkai Seinenbu Hensan Shuppan Iinkai, *Kita no Umi wo Watatte – Karafuto Hikiagesha no Kiroku* (Crossing the Northern Sea – The Chronicles of Karafuto Repatriates), Tokyo: Daisan Bunmeisha, 1976. An online collection of personal experiences of repatriates, soldiers, and detainees published by the Heiwa Kinen Tenji Shiryokan (Peace Memorial Museum) can be accessed online at the following address: www.heiwakinen.jp/library/shiryokan/heiwa.html.
16 In recent years, a number of these stories have been serialised on screen. In 2014 and 2015, TBS (Tokyo Broadcasting System) produced special drama series that serialised the war's end and repatriation of Japanese in Manchuria, in particular focusing on female and child characters, titled *Reddo Kurosu – Onnatachi no Akagami* (Red Cross – the Red Conscription Papers of Women) and *Tooi Yakusoku – Hoshi ni natta Kodomotachi* (Distant Promise – the Children in the Stars).
17 The most recent contribution of this group is particularly rich in scope; see S. Araragi ed., *Teikoku Igo no Hito to Idō.*
18 K. Katō, *Kaigai Hikiage Kankei Shiryō Shūsei* (Materials Related to Overseas Repatriation), Tokyo: Yumani Shobō, 2002.
19 Watt. *When Empire Comes Home*, Chapter 3.
20 Such efforts were expanded after incidents of repatriate non-compliance at repatriation centres; see SCAP GHQ G-2 Far East Command Doc. 000.1 Jan – Dec 1948: available from the National Diet Library Materials on the Allied Occupation of Japan, http://dl.ndl.go.jp/?__lang=en#senryo.
21 Watt. *When Empire Comes Home*, p. 77.
22 Ibid., p. 173.
23 Ibid., pp. 173–176.
24 T. Nakamura, *Lectures on Modern Japanese Economic History 1926–1994*, Tokyo: LTCB International Library Foundation, 1994, p. 176.
25 K. Odaka, "Hikiagesha to Sensō Chokugo no Rōdōryoku" (Repatriates and the Initial Postwar Workforce), *Tokyo Daigaku Shakaigaku Kenkyū Kiyō*, 4/1996, p. 138.
26 F. Edding, *The Refugees as a Burden, a Stimulus, and a Challenge to the West German Economy*, Dordrecht: Springer, 1951, p. 51.

27 I. Connor, *Refugees and Expellees in Post-War Germany*, Manchester: Manchester University Press, 2007, pp. 42–44.

28 For more details on these projects, see Sengo Kaitakushi Hensan Iinkai, *Sengo Kaitakushi* (The History of Postwar Land Reclamation), Tokyo: Zenkoku Kaitaku Nōgyō Kyōdō Kumiai Rengōkai, 1967.

29 Odaka, "Hikiagesha to Sensō Chokugo no Rōdōryoku", p. 139.

30 A. Yanagisawa, *Nihonjin no Shokuminchi Keiken – Dairen Nihonjin Shōkōgyōsha no Rekishi* (The Experience of Japanese in the Colonies – the History of Japanese Businessmen in Dalian), Tokyo: Aoki Shoten, 1999, pp. 311–329.

31 S. Ivings, "Colonial Settlement and Migratory Labour in Karafuto 1905–1941", PhD Thesis, London School of Economics, 2014, pp. 34–37.

32 For an excellent illustration of Japanese settler society in Korea see J. Uchida, *Brokers of Empire: Japanese Settler Colonialism in Korea 1910–1937*, Cambridge, MA: Harvard University Asia Centre, 2011.

33 J. Bull, "Occupation-era Hokkaidō and the Emergence of the Karafuto Repatriate", in S. Paichadze and P. Seaton, eds., *Voices From the Shifting Russo-Japanese Border*, Abingdon: Routledge, 2015, pp. 65–67.

34 Zenkoku Karafuto Renmei, *Karafuto Shūsenshi* (A History of the End of the War in Karafuto), Tokyo: Zenkoku Karafuto Renmei, 1973, p. 337.

35 Ibid., pp. 380–381. Also see Y. Kimura, "Dasshutsu to Iu Hikiage no Hōhō: Karafuto kara Hokkaidō he" (Repatriation by Fleeing from Karafuto to Hokkaidō), *Hokkaidō Tohoku Shi Kenkyū*, Vol. 9, No. 1, 2013.

36 SCAP GHQ G-2 Far East Command Doc. 091.3 Russia Jan – Dec 1946, section entitled "Informal Report of Conditions in Karafuto", 30/1/1946, available at the National Diet Library Materials on the Allied Occupation of Japan, http://dl.ndl.go.jp/?__lang=en#senryo.

37 Bull, "Occupation-era Hokkaidō and the Emergence of the Karafuto Repatriate", pp. 67, 70–74.

38 SCAP GHQ G-2 Far East Command Doc. 091.3 Russia Jan – Dec 1946, section entitled "Informal Report of Conditions in Karafuto", 30/1/46.

39 See: Y. Tonai, "Soviet Rule in South Sakhalin and the Japanese Community, 1945–1949", in S. Paichadze and P. Seaton, eds., *Voices From the Shifting Russo-Japanese Border*, pp. 96–99.

40 Ibid.

41 Zenkoku Karafuto Renmei, *Karafuto Shūsenshi*, pp. 581–582.

42 Ibid., pp. 602–603.
   Nonetheless, it is known that some of those resettled in the northeast – including Karafuto Ainu, initially settled in Fukushima prefecture – eventually relocated to Hokkaidō where work appeared to be more readily available. For more details on the repatriation of Ainu from Karafuto, see M. Tamura, "Karafuto Ainu no Hikiage" (The Repatriation of Karafuto Ainu), in Araragi, S, ed., *Nihon Teikoku wo Meguru Jinkō Idō no Kokusai Shakaigaku* (International and Social Studies of Migration in the Japanese Empire), Tokyo: Fufuta Shuppan, 2008.

43 Ivings, "Colonial Settlement and Migratory Labour in Karafuto 1905–1941", pp. 133–148.

44 Y. Kimura, "Sengo Karafuto kara no Hikiagesha to Hokkaidō – Toshibu to Tankō Toshi wo Chūshin ni" (Postwar Repatriates from Karafuto in Hokkaidō: Cities and Mining Towns), *Hokudai Shigaku*, Vol. 54, No. 1, 2014, pp. 44–45.

45 Bull, "Occupation-era Hokkaidō and the Emergence of the Karafuto Repatriate", p. 69.

46 J. Bull, "The Making of Karafuto Repatriates", PhD Thesis, Hokkaidō University, 2014, p. 255.

47 Karafuto Kyōkai, *Karafuto Hikiage Dōhō no Genkyō* (The Current Condition of our Fellow Karafuto Repatriates), Unpublished Report, 25/10/45, reproduced in Katō, *Kaigai Hikiage Kankei Shiryō Shūsei*, Vol. 30, Tokyo: Yumani Shobō, 2002, pp. 190–191.

48 Ibid., pp. 192–195.
49 Ibid., pp. 191–192.
50 The 1946 data is drawn from Hokkaidō-chō, *Hokkaidō Gaikyō* (Overview of Hokkaidō), Sapporo: Hokkaidō-chō, 1948, pp. 287–290. The 1950 data is drawn from Bull, "Occupation-era Hokkaidō and the Emergence of the Karafuto Repatriate", p. 69.
51 Calculated from data presented in Bull, "Occupation-era Hokkaidō and the Emergence of the Karafuto Repatriate", p. 69, Table 3.4.
52 Kimura, "Sengo Karafuto kara no Hikiagesha to Hokkaidō", pp. 47–49.
53 Ibid., p. 53.
54 Kōseishō Hikiage Engo Kyoku Mikikan Chōsabu, *Hikiagesha Zaigai Jijitsu Chōsa* (Factual Investigation of Overseas Repatriates), Tokyo: Kōseishō, 1956. These documents are unpublished survey returns available upon request at the annex of the National Archives of Japan (*Kokuritsu Kōbunshokan*).
55 Bull, *The Making of Karafuto Repatriates*, Chapter 5.
56 For more on this, see the chapter in this volume by Mark Metzler.
57 Nakamura, *Lectures on Modern Japanese Economic History 1926–1994*, pp. 152–153.
58 Kimura, "Sengo Karafuto kara no Hikiagesha to Hokkaidō", pp. 60–62.
59 Ibid. Also see the chapter in this volume by M. Metzler.
60 Calculated from data presented in Bull, "Occupation-era Hokkaidō and the Emergence of the Karafuto Repatriate", p. 68.
61 See chapter in this volume by William Tsutsui.
62 Kimura, "Sengo Karafuto kara no Hikiagesha to Hokkaidō", p. 57.
63 The repatriate rate was calculated using the HZJC sample and the national rate was calculated using data from chapters 2–17 and 23–37 of the Historical Statistic of Japan, available from the following link: www.stat.go.jp/english/data/chouki/index.htm.
64 For more on this organisation and its emergence, refer to Bull, *The Making of Karafuto Repatriates*, especially Chapter 2.
65 Watt, *When Empire Comes Home*, p. 6.

8 Good wife, wise mother, and Americanised consumer

The forced social democratisation of the private sphere in Occupied Japan

Zsombor Rajkai

Introduction

After its defeat in World War Two, Japan managed to create a strongly develop-ing economy that also promoted relative social stability. Following the economic growth at the turning point of the nineteenth and twentieth centuries during the Meiji period (1868-1912), the postwar socioeconomic transformation can be con-sidered the second 'miracle' in Japan's century-long modern history. The Occupa-tion (1945-1952), as a brief yet epoch-making period after World War Two, played a fundamental role in this process. Despite the wide range of research on the Occupation period, however, general understanding about how and to what degree the Occupation contributed to the renewal of Japan after World War Two varies according to the investigated aspect or aspects of the history of the period. One less studied, though essential, element here that also concerns the study of Japan's economic history is the 'forced' democratisation of the private sphere (family and gender relations). This change was a central contribution to the establishment of the modern Japanese family through its promotion of gender-biased working pat-terns in marital relations, in particular the *salarimanisation* and *housewifisation* of the working-age population. The former term refers to a process during which more and more Japanese men started to work for a regular salary through stable employment, whereas the latter pertains to the process during which the major-ity of Japanese women became principally engaged in domestic matters, such as housework and child raising. This led to an unprecedented change in Japanese working patterns, since married couples previously spent far more time together, both at home and outside the home (working together), in pre-modern Japan.[1]

The modern Japanese family, with its remarkable gender-biased role/employ-ment division, became the fundamental socioeconomic unit in modern Japan, bringing about new micro-level economic practices that ultimately manifested into unprecedented consumerism – one of the main pillars of Japan's 'miraculous' postwar economic development. The modern family became strongly intercon-nected with the rise of consumerism during the first 30 years of postwar economic growth in Japan. Due to further industrialisation after World War Two, house-hold electric goods, such as washing machines, refrigerators, and televisions (1955-1964) – also called the 'Three Sacred Treasures' (*san shu no jingi*) – and later items, such as cars, coolers (air conditioners), and colour televisions (1965-1974) – also called the 3Cs – started to be produced on a large scale.[2] These all targeted the 'nuclear' family as the basic unit of consumerism, significantly easing the workload of Japanese housewives and helping average households to realise some elements of the then widely admired American way of life.[3] The formation of gender-biased marital working patterns – a typical characteristic feature of the modern family in general – was, however, a long process, lasting from the Taishō period (1912-1926) to the 1970s. Thus, the birth of the modern family in Japan cannot be attributed solely to the Occupation period. Yet, it becomes a highly important question as to how the Occupation period – as a transitional period both in terms of change and continuity – contributed to the formation of the modern Japanese family that later so deeply affected socioeconomic relations during the postwar era. This question can only be answered when the Occupation era is studied in a wider context as a sort of connecting period between the preceding and succeeding decades. This chapter addresses the making of the modern Japanese family and pays attention to the roles envisaged for women and the economic impacts of these changes. This chapter also discusses several related issues, such as the Japanese family and social change from the Meiji period onwards, Occupation policy, the occupiers' understanding of Japan in general, as well as the impact of their policies in the long run.

Socioeconomic modernisation: the creation of a new middle class

After World War Two, Japan experienced an enormous socioeconomic transformation with two striking aspects at its core: land reform and salarimanisation. Both represented remarkable milestones in the modern history of Japan's society and economy. Japan's large-scale social modernisation started in the Meiji period, which – by employing the (Western) concept of the *citizen* – ended the Edo period's formal legal inequalities in terms of rights and duties of the population, and promoted a rapid transformation of the previous social structure. In this process, the elite class of Edo Japan was gradually – but also in a very short timeframe – deprived of its formal social privileges, and by the end of the nineteenth century, Japan had developed capitalist, socioeconomic conditions with a rapidly forming working class, along with a new managerial elite and modern bureaucracy. At the same time, there was also a new middle class forming in urban settlements that was not a historical continuation of the former middle class of the Edo era. This so-called 'old' middle class included independent farmers as well as owners of small retail premises, who in many cases struggled to adapt themselves to the new social conditions of Meiji Japan. The source for the 'new' middle class included young people from rural settlements who moved to the cities and worked as employees for a regular salary.[4] Many of them, however, kept strong ties with their families back in the countryside, thus acting more like urbanised peasants – at least in the beginning.[5] As a result of the remarkable urbanisation of the pre-war period, this new middle class gradually grew, although this process was later hindered during the war. At the end of World War Two – 80 years after the establishment of modern Japan in 1868 – Japan's demographic structure still presented a 'traditional' pyramid form, and nearly half of the population still lived in rural settlements, mainly working as tenant farmers.[6] The Occupation's General Headquarters (GHQ) saw the class of rural landowners as a hindrance to the democratisation of the country, believing that they were also partially responsible for the rise of militarism in the 1930s. Therefore, GHQ decided to carry out wide-ranging land reform as the third pillar of the economic democratisation program – together with the liberalisation of working practices and economic deconcentration.[7] By 1949, around 80 percent of the tenanted holdings, almost two million hectares of arable land, had been redistributed to independent (previously tenant) farmers, and only seven percent of farmers remained without land.[8] The former landowners were only allowed to keep a few acres of land which they were able to cultivate by themselves, with a small area permitted for renting out.[9] This affected the former rural aristocracy in a negative way, with them losing both a remarkable portion of their property and also their previous elite status. In contrast, the independent farmers' living conditions improved significantly, and, matching with GHQ's expectations, they became a new rural middle class and, in many cases, strong supporters of the new Japan.

The other main characteristic feature of Japan's socioeconomic modernisation was the process of salarimanisation, which took place on a full scale level between the 1950s and 1970s. This was accompanied by another remarkable process: the housewifisation of Japanese women. This process proceeded simultaneously with the trend toward nuclear families, along with a decrease in the number of children (down to around two per mother by the mid-1950s).[10] Together these changes constituted the three main characteristic features of the postwar Japanese family system – at least in an 'ideal' sense.[11] This postwar 'ideal' nuclear family model included a married couple and two children, with a strong gender-biased role division between the spouses (the husband acting as the breadwinner and the wife as a housewife) and formed one of the core bases of the emerging consumer economy. It was also characterised by an increased consciousness of blood relationships, the privacy of family relations, as well as by an increase of child-centric attitudes that contributed to the formation of an education-focused society based on individual achievements.[12] This model, however, was not uniquely Japanese, and echoed the then general family model found in urban middle-class families in developed Western countries. Thus, Japan was thought to be simply following the general path of socioeconomic modernisation in a similar fashion to Western societies.[13] In fact, despite such alleged Western links, this model did not emerge for the first time during the postwar period in Japan. Its first appearance can be traced back to the Taishō period, when the formation of a new lifestyle among urban middle-class families was ongoing through salarimanisation,[14] though the proportion of salaryman-type families was still relatively low at the time. Along with this process, a significant symbolic change to the idealised image of womanhood was ongoing through the emergence of a new form of idealised motherhood through the slogan of *ryōsai kenbo* (good wife and wise mother), which promoted women staying at home and becoming more deeply engaged in household matters such as housework and child raising.[15] This idea also opened the way for many Japanese women to improve their social status – at least in terms of public praise won through adhering to this image.

The Occupation's contribution to Japan's ongoing socioeconomic modernisation took shape through the democratisation of family and gender relations. Within three years of Japan's capitulation in 1945, a new constitution (1947) and civil code (1948), both emphasising democratic values regarding family and gender relations, were declared to replace the former – allegedly undemocratic – Meiji constitution (1890) and civil code (1898). In this democratisation process GHQ, some members of which viewed themselves as liberators of Japanese women from 'feudal' oppression, put a great emphasis on the improvement of women's social and economic conditions in postwar Japan.[16] Women became both a target of, and a tool for, the realisation of democracy, and this also had a significant impact on Japan's postwar economic history. The American plan to *use* women for creating a peaceful and democratic society in Japan, however, was not a unique phenomenon confined to Japan. A similar attempt by the United States was also seen in occupied Germany, which inspired General MacArthur to execute a similar plan in Japan.[17] There were several reasons for employing women within defeated Japan's postwar democratic transformation. Firstly, men were diminished in number, exhausted, and potentially embittered by wartime military service, thus seemingly less reliable as a potential source of support for democracy. Secondly, pre-war Japan's *imperial familism* (*tennō kazokushugi*, see below) was viewed by many as a cause of the war, under which Japanese women had suffered as victims. Thus, the employment of women, both in a policy and economic sense, was an essential tool for fighting against what GHQ perceived as the remnants of 'feudalism'.[18] The promotion of democracy using women had another strand too, the struggle against 'communism'.[19] The emerging Cold War between the capitalist and socialist (communist)[20] blocks of countries not only had political and economic aspects, but also cultural dimensions. Women were used on both sides to show the cultural supremacy of the capitalist or socialist block – only in different ways. In the newly forming socialist countries, women were an essential part of the state's plan to replace and renew previous social relations (which, somewhat oxymoronically, were both pre-modern/feudal and capitalist in their view) in order to create a society with no historical precedence. In contrast, in countries with capitalist socioeconomic conditions, the purpose was to maintain and strengthen already existing modern capitalist conditions in the name of democracy.[21]

An interesting question for contemplation is whether the Occupation period merely strengthened already ongoing processes from earlier periods, or if Japan could ever have carried out a similar socioeconomic modernisation in the long run without the Occupation. Eiji Takemae suggests that pre-surrender Japan in general had not been prepared for the enormous change that awaited it after the end of the war, and argues that in regard to feminism in wartime Japan: 'while endogenous input was a necessary ingredient in the formula for change, it was not sufficient of itself".[22] Nonetheless, before examining the reforms of the Occupation period, it should be clarified that Japan's salarimanisation and housewifisation, while rooted in the Taishō period, were not historically unique phenomena but closer to universal aspects of capitalist modernisation, and thus it can be assumed that Occupation policy, rather than creating change in itself, *merely* contributed to the already ongoing process of salarimanisation and housewifisation in this case. A detailed discussion, however, is in order to make clear the validity of this assumption and how exactly the Occupation period contributed to this already ongoing change.

Ambiguous reforms during the Occupation period

The occupiers' view of Japan, along with the reforms they decided to impose upon the Japanese, is a crucial angle in understanding the contribution of the Occupation to the changes of the early postwar period in both economic and societal terms.

During the first half of the twentieth century, there were two different schools of thought regarding America's relationship to Japan. One argued for the employment of a mild approach and even for a partnership with Japan. The other one, pursued by the Office of War Information, stressed the use of somewhat harder policies, and argued for the necessity of re-education and re-orientation in order to pacify and democratise Japan in the postwar era.[23] The MacArthur administration initially followed this latter stream. MacArthur himself looked at the Meiji period as the cause of all problems that contributed to the emergence of militaristic pre-war Japan, and thus, there was no room within his ideas about policy for resurrecting the socioeconomic conditions which existed before militarism took power from the 1930s. Instead, the three *d*'s – the demilitarisation of Japanese society, the democratisation of the political process, and the decentralisation of wealth and power – became fundamental slogans for early Occupation policy.[24] In reality, however, pre-war Japan showed very complex social conditions, in which pre-modern and modern socioeconomic elements, militaristic and democratic thoughts and values, along with anti- and pro-Western attitudes were all present, forming a highly complex and varicoloured intellectual landscape. However, these antagonistic conditions and values were never of the same strength at one time, but were continually wrestling with one another, with temporary victories and defeats over time. Edwin O. Reischauer argued that from the very beginning of the Meiji period, Japan seemed to show a periodic shift of anti and pro-Western attitudes over a cycle of 20 years or so, suggesting that after modernisation, a serious loss of a firm orientation in terms of cultural identity took place in Japan.[25] Whether this position is nuanced enough to be truly accurate is debatable, but Japan appeared to be on the horns of a dilemma as to whether it should identify itself as an Asian country or orient itself towards the West. This internal dilemma manifested itself in different ways, not only as time progressed, but also across spatial and social divisions. People in urban settlements were obviously more exposed to Western influence than the majority of the population living in rural areas. Thus, Japan by the 1930s had become a so-called double society, where people living in the same country existed in clearly distinct social positions.[26] This seems to be one price of the rapid and very complex socioeconomic and political transformation of the country during the Meiji period. Most in GHQ seemed to have only a limited understanding of the complexities of pre-war Japanese society, labelling much of it 'feudal' despite its many modern aspects. Although GHQ did make use of Japanese people who were familiar with the West through their education, along with Japanese Americans and also other Americans who were highly familiar with Japan, it seems to have failed to take into account the true complexity of pre-war Japanese society.

One of the first major concerns of GHQ in terms of demilitarisation was to democratise the pre-war Japanese family system. This was not simply just for the democratisation of gender relations in social, political, and economic ways, but was due to the American assumption that the pre-war Japanese family system was partially responsible for Japan's militaristic behaviour. One idea expressed here was that imperial familism stressed a subordinate relationship between the Emperor (father) and citizens (children), just like in a patriarchal family. Another stressed the importance of the vertical (subordinate) relationship between parents (especially the father) and children as the key relationship within the family over the horizontal marital (conjugal) relationship. The postwar American standpoint was that the vertical subordinate relationship within Japanese families on the (everyday) micro-level was related to the official ideological stress on the vertical (subordinate) relationship between the Emperor and citizens on the macro-level, and thus, both needed to be abolished. The Japanese *ie* (pre-war family/household) system was abolished in the new civil code, and it was replaced by Article 24 of the new constitution that emphasised the importance of (democratic) marital (conjugal) relations over vertical (subordinate) family relations. However, whereas the economic and social democratisation of the family seemed to be indispensable for *pacifying* Japan from an American point of view, GHQ must have failed to see the formation of a double (both pre-modern and modern) structure of Japanese families – analogous to the double social structure at the macro-level – from the Meiji period. On one hand, Imperial Japan had stressed strict vertical family relations from the end of the nineteenth century, with a great emphasis on patriarchal authority and the practice of primogeniture typical of samurai families before the Meiji period. Meiji Japan also standardised and extended this family model to all its citizens through the Civil Code. In this ie family model, the wife was completely legally and economically subordinate to her husband, and her main duty was to do the housework, as well as to produce a male heir. This was also the time when the ideology of 'good wife and wise mother' was articulated as an important slogan for women in Meiji Japan to improve their social status. Under this idea, conjugal relationships formed from an emotional aspect were not emphasised, and a stress was placed instead on instrumental duties. On the other hand, another idea, borrowing the English word 'home' (*hōmu* or *katei*), also started to penetrate into Japanese society in this era. This put stress on the romantic aspect of marital relations and was rather critical towards the subordinated position of women in the family.[27] The word hōmu was first used in Japan by Protestant social

reformers as a contrast to the ideas typical of the vertical relations of the ie system, thus making the two concepts (ie and hōmu/katei) appear antithetical (indig-
enous and foreign, feudal and modern) to each other – at least in the beginning.[28]
Nonetheless, the two concepts coexisted later in a sort of synthesis, because they
in fact did not necessarily exclude each other, with the ie system mainly stressing
heredity, and hōmu referring to the spatial area and romantic elements of marital
relations.[29]

This double structure, however, becomes even more complex when looking
at the spatial (internal) arrangements of Japanese houses during the pre-war era.
By the 1920s, two typical household types had emerged in Japan. One referred to
households where people sat by the fireside (*iroritan no aru ie*), and the other one
pertained to a household where there was a common room for family members to
eat together (*cha no ma no aru ie*), usually next to the kitchen.[30] The former was
typical of the ie family, in which the eldest son stayed with his (elderly) parents
in the parental home (*jikka*) in the countryside, whereas the latter was typical of
the katei family, in which non-first born sons – while being officially registered
as a resident and holding a close relationship with the parental home – moved
to urban settlements and started their own families (of two generations).[31] In the
beginning, the parental home played a more significant role in their relationship,
but later the stress shifted to the families of non-firstborn sons as their number in
urban settlements increased over time. The nuclear families of non-firstborn sons
in urban settlements significantly contributed to the formation of the new urban
middle class. This double structure of Japan's pre-war family system was tacitly
approved of by the pre-war Japanese authorities.[32] Thus, when the Occupation
decided to abolish the Japanese pre-war ie family system and to replace it with a
new one in the name of democratisation, the new family form for replacing the ie
system was de facto already present.

The family reform pursued by the Occupation was also not one which sought
complete change. Though GHQ forced the abolition of the pre-war ie system, it
did not abolish another institution related to family, i.e., the institution of household (or family) registration (*koseki seido*). The family registration system had
already been present in Japanese history before the Meiji period, but it is Meiji
Japan that extended its use to all citizens as an essential element of the family
system.[33] During the Meiji period, the family was the basic social unit instead of
the individual. According to this system, each citizen had to belong to an official
family household – usually the household of the father or the husband – and was
often unrelated to the person's place of birth or actual residence. This system,
from the time of the Meiji Civil Code, also barred the possibility of married couples being registered under two different family names.[34] This later became the
subject of heavy critiques by those who saw the family registration system as a
hindrance to the realisation of gender equality.[35] Thus, the MacArthur administration promoted family change (the spread of nuclear families) through the abolition of the pre-war (three-generational) ie system, whereas it also contributed to
the maintenance of certain pre-war elements that were later viewed as undemocratic, such as patriarchal family relations. By maintaining the family registration

system, the Occupation actually reinforced the family as the basic social unit in Japan, although this time, it was a different – partially old, partially new – family system.[36] According to later critiques, the patriarchal character of the postwar Japanese family did not disappear; only the role of the patriarch changed from the father (of a three-generational household) to the husband (in a nuclear family).[37]

The survival of certain pre-war elements of the Japanese family system is sometimes viewed as a result of the prioritisation of economic goals by the United States during the Occupation period. However, it is also argued that such an assumption could be an overstatement, in that while economic stability was considered necessary for postwar social stability, there was also enough room for the Japanese people to shape their own fate.[38] Nonetheless, it can be concluded that the family reforms instituted by GHQ were key policies in the formation of a basic element of the future Japanese economy: the consumerism-focused nuclear family. Furthermore, the expected role of women in the new Japan also became an important factor in the study of both the family reforms of the occupiers and their consequences for postwar Japan's work environment and the position of women within it.

Democratisation and Americanisation: the making of the modern Japanese woman

In viewing themselves as the liberators of Japanese women from pre-war 'feudal' oppression, many within GHQ expected Japanese women to be a key element in the new postwar Japan. Towards the end of World War Two, numerous women were already working in various workplaces to compensate for the labour shortage, and this large number of working women had great potential to serve as a base for improving women's social conditions in the postwar era, in spite of the fact that several Japanese feminists collaborated with the then present military/ bureaucratic government.[39] Nonetheless, pre-war Japanese feminists continued to play a role after the end of the war too. For instance, three powerful feminists – Ichikawa Fusae, Akamatsu Tsuneko, and Kawasaki Natsu – founded the Women's Postwar Counter-Measures Committee (*Sengo Taisaku Fujin I'inkai*) on 25 August 1945 and urged the implementation of universal suffrage, something soon accomplished with the support of the occupiers. As a result of Japan's first postwar elections, 39 women took their seats in the Lower House of the Diet in 1946.[40] In the following year, 23 women were elected to prefectural assemblies, 74 to city councils, and 707 to town assemblies.[41] In drafting the new constitution, there were eight subcommittees, among which the Civil Rights Subcommittee became essential in articulating a model of gender equality. Beate Sirota, one of the three committee members,[42] drafted two articles for the new constitution that guaranteed equality both in society (Article 14) and within the family (Article 24).[43] Article 14 forbids any discrimination in political, economic, and social relations in terms of race, sex, social status, or family origin, whereas Article 24 stresses equality between the two sexes regarding family issues such as spousal selection, divorce, inheritance, and property rights. Furthermore, Article 4, in the Labour

Standards Law (*Rōdō Kihonhō*) of 1947 clearly emphasises equal payment for both sexes. These articles together laid the legal foundation of gender equality in several aspects and thus opened the way to create a society with true gender equality. In reality, however, this legal foundation in many aspects, including economic ones, proved to be rather nominal.[44]

However, from a political viewpoint, women were not only given the legal right to vote, but were also personally addressed and encouraged to use their political rights. For instance, Lieutenant Ethel Weed, an appointed Women's Information Officer in SCAP's Civil Information and Education Section,[45] met numerous Japanese women of different backgrounds between 1945 and 1946 and attempted to convince them of the value of grasping the chance to become politically engaged by using their newly obtained right to vote.[46] Weed also helped Japanese women's rights activists to establish a government bureau, the Women's and Minors' Bureau, to improve women's social conditions – a pre-war demand of Japanese feminist activists. This bureau became an essential organ for organisations such as the League for Democratising Family Law and the Women's Democratic Club.[47]

Education also played an enormous role in the alteration of women's roles in the country. Japan's pre-war education system, with its multiple tracks that were thought to create educational differences, was replaced with a one track system based on the American model.[48] Nonetheless, educational reforms did not happen in a unilateral way, and the Americans gave major opportunities to the Japanese in drafting educational policies. As a response to a directive from Washington, a Committee of Japanese Educators was established.[49] This committee, among others, oversaw a concerted effort to promote women's education. For example, in 1950, 148 junior colleges were founded, with about 75 percent of them accepting only female students. In addition, the 34 pre-war women's colleges were given university status, and although the percentage of female students in tertiary education in total was still only ten percent, their ratio steadily increased in the following years.[50]

The Civil Information and Education Section (CIE) within GHQ also played an enormous role in the shifting status of women. The CIE was not simply responsible for transmitting information, but also values through media such as the radio, newspapers, and films. A popular radio program called 'Women's Hour' presented values related to the new ideal womanhood discussed above. Women who frequently listened to radio programs like 'Women's Hour' became potential advocates of the new urban middle-class consumer family model.[51] Nonetheless, the most reliable contacts among Japanese women for GHQ were those who were already familiar with Western culture and also those who were Christian. Well-educated women familiar with Western culture were expected to protect and project Western-style capitalist values.[52] Such women were not necessarily that limited in number, since from the time of the Taishō period, young people in urban settlements were more obviously exposed to Western ideas.[53] Although the numbers of highly educated women with significant exposure to Western culture remained relatively small, they served as a significant source of core support for change during the Occupation period.

However, the model that America provided women through these forms of re-education and re-orientation was not without its contradictions. On one hand, GHQ policy stressed both the necessity of Japanese women's social and economic advancement (high level of education, political activity, as well as their work outside the family). On the other, their role as a wife and mother taking care of household issues was encouraged. There was an obvious emphasis on the latter, especially when compared to work outside the family/home. Women's expected primary obligation was related to the household both as a wife and as a mother, whereas they were also expected to contribute to the national economy through practicing consumerism. In doing so, Japanese women were shown a model of the then existing lifestyle typical of American urban or suburban middle-class families and were provided with the possibility to change their social status by following the American way of life – as well as through the modernisation, rationalisation, and electrification of the household.[54] Thus, this policy, despite its beneficial outcomes, could be viewed as America – based on orientalist assumptions – approaching the reform of the lives of Japanese families and women from a supposed superior (and ironically paternalistic) position.[55] GHQ policy expected women to be well educated and politically engaged (but not further question the existing social order), and to fulfil the role of a good wife, mother, and American-style consumer. Based on this expected role of women, it can be argued that the model provided to Japan with was one more of late-1940s American ideas about gender equality and consumerism rather than that of true democracy or equality.[56]

Conclusion

Despite significant Japanese support for the democratisation of Japan, the Mac-Arthur administration's direct intervention into Japan's family system caused a certain level of frustration and debate among Japanese intellectuals. On one hand, there were people such as Kawashima Takeyoshi, a legal sociologist, who stressed the necessity of reforming the institution of family in Japan to benefit the democratisation of the whole country. Based on empirical research on the actual conditions of rural Japan, Kawashima distinguished two types of family in Japan – a samurai family type and a rural family type – and pointed out the deceptiveness of pre-war Japan's patriarchal state.[57] On the other hand, there were also scholars who felt concerned about the applicability of modern Western concepts when reforming the institution of family in Japan. Such concerns were especially present in the field of family research that even led to two parallel – though distinct – waves of academic debate in early postwar years. One debate referred to the applicability of the concept of the nuclear family. The nuclear family model including two generations and – at least in an ideological aspect – emphasising democratic social and economic marital relations over vertical patriarchal family (parent-child) relations was imposed on Japan by the occupiers, but scholars like Yamamuro Shūhei,[58] for instance, had concerns about its usefulness in a Japanese context. The other debate went even further in arguing against the Westernisation of the Japanese family by stressing Japan's national particularity. The most notable figure espousing this standpoint was Aruga Kizaemon,[59] who argued that the Japanese ie was not only uniquely Japanese, but it was more like a 'unit for livelihood protection' (*seikatsu shūdan*) rather than a family as it is understood in general. Thus, as an extension of his argument, it also becomes impossible to carry out a cross-cultural comparison between the Japanese ie and *family* in other societies.[60] Later, the theory of a Western-style modernisation of the family was accepted by the majority of Japanese family researchers, and the Japanese ie was positioned as a semi pre-modern Japanese family system – a sort of anachronism. Consequently, the academic debates mentioned above were rather pushed to the background. Yet, they have not disappeared completely, and some studies recently have had recourse again to early postwar theories, aiming to show the unique characteristics of, and the coexistence of modern and traditional within, the contemporary Japanese family system. There was also no similar (direct) intervention by the United States into the institution of family in other societies in East Asia after World War Two, and thus, no other country in East Asia was exposed to an identical challenge to national identity or social structure under American influence as was Japan. Nonetheless, it must be mentioned that although America stressed the necessity of changing the institution of family, the development of family studies within Japan enjoyed a great degree of freedom after World War Two, while such a freedom of research was much less obvious in other parts of East Asia. Perhaps because of these historical conditions, academic debates on the concept of family have remained a somewhat marginal issue in other East Asian societies.[61]

Besides the abovementioned frustration among Japanese intellectuals, generally speaking, the impact of the Occupation period on the formation of postwar Japanese society (and, by extension, its economy) had two characteristic features that manifested themselves in different forms. First, the Occupation period is divided by some into two eras. During the first phase (1945-1947), the aforementioned era of the three *d*'s, the demilitarisation of the society, democratisation of the politics, and decentralisation of wealth and the economy, allegedly stood in the centre. From 1948 onward, this era was then replaced by what some call the 'reverse course' – typified by many as being embodied by the so-called three *r*'s – reconstruction of the economy, the rehabilitation of purgees, and what some refer to as the 'rearmament' of the country.[62] However, in this case, it is hard to speak about such a 'reverse course' when it comes to the fundamental legal and institutional reforms related to the democratisation of family and gender relations, as these were not reversed even after 1952. Second, though Japan between 1945 and 1947 was arguably more exposed to active Occupation policy reforms than later, the Occupation was carried out from the start in a rather indirect way, relying on the already existing structures of the Japanese state. However, not just bureaucrats or educators played significant roles in promoting the reforms, but Japanese feminists, too, who – taking up subjects that had already been on their agenda before the end of the war – urged the realisation of legal reforms on behalf of women. The expectations towards Japanese women by the occupiers, however, were not without contradictions. On one hand, they emphasised the necessity of women's education, along with their political as well as social participation in favour of making Japan a 'democratic' country. On the other hand, by introducing a model of the American life, GHQ also put a great emphasis on a woman's role as a house-wife, stressing that this could now be achieved more easily with the modernisa-tion of the Japanese lifestyle through the rationalisation and electrification of the household.[63] Thus, it can be said that postwar Japanese women were expected to be active both inside and outside the home in the occupiers' official rhetoric. However, there was a rather obvious stress on women's household responsibilities as the primary duty within these two roles.[64] This further promoted the spread of gender-biased role divisions in marital relations that significantly affected pat-terns of work and consumption, and therefore Japan's postwar economic history as a whole. Based on the occupiers' official propaganda regarding the involve-ment of Japanese women in the renewal of postwar Japan, it can be argued that the Occupation period, by putting a categorical end to Japan's pre-war militarist system and employing a strong anti-communist rhetoric, significantly contributed to the spread of the modern salaryman-housewife family model that became the basic socioeconomic unit of postwar Japan.

Notes

1 It is a popular belief in Japan that the 'husband (breadwinner)–wife (housewife)' gen-der-biased role division refers to pre-modern marital relationships. In fact, whereas wives have been in charge of child raising and housework throughout Japan's history, this was not their only engagement during pre-modern times. Women worked with their husbands together in the fields in peasant families, in the workshop in craftsmen's families, and in the shops in merchant families – i.e., in approximately 90 percent of Japanese households in total; thus, the scope of their work was broader than just being in charge of child raising and housework. It was not before the appearance of the modern family that many women became mainly focused on household issues, which later led to the birth of the popular term *sengyō shufu* (professional housewife) during the postwar years. See: Z. Rajkai, "Kindai Kazoku no 'Dentōka': Seiyakuwari Bungyō ni Kakawaru 'Dentō no Hatsumei' – Kyōtoshi ni Okeru Kikitori Chōsa kara" ('Traditionalisation' of the Modern Family: Modern Divisions of Role and an Invented Tradition – From a Survey in Kyoto City), *Kyoto Journal of Sociology*, Vol. 11, 2003, pp. 119–133 for a detailed discussion of the reasons for the emergence of this popular belief.
2 For more on the adoption of household electrical goods, see: A. Gordon, "Consump-tion, Leisure and the Middle Class in Transwar Japan", *Social Science Japan Journal*, Vol. 10, No. 1, 2007, pp. 16–19.
3 A. Miura, *The Rise of Sharing: Fourth-Stage Consumer Society in Japan*, Tokyo: International House of Japan, 2014. Miura divided the history of consumerism in Japan into four periods. The first period (1912-1941) refers to consumerism practiced by only ten to 20 percent of Japan's total population in pre-war urban areas, whereas the second period (1945-1974) pertains to the above-mentioned consumerism charac-terised by *quantity* through mass production. The third period (1975-2004), however, rather stressed *quality* by focusing on individual needs through the spread of brand-name goods that also gave preference to career women over housewives. According to Miura, there has been a remarkable shift since around 2004 from individualism to altruism, from brand-name goods to simplicity and casualness, and also from stressing private possession to sharing.

4 E. O. Reischauer, *Japan: The Story of a Nation*, Tokyo: Tuttle Publishing, 2004, p. 110.
5 Ibid., p. 133.
6 In 1946, Japan's total population was approximately 76 million people, within which the farm households' population included about 34 million people. Statistics Japan, www.stat.go.jp/data/chouki/07.htm, accessed 30/9/2016.
7 See Steven Ericson's chapter in this volume for more on economic deconcentration. E. Takemae, *Inside GHQ: The Allied Occupation of Japan and Its Legacy*, New York: Continuum, 2002, p. 339–346.
8 Ibid., p. 344.
9 See Juha Saunavaara's chapter in the current volume for more on the amounts of land permissible to be retained by landlords.
10 The total fertility rate stabilised at around two children per mother between the 1950s and the 1970s. Ministry of Health, Labour and Welfare, www.mhlw.go.jp/toukei/saikin/hw/jinkou/kakutei13/index.html, accessed 30/9/2016, for reference. This period is also regarded as the one in which the establishment of the modern Japanese family from a demographic point of view took place.
11 E. Ochiai, *The Japanese Family System in Transition: A Sociological Analysis of Family Change in Postwar Japan*, Tokyo: LTCB International Library Foundation, 1997.
12 The strong class consciousness of promoting education towards one's child(ren) first appeared during the Taishō Period within the new middle urban families, accompanying the appearance of the first modern housewives. Y. Sato, "Taishōki no Shin Chūkansō ni Okeru Shufu no Kyōiku Ishiki to Seikatsu Kōdō: Zasshi 'Shufu no Tomo' wo Tegakari toshite" (The Education Consciousness toward the Child and the Living Behaviour of the Housewife in the New Middle Class in the Taishō Era: By the Analysis of the Magazine 'Shufu-no-Tomo'), *Nihon Kasei Gakkaishi*, Vol. 55, No. 6, 2004, pp. 479–492.
13 Talcott Parsons, an American sociologist, during the arguable peak of American optimism after World War Two, envisioned a sort of universalist path of modernisation (a kind of convergence model on a global scale), suggesting that non-Western societies were following a path of social change similar to Western experience. Parsons's ideas, though not without caveats, were also later accepted by several social scholars in early postwar Japan.
14 Also see: Reischauer, *Japan: The Story of a Nation*, p. 137.
15 Koyama Shizuko genuinely showed that the ideology of ryōsai kenbo was a modern construction and not a traditional Japanese ideology. S. Koyama, *Ryōsai Kenbo: The Educational Ideal of 'Good Wife, Wise Mother' in Modern Japan*, Leiden: Brill, 2013.
16 Y. Tsuchiya, *Shinbei Nihon no Kōchiku: Amerika no tai Nichi Jōhō, Kyōiku Seisaku to Nihon Senryō* (Constructing a Pro-U.S. Japan: U.S. Information and Education Policy and the Occupation of Japan), Tokyo: Akashi Shoten, 2009, pp. 18–19.
17 Ibid., pp. 204–205.
18 For a detailed analysis on the problems of employing the term 'feudal' in this context, see: L. Hein, "Revisiting America's Occupation of Japan", *Cold War History*, Vol. 11, No. 4, November 2011.
19 Tsuchiya, *Shinbei Nihon no Kōchiku*, p. 199.
20 It seems to be a popular practice both in academic writings and in the media to call postwar socialist countries *communist*. This, however, needs correction. Whereas most of these countries were/are led by a political party that calls itself communist, none of these countries ever realised communism per se, even according to their own beliefs. These countries aimed at reaching communism through the building of state socialism first as an imagined transitional historical stage between capitalism and communism, but most of them either collapsed or turned to alternative systems before realising the idealised stage of communism.
21 The expected role of women significantly differed in the socialist and capitalist blocs. The main difference manifested itself in their expected contribution to the national

economy. In socialist countries, there was a great emphasis on women's full-time work in the name of gender equality. Based on a Marxist interpretation of equality, the state in socialist countries believed that women could be fully equal to men only if they were provided with an independent economic status. In contrast, in many capitalist countries in the early postwar era, women's full-time employment was much less obviously encouraged, and there was more stress on their role concerning household work. Thus, though women were *used* in both socialist and capitalist countries for postwar campaigns in the emerging cultural Cold War, their expected roles referred to different socioeconomic models. Japan's postwar fate in this regard, and others, was decided by the fact that it was occupied principally by the United States, and not by the Soviet Union.

22 Takemae, *Inside GHQ*, p. xlii.

23 Tsuchiya, *Shinbei Nihon no Kōchiku*, p. 17.

24 J. L. McClain, *Japan: A Modern History*, New York: W.W. Norton and Company, 2002, p. 550. Also see: Reischauer's, *Japan: The Story of a Nation*, Takemae's, *Inside GHQ: The Allied Occupation of Japan and Its Legacy*, as well as J. W. Dower, *Embracing Defeat: Japan in the Wake of World War II*, New York: W.W. Norton and Company, 2000, and T. French, *National Police Reserve: The Origin of Japan's Self Defense Forces*, Leiden: Global Oriental, 2014 for detailed discussions regarding the 'reverse course'.

25 Reischauer described Japan's path to modernisation by employing the metaphor of a *pendulum*. According to Reischauer, Japan's self-definition from the end of the nineteenth century depended on its self-perception in relation to Western countries, which changed every 20 years: from a pro-Western attitude to an anti-Western attitude that then swung back to a pro-Western attitude again and vice-versa. See: Reischauer, *Japan: The Story of a Nation*, p. 120 for details. A similar description of Japan's socioeconomic modernisation is provided by Andrew Gordon in his discussions of the history of the Japanese-style labour management. A. Gordon, "The Invention of Japanese-Style Labor Management", in S. Vlastos, ed., *Mirror of Modernity: Invented Traditions of Modern Japan*, Berkeley: University of California Press, 1998, pp. 19–36.

26 Reischauer talks about a 'double structure' of the economy. Reischauer, *Japan: The Story of a Nation*, p. 150.

27 Y. Nishikawa, "Sumai kara Miru Nihongata Kindai Kazokuron" (The Theory of the Japanese-style Modern Family Seen through the Living Place), in M. Inoue, ed., *Kazoku Shakaigaku wo Manabu Hito no Tameni* (For Those Who Want to Study the Sociology of Family), Kyoto: Sekai Shisōsha, 2010, p. 45.

28 J. Sand, "At Home in the Meiji Period: Inventing Japanese Domesticity", in S. Vlastos, ed., *A Mirror of Modernity: Invented Traditions of Modern Japan*, Berkeley: University of California Press, 1998, p. 192.

29 Sand, "At Home in the Meiji Period", p. 192.

30 Nishikawa, "Sumai kara Miru Nihongata Kindai Kazokuron", p. 34.

31 Ibid., p. 37.

32 Ibid., pp. 37–38.

33 Japan's ambiguous attitude to modernisation during the Meiji period is well reflected in its choice of model for the articulation of a modern civil code. Japan first drafted a civil code based on the French model in 1890 and intended to implement it in 1893. Very soon, however, a severe opposition emerged from those who were more familiar with the English and German law, stressing that the drafted civil code was too *liberal* for Japan and that it would destroy Japanese values such as loyalty or filial piety. Behind these concerns was the fear that Japan was undergoing a social change in which the family was becoming weaker, being gradually replaced by the individual as the new social unit. Thus the implementation of the draft was postponed, and its contents became the subject of reconsideration. As a result, the family was made the social unit

of modern Japan and was modelled after the samurai family structure. Despite the fact that there were remarkable differences in the family system according to regions and social classes, the Meiji government aimed to unify the whole society under a uniform family system through the revised civil code that took effect in 1898. This uniform (samurai-like) family system gave considerable power to the head of the family over other family members and made the eldest son the heir of the family property on the basis of the same principle.

34 Interestingly, at the beginning of the Meiji period, no constraint like this was imposed on Japanese citizens from above. Though the citizens of Meiji Japan were first (1871) allowed to, then later (1875) forced to, choose a family name, from 1876 on, Japanese women were banned from changing their family name to that of their husband after getting married, despite the fact that in reality, it had already become a sort of custom among Japanese women to follow their husband's family name. See: "Waga Kuni ni Okeru Shi no Seido no Hensen" (Change in the Institution of Surnames in Japan), official homepage of the Japanese Ministry of Justice (MOJ), www.moj.go.jp/MINJI/minji36-02.html, accessed 30/9/2016, for reference.

35 Another ambiguous attitude of Japan to modernisation during the Meiji period can be recognised in its educational orientation. Whereas there was no uniform education system in the first half of the Meiji period, it became a more and more urgent task to create a national education policy. By the end of the nineteenth century, two different ideologies were competing regarding educational principles. One stressed that education should focus on individual abilities and interests and denied the necessity of a standardised education system through standardised textbooks and curricula, believing that *thinking* should be given priority. In contrast, the other ideology emphasised the necessity of a standardised education policy that provided the students with uniform knowledge through standardised textbooks and curricula in order to foster national sentiments and thus to make Japan a strong modern country parallel to Western countries at the time. The Meiji government employed the latter. Reischauer, *Japan: The Story of a Nation*, pp. 107–108; also see: McClain, *Japan: A Modern History*, pp. 260–267. In 1903, the government demanded that all primary schools should use the same textbooks. Ibid., p. 264.

36 However, whereas family was viewed as the basic social unit, it was done so by emphasising the importance of conjugal sex. Theodoor H. van de Velde's book stressing that sex is essential to marriage was translated in its entirety under the title *Kanzen Naru Kekkon (The Complete Marriage)* and became a very popular book in 1946. In fact, a part of van de Velde's book had already been translated in 1930 under the title *Kanzen Naru Fūfu* (*The Complete Couple*) by a left-wing translator, but it gained full attention only after World War Two. In 1949, a new monthly magazine titled *Fūfu Seikatsu* (*Married Life*) was launched too, which contributed to the end of the genre of *kasutori* magazines – cheap erotic magazines that appeared right after the end of the war. The establishment of magazines for 'housewives' was, however, not an entirely Occupation trend, since a pre-war magazine in the early 1930s called *Hanashi* (*Story*) had already addressed sexual practices, but the boom of such titles took place after the war. *Fūfu Seikatsu* was later followed by other magazines such as *Fūfu Nikki* (*Couples' Diary*), *Modan Fūfu Jitsuwa* (*Modern Couples' True Stories*), *Fūfu Sekai* (*Couples' World*), *Shin Fūfu* (*New Couples*), *Fūfu no Shinshitsu* (*Couples' Bedroom*), *Fūfu no Seiten* (*Couples' Sex Manual*), *Kanzen Naru Fūfu Seikatsu no Tomo* (*Complete Couples' Life Companion*), *Aijō Seikatsu* (*Love Life*) and *Romansu Seikatsu* (*Romance Life*). This new trend divided Japanese postwar society, yet it also indicated the dawning of a new age and contributed to the realisation of greater gender equality regarding marital relations. See: Dower, *Embracing Defeat*, pp. 162–167, for more details.

37 Y. Nishikawa, "Kindai Kokka to Kazoku: Nihongata Kindai Kazoku no Ba'ai" (The Modern State and Family: In the Case of the Japanese-style Modern Family), in

S. Inoue et al., eds., *Gendai Shakaigaku 19: 'Kazoku' no Shakaigaku* (Modern Sociology 19: Sociology of 'Family'), Tokyo: Iwanami Shoten, 1996, pp. 80, 88.

38 M. Toyoda, "Review Essay: Information, Re-education and Re-orientation Policies in the US Occupation of Japan", *Social Science Japan Journal*, Vol. 15, No. 2, 2012, p. 257. Also see: Tsuchiya, *Shinbei Nihon no Kōchiku*, pp. 203, 209.

39 Takemae, *Inside GHQ*, p. xiii.

40 Nonetheless, whereas ten women took seats in the Upper House in the same year in 1947, only 15 women were elected in the Lower House for the first time. Ibid., p. 321.

41 Ibid., p. 304.

42 Sirota was just 22 years old at the time, but she was raised in Japan and could speak fluent Japanese. Dower, *Embracing Defeat*, p. 365.

43 In doing so, the new Japanese constitution became more progressive, at least on paper, than the American constitution, which did not include similar articles specifically protecting women. Ibid., p. 369.

44 For instance, equality in employment remained a subject of debate for decades, and it was not before 1985 that the Equal Employment Opportunity Act was finally passed in order to help realise gender equality – again at least in a theoretical sense. Another example refers to remarriage. The Meiji Civil Code forced women after divorce to wait for at least six months before getting married again, whereas there was no such legal requirement for men. The reason was that the father of a child could not be identified if the woman was pregnant in the meantime. This length of time, however, was reduced to 100 days on 6 July 2016. Annette Marfording, in studying the history of gender equality in postwar Japan, has argued that the law by itself had little affect on the actual social conditions in Japan. A. Marfording, "Gender Equality under the Japanese Constitution", *Verfassung und Recht in Übersee / Law and Politics in Africa, Asia and Latin America*, Vol. 29, No. 3, 1996, pp. 324–346.

45 She took an active role in articulating a sort of policy alliance with Japanese women. Takemae, *Inside GHQ*, p. 128.

46 Weed was not alone in doing so. She and her colleagues selected 27 women to teach Japanese women throughout the country about their rights under the new constitution, and this greatly encouraged grassroots women's movements. The MacArthur administration included 453 women, and this fact also seemed to be inspiring for local women's political activity in the new Japan. Ibid., pp. 127–129.

47 Ibid., 330. The new Civil Code reformed former discriminatory clauses regarding family relations such as marriage, divorce and property rights, along with male primogeniture. Nonetheless, a Nationality Law was articulated by the Ministry of Justice in 1950 that banned the holding of more than one citizenship. The same law also banned the provision of citizenship to children of Japanese mothers and granted citizenship only to children that were born to Japanese fathers. In doing so, this law stressed pre-war patrilineality. The law was amended only in 1985, and from that time on, children born to Japanese mothers can also obtain Japanese citizenship. Ibid., pp. 498, 528.

48 I.e., six years for primary education, three years for junior high school education, and three years for senior high school education – the so-called 6–3–3 model.

49 In other words, it was not a direct decision of GHQ. The members of the committee were not only already famous in the world of education in Japan at the time, but many of them had educational experience in Western countries. Ibid., p. 355.

50 Ibid., p. 366.

51 M. Okahara, *Amerika Senryōki no Minshuka Seisaku: Rajio Hōsō ni yoru Nihon Josei Saikyōiku Puroguramu* (Democratisation Policies during the US Occupation Period: Radio Broadcasting Programs for the Re-education of Japanese Women), Tokyo: Akashi Shoten, 2007. Also see: Toyoda, "Review Essay", p. 257.

52 Tsuchiya, *Shinbei Nihon no Kōchiku*, pp. 210–211. See Thomas French's chapter in the current volume for more on the impact of the 'demonstration' of motor vehicles on consumer behaviour.

53 For instance, as noted above, Western concepts of marriage based on love rather than on arrangement started to spread among urban young people, and so did the Western notion of the *modern girl*, called *moga* in Japanese. Likewise, people in urban settlements became familiar with Western movies, arts, dance, literature, sports and cafés (Reischauer, *Japan: The Story of a Nation*, p. 145). In the nineteenth century, schools providing middle and higher education admitted only men, and this created dissatisfaction among women. Ambitious women thus had to go to private schools that were run by Christian missionaries. Tsuchiya, *Shinbei Nihon no Kōchiku*, p. 199. However, from the beginning of the twentieth century, middle school education for women became available, whereas at the same time, several women's colleges were also opened, of which the first was established in 1901. Reischauer, *Japan: The Story of a Nation*, p. 146.

54 Tsuchiya, *Shinbei Nihon no Kōchiku*, pp. 213–221. Gordon, "Consumption, Leisure and the Middle Class", pp. 16–19.

55 Toyoda, "Review Essay", p. 258.

56 Ibid., p. 257. Also see: Tsuchiya, *Shinbei Nihon no Kōchiku*, p. 218.

57 T. Kawashima, *Nihon Shakai no Kazokuteki Kōsei* (Familialistic Structure of Japanese Society), Tokyo: Gakusei Shobō, 1948. Also see: T. Kawashima, *Ideorogii toshite no Kazoku Seido* (The Family Institution as Ideology), Tokyo: Iwanami Shoten, 1957.

58 S. Yamamuro, "Kakukazokuron to Nihon no Kazoku (1)" (The Theory of the Nuclear Family and the Family of Japan (1)), *Ke-su Kenkyū*, Vol. 77, 1963a, pp. 23–32, and "Kakukazokuron to Nihon no Kazoku (2)" (The Theory of the Nuclear Family and the Family of Japan (2)), *Ke-su Kenkyū*, Vol. 78, 1963b, pp. 9–22.

59 K. Aruga, "Kazoku to Ie" (Family and *Ie*), *Tetsugaku*, Vol. 38, 1960, pp. 79–110.

60 Z. Rajkai, *Kyōgō Suru Kazoku Moderu Ron* (The Theory of Competing Family Models), Kyoto: Kyoto University Press, 2014, pp. 41–43.

61 M. Amano, "The History of Family Research in Japan", in I. Shrubar and S. Shimada, eds., *Development of Sociology in Japan*, Wiesbaden: VS Verlag für Sozialwissenschaften, 2005, pp. 175–190; and E. Ochiai, "Paradigm Shifts in Japanese Family Sociology", *International Journal of Japanese Sociology*, Vol. 22, No. 1, 2013, pp. 104–127. The American intervention into Japan's family system during the Occupation period had another major impact too that did not manifest itself immediately. By removing imperial familism, not only was the pre-war social system officially denied, but the term *familism* per se also became a difficult and undesirable concept to describe Japan from a cultural point of view. Despite the fact that both right after World War Two and again recently, there are researchers questioning the modernisation of the Japanese family from a Western point of view, and emphasising the uniqueness and significance of it, the term *familism* has not become a widely used concept in describing Japan's social and cultural characteristic features. This stands in contrast to (for instance) the South Korean scholarship that often uses the term *familism* to distinguish the social conditions of the South Korean society from Western (especially North American) individualism in order to construct a (South) Korean national identity. The conceptualisation of national or cultural identity through the family is also typical of Chinese and Taiwanese academic works, although it must be mentioned that especially the Taiwanese scholarship seems to have less recourse to the term *familism* than that of South Korean scholars. The connotation of the term *familism*, however, differs in the Chinese, Taiwanese, and South Korean academic writings significantly. In China *family* (family-centredness) is often used to distinguish China's cultural orientation from Western individualism, just like in the case of South Korea or Taiwan, but it seems to be difficult for the Chinese scholarship to give full credit to the term *familism* because of its connotation to feudal social conditions. Such a connotation, however, seems to be a minor problem for scholars in South Korea or Taiwan due to the fact that these societies did not go through the social reorganisation regarding family after World War Two that China or Japan – though in different ways – had to due to internal or external influences. Nonetheless, it must be noted that the alteration of the pre-war

Japanese family system by the Americans during the Occupation period helped Japan to generate significant paradigm shifts later in family research. These paradigm shifts in Japanese family research became so *successful* that the American family research currently seems to be lagging behind it in certain aspects. See: Rajkai, *Kyōgō Suru Kazoku Moderu Ron*, pp. 16, 221. The historical roots of this can be traced back to the Occupation period which allegedly *lifted* the obstacles of traditionalism regarding the family.

62 See: T. French, "Contested 'Rearmament': The National Police Reserve and Japan's Cold War(s)", *Japanese Studies*, Vol. 34, No.1, May 2014.
63 Gordon, "Consumption, Leisure and the Middle Class", pp. 16–19.
64 Tsuchiya, *Shinbei Nihon no Kōchiku*, p. 217.

Index